Social Clubs for the Aging

Social Clubs for the Aging

—Including—
Twenty-four Programs
for Nine Clubs

VOLUME I

By   **185688**

TONI MERRILL, M.A.

Activity Program Consultant in County Homes
Editor of the OLDSTER
Wisconsin Department of Health and Social Services
Division of Family Services
Madison, Wisconsin

With a Chapter by   *HQ 1061*

Helen Clarke   *M4*
      V. 1

Emeritus Professor
University of Wisconsin, School of Social Work
Madison, Wisconsin

CHARLES C THOMAS · PUBLISHER
Springfield · Illinois · U.S.A.

Published and Distributed Throughout the World by

CHARLES C THOMAS • PUBLISHER

BANNERSTONE HOUSE

301-327 East Lawrence Avenue, Springfield, Illinois, U.S.A.

With THOMAS BOOKS *careful attention is given to all details of manufacturing and design. It is the Publisher's desire to present books that are satisfactory as to their physical qualities and artistic possibilities and appropriate for their particular use.* THOMAS BOOKS *will be true to those laws of quality that assure a good name and good will.*

Printed in the United States of America

C-1

This book about the oldsters is dedicated to the youngsters: Suzanne, Kathryn, Peter, Stephen, Christine, Lissa, Betsy, Andrew, Leslie, Stephie, Mary, Mark, Barbara, Todd, Susan, Janet, Sue, Nan, Liz, Laura, Kathy, Larry, Gaile, Beverly, Marlene, and Jeannine.

INTRODUCTION

THE originating impetus for this book was the need for resource material for clubs for the elderly. It was written for leaders with no training who, with the use of this book, could direct social groups for the aging, particularly in Homes for the aging. Wisconsin county home activity programs are developing social and special interest clubs with original and successful ideas, many of which are included herein.

The writer is the activity program consultant for Wisconsin county homes and editor of the *Oldster,* a newsletter whose purpose is to exchange activity program ideas for the aged and infirm.

An attempt has been made to present material in the easiest possible "how-to-do-it" form, especially considering the inexperienced and untrained leader.

To organize social clubs, service and special interest clubs, and a resident council, it should be helpful to have a number of programs set up in detail, described and ready, to encourage a leader in taking the first and succeeding steps. The book gives a variety of sustained programs for founding a club and getting the machinery in full gear. The assembled resource material is designed to make this task easy. Over 350 program activities are described, along with goals and motivation techniques. Whether the clubs have officers or not, goals and achievements could be decided by the club members.

Following the initial organization, nothing should prevent a continuing thriving club from meeting on a regular basis, though wisely on a small scale as a start.

With stimulation and groundwork, it is predicted that flourishing social groups in nursing homes and hospitals will soon be well established.

The Framework

Characteristics of residents in the Homes for whom these social clubs were designed were men and women in equal numbers, whose average age is eighty-two, who vary in types of care needed from bed-bound, room-bound, semiambulatory to ambulatory, with a broad area of psychological abilities and backgrounds.

It can be assumed that all residents and patients have physical handicaps; in each instance, it must be determined first what the potential club member is physically able to accomplish. Once this is decided it is essential to learn what interests an individual has, what in his background suggests his greatest pleasures, what will absorb the loneliness of his lengthy days apart from friends and relatives and from all that is familiar.

Strangely enough, residents sometimes sit in the same dining room at the same table without even knowing one another's names or having any conversation with their companions. How is this possible with mobile people who can see and hear and speak! Have they given up in desperation, only waiting to die?

Often, a craft program, though it may reach only 20 percent of the resident census, is the extent of activity in a nursing home. In one instance, it was said that the activity aide who was ill and away from work for six weeks was never missed; the same twenty-six women residents who spent their days in the craft shop on their own special projects continued just as they always had, finding their own supplies and materials and helping one another as previously. "We never missed her," the administrator said again.

Is it fair for the leader to spend full time on only 20 percent of the residents? This illustration seems to indicate that when the craft program was well enough developed, the leader should have reached out to expand activity in other recreational areas, in social groups for example, by which portions of the other 80 percent of the census might be found and awakened.

Objectives of Book

Making life interesting again, learning names and "getting acquainted" can be developed in social groups through games, discussions, trips, studying a common theme together, participating in all kinds of projects including those for the Home, the community, or even for foreign lands!

The objectives of the book are to instruct the leader as to possible types of club activities, spelling them out step by step, to provide resource and reading material, suggesting ways of establishing a permanent and stable social group.

Methods of Presenting Materials

Since residents are slowed down physically and often mentally, sophisticated intellectual stimulation is not proposed in most club activities. It is the unique resident who can quote Shakespeare, who can explain the space program, or who receives an alumni magazine. The more capable resident should not be ignored but utilized to work at his maximum on committees or perhaps as an occasional leader conducting a poetry reading class or a book review group, or taking responsibility for some study with specially selected residents. Finding and applying a resident's abilities, talents, and knowledge is the job of the appointed leader.

The order of procedure in the club need not be followed as presented in these chapters; naturally, seasons of the year, the Home's physical facilities, community opportunities, supplies and materials available, characteristics of the club members, their inclinations, and other considerations must be deliberated, the activity tried, adapted and prepared, and timed for use.

The sequence of programs as here presented is not inevitable.

There should be no distinction between clubs and interest or skill groups; they can be all or one.

Some club records are random samples, some are business meetings, some program activities, and some extensive chronological reports.

The club purpose, generally, is sociability plus a designated type of activity and interest.

There is no reason why the same favorite game or stunt couldn't be played briefly each time, or the same favorite craft project pursued for awhile at each meeting if this is what members are happiest doing; however, it is presumed that many of these program ideas will introduce diversity.

Each activity is an experiment, to be discarded or repeated as the group chooses. Much of the program material is obviously applicable to many types of social groups.

The club goals, motivation techniques (all of those submitted here were presented by activity staffs in county homes), and even the programs themselves are not necessarily limited to one single club, but usually can be adapted and applied in almost limitless ways.

The method of presentation is hopefully structured to reach out as an electric current which will spark each member—no one knows or can predict how—and is an attempt which either fails to catch on or gloriously follows through. But if interest lags, opportunity for another and still another "go at it" is provided the leader.

Hopes and the Future

One can consider club meetings successful when residents depart at the close, chatting together as they have not before, when they surprise the leader by offering assistance in "cleaning up," volunteer to report on a magazine article for the next meeting, laugh for the first time that week, and testify that they feel better now than they have, that they've made friends they can talk with between club meetings, or that they now have what they've missed most in the Home—a club to belong to!

For Whom Is the Book Planned?

The book is slanted to resident leaders and staff and community volunteers working in hospitals and nursing homes, but it is also for social workers, city recreation staff assigned to "golden age" retirement clubs, and social groups of all ages in any setting, who need resource material.

It can be used in educational activities, for recreation students in Homes and institutions, for college social work majors, and for training courses of various kinds.

The book is designed to help volunteers and professional recreation leaders do a good job in institutions for the aging, public and private nursing homes, and hospitals for the chronically ill and disabled. Perhaps it can also be beneficial to leisure-time workers generally and to teachers and students of various aspects of gerontology.

The body of the book contains excerpts and entire records of social groups from Wisconsin public county homes, and has many program suggestions. They, together with the author's comments and interpretations, illustrate the great variety of programs, activities, and facilities available and the multiplicity of skills exercised.

The leader need not be an authority or even especially knowledgeable in subjects of fin and feather, homemaking, gardening, or any other specialty. He is there to set the time and day, support and strengthen the group as to members and program material, plan for and work with committees, and arrange for materials and supplies for the following meeting. Perhaps he is there most of all to ask the questions and learn from the members, many of them certainly knowledgeable and experienced, who will flourish in the ego-building process.

ACKNOWLEDGMENTS

A PPRECIATION goes to Miss Helen Clarke, Professor Emeritus of the University of Wisconsin, who wrote the part on "Gerontological Theory" and who read the manuscript many times, making encouraging and important suggestions about rewording, reorganization, and additional material.

Gratitude is given to the county home staffs and residents, all of whom contributed in small or large ways to the content of the book. Material is frequently taken from records, the author's observations, talks at Home institutes by county home staffs, or visits by the consultant, and Home newsletters.

Book lists recommended for reading aloud in "Automobile Club," and "Fin and Feather Club" were compiled by the Madison Public Library, Madison, Wisconsin; all others were taken from "Let's Read Aloud," Milwaukee Public Library, Milwaukee, Wisconsin, books from these lists actually having been read aloud to oldsters in nursing homes, to their delight.

Many of the ideas from "How to Lead a Club" came from a paper cover brochure, "Senior Age Clubs, a Guideline of Creative Group Activity for the Older Citizen," used with permission by the author, Jerome Kaplan, Editor-in-Chief of *The Gerontologist*.

T.M.

Recreation accepts people at their own levels of skill and commences with their interests. Its concern is with the individual and his wants as a person.

G. Ott Romney—*Off the Job Living*

California Homecoming Queen

This season's Homecoming Queen at Southern California's Oceanside Carlsbad College was elected in a landslide victory (270 out of 300 votes) in recognition of her status as the most exuberant co-ed on campus.

As a sophomore English major, Irene Horvath writes fashion and book review columns for the college newspaper, has several novels waiting to be edited and one already in the hands of a literary agent, is active in the Spartan Club, sells tickets for campus functions, makes clothes for her family, studies fifteen to twenty hours weekly to keep up with her full-time academic load, sleeps eight and a half hours every night, never takes a nap, and is never tired.

Irene has an active life of accomplishment already behind her: she was unable to walk until age four because of polio; she published a book of poetry at nine; she was a recognized fashion designer at fifteen; she has been married and widowed, she has ventured into the business world as a store owner; and recently (in order to pursue her chosen career of creative writing) she returned to school.

The first known college Homecoming Queen who is also a Social Security old-age beneficiary, Irene celebrated her seventy-second birthday last summer.

—*Aging,* December 1959
Department of Health, Education and Welfare

CONTENTS

PART I

GERONTOLOGICAL THEORY

HELEN CLARKE

PART II

DEVELOPING COMPREHENSIVE CLUB PROGRAMS

PART III

HOW TO LEAD A CLUB

PART IV
SAMPLE PROGRAMS

Social Clubs for the Aging

PART I

GERONTOLOGICAL THEORY

HELEN CLARKE

Questions and Responses

GERONTOLOGICAL THEORY

THIS preliminary chapter is intended to supply a background or theoretical structure for the decisions and actions of the leader and for the guidance of his relationships with group members. It makes a basic assumption that an effective leader of a social group is one with some degree of program "know-how" based upon sound principles. He synchronizes practical knowledge and experience with theories. He has perceptions of what makes individuals, groups, and society click, and he utilizes insight and understanding of the behavior of others and of himself. He has a sense of proportion and of values, and an ability to stand off and look critically at what he and others are doing and to benefit from such evaluation.

This and the next chapter concentrate on several aspects of knowledge available to social group leaders and pertinent to effective performance. I shall ask several questions and attempt exploratory answers. These questions and answers are suggestive; they are not definitive nor exhaustive. There is a vast literature on each topic which the reader may choose to explore. Reference to a few sources is made at the close of this general statement. Many more references are available in the body of the book.

QUESTIONS AND RESPONSES

I. What Are Gerontology and Geriatrics?

Gerontology is the scientific study of the processes and phenomena of the aging. Our concern in this book is exclusively with *human* gerontology. Geriatrics is the scientific study of the diseases, the physical and psychological conditions, of the aging.

The scientific study of aging is a 20th-century phenomenon and has come about because of increases in the numbers of the aging and the rapid changes in environmental conditions affecting them. Current knowledge about the aging and their situations can be organized around four classifications: biological, psychological, sociological or situational, and sociophysiological or be-havioral developments.

Biological aging goes on from birth to death. As people ap-proach and reach the older ages, there is an increase in long-term chronic diseases, such as heart disturbances and arthritis, suscep-tibility to acute diseases, slowing down in performance and ac-curacy, decline in energy, reduction in the power of concentration.

Psychological aging may involve changes in the central nervous system in perceptual capacities, in ability to organize and utilize one's self and resources. Psychologists are concerned with per-sonality and behavior changes as well as with biological and en-vironmental changes.

The third category of aging has to do with changes in *situa-tions,* whether as a member of an occupation, of a family, of a community, or of various kinds of social groups. Changes may occur abruptly as with retirement or death of a spouse, or slowly as in case of chronic disease.

The *behavioral* aspect of aging is concerned with the meaning to the individual of the other three changes. It encompasses the reactions he has to himself and his self-image, and to his feeling about retirement and the likely diminution in income. Changed roles and status affect his relationships with family, neighbors, as-sociates *ad infinitum.*

Indexes of books dealing with the study of the aging list many conditions and problems, for example:

Historical Perspectives on Problems of Aging

Environmental Changes

Modern Viewpoints toward Aging and the Aged

Problem Areas as Health, Income, Housing, and Leisure Time

Physical and Psychological Characteristics of the Aging Population

The Impact of Aging on Individual Activities and Social Roles

Retirement, the Emerging Pattern

The Subculture of the Aging

Are the Aging a Minority Group?

Expanded knowledge about aging furnishes a base for adapta-tions of living patterns and for modification of social attitudes and institutional facilities. Readers of this book are not expected to become gerontological experts, but rather they are encouraged to appreciate how many aspects of the aging process there are. Development of the inquiring point of view *is* an objective.

Gerontological publications and literature about the elderly point up the fact that there is an enormous variation in time of onset of the various changes in aging individuals and in the circumstances affecting them. Who has not heard of such characters and personalities as King Lear, Franz Hals, Rubens, Toscanini, Verdi, Wagner, Schweitzer, Justice Oliver Wendell Holmes, Jr., and his medical and literary father. All these men lived to a ripe old age and were, on the whole, productive until their deaths. No one of them is typical but all, except King Lear, found ways of more or less satisfying their desires and of making contributions to their society. Few of the aging will achieve the renown of these men, but many will make contributions to their communities and in turn derive benefits.

It is possible and often desirable to generalize concerning situations and problems confronting the aging. However, no one working with older citizens should expect individuals to conform to a preconceived pattern or stereotype. Individual older persons vary as much as infants, adolescents, and young and middle-aged adults. All who live and work with the aging will benefit from comprehensive knowledge of the aging processes and from keen and sympathetic observations of them as individuals performing their daily routines.

II. What Is Demography and What Is Its Importance to Those Working with the Aging?

Demography is the statistical study of factors such as fertility, sex, mortality, disease, marital status, and geographical distribution which determine the changing composition and characteristics of human populations. Most demographic analysis is made in the context of age structure.

There is an extensive and expanding body of demographic information about the aging. The following sample of studies shows the diversity and range of subjects analyzed:

Age Classifications Throughout the World by Country, Regions, Area

Population in the United States by Age and Sex at Various
Times

Factors in Increases of Numbers of Older Persons and Race,
Sex, Country

Relation of Birth and Death

Changes in Age Sex Composition

Changes in Proportion of Middle-Aged to Older Persons

Urban, Rural, Urban-Suburban Differences in Population

Out of the masses of accumulated data on the aging, this introductory statement includes only a few highlights. Readers will recognize that figures differ at different times, that research design affects findings, and that interpretations vary depending upon purpose and frame of reference. The facts selected are intended to provide a comprehensive but simplified picture of the size and characteristics of the aging population in the United States.

1. How many older Americans are there? One in every eleven persons in the United States is sixty-five or over, a total of eighteen and a half million men and women.

In this century, the percentage of the United States population aged sixty-five and over more than doubled (from 4.1% in 1900 to 9.4% in 1965), while the number increased sixfold (from three million to more than eighteen million).

Women outlive men. There are about 129 older women per 100 older men. Life expectancy at birth is 73.7 years for females and 66.7 for males. Life expectancy for women is still increasing faster than for men.

2. Where do older Americans live in the United States? During the next twenty years, the older population of the United States is expected to increase almost 40 percent to twenty-five million. It will grow to over two million in two states (California and New York) and will number over one million in five other states (Florida, Illinois, Ohio, Pennsylvania, and Texas).

3. What are the living arrangements of older persons? The big majority of older men and women live in families. Only one in twenty-five lives in an institution.

Two thirds of the men, but only one third of the women, live in families with their spouse.

About one third of the women, but only one sixth of the men, live alone or with nonrelatives.

4. What is the marital status of older persons? Most older men are married; most older women are widows. There are almost four times as many widows as widowers.

About two fifths of older married men have wives *under* sixty-five years of age.

5. What is the economic situation of older persons?

Some are well off.

About 350,000 couples (sixty-five plus who are heads of families) have incomes of $10,000 or more.

Close to 940,000 older couples have incomes from $5,000 to $10,000. A little less than a third of the nonmarried have assets of $5,000 or more.

Many are not well off.

Some 2.6 million older couples (more than half) have incomes under $3,000.

Among older couples, more than one sixth have no assets of any kind or assets of less than $1,000 except for equity in their home. More than a quarter of nonmarried older persons have no assets at all and another tenth have no assets except for home equity.

The largest single source of their total income is still earnings from employment, even though fewer than one in five are in the labor force.

6. How many older persons work? More than three million, or 17 percent, are in the labor force, either working or actively seeking work.

They make up 4 percent of the United States labor force.

More than a quarter (two million) of the older men but only a tenth (one million) of the older women are in the labor force.

7. How much do older persons spend? Of their total income of over $40 billion a year, almost all is used for current expenditures.

Their heaviest dollar outlays are for housing and household operations, food purchases, and transportation.

Older people spend proportionately more than younger people on housing and household operations, health care, and food purchased for preparation at home.[1]

---

[1] "Facts about Older Americans," United States Department of Health, Education and Welfare, Administration on Aging, Publication #410, May, 1966.

It is only as our demographic information has increased in quantity and quality that the United States has been able to scientifically analyze expectations about the place of the aging in society, their needs, and the essential resources for meeting them. Since the passage of the Social Security Act in 1935 there have been governmental resources for the amassing of quantitative information about many blocks of people, including the aging, not formerly available. The Census Bureau and other public and private resources today provide masses of factual information about our population.

III. What Is Retirement and What Are Its Effects?

Retirement is a break in an individual's work life, a severing of occupation and career activities. There are other conditions of retirement, e.g. concerning child rearing, housekeeping, committee activity. But gerontological literature usually defines it as voluntary or involuntary withdrawal from paid employment.

Retirement is a phenomenon of modern industrial society. Formerly, older persons were expected to perform useful functions all their lives. If they could no longer carry on some acceptable activity, they became the responsibility of the kin group. In some cultures, if family could no longer be responsible for the old and helpless, arrangements could be made for their neglect, abandonment, and even death.

The explosion in the 19th and 20th centuries of technological and scientific information enormously expanded production, and had as one of its consequences the phenomenon of retirement. Displacement of older persons was considered essential so as to assure employment of younger persons. Further, the great increase in the numbers of the aging and the inevitable diminution of their energies and skills, argued for their retirement from employment.

Expanded industrial production also brought about increased earnings, profits, savings, taxes, and public revenue which have made possible greater assurance of security and satisfaction for many of the aged. It is only prosperous societies like ours which can supply multiple services for the many classifications of persons with special characteristics and problems, such as the aging.

There is a contradiction in the phenomenon of retirement. At one and the same time, society expects and even demands retirement—usually at sixty-five or often even earlier—and accompanies it with indifference, condescension, commiseration. Ironically, retirement is verbally held out to be a necessary and desirable event, but is actually looked upon as a period of dwindling utility to society and of reduced satisfactions to the individual. The "work ethics" of early America is still with us and dominates attitudes regarding retirement.

Social attitudes and social conditions clearly affect the degree of anticipation or reluctance to enter into retirement. Perhaps no less important is the personality of the retired individual. If he does not think of retirement as an ambiguous period but looks forward to choice of activity and fewer pressures, the adjustment process may very well be pleasurable and the results satisfying both to society and to the individual.

IV. What Is the Significance of Leisure for the Retired Elderly?

Retirement brings leisure. Unless the aging retired person has full or partial employment, his life is composed of 100 percent leisure. What he does with it depends upon many factors, such as past experiences, opportunities, physical and psychological energies, income, desires. It may be considered as freedom from work or deprivation of the opportunity to work; as the chance to choose activities or as coerced idleness. It need not be considered as inevitably leading to an unfruitful, dreary life with death as the desirable end. Retirement leisure, in other words, may be thought of by the retired person and by society as a liability or an asset.

It is normal that with aging, individuals should more or less expect disengagement, meaning withdrawal from high-powered, strenuous activities and from some personal contacts. Disengagement is reduction in the level of activities and in the number of relationships. It need not imply a sterile existence. Choice is not between activity and inactivity but between types and amounts of activity and range of associations.

Aging people can help themselves find satisfying leisure experience and those who work and associate with older people can help them achieve a rich retirement by examining various aspects of their lives, such as follow:

1. Analysis of what resources and opportunities are available to them.

2. Discovery and definition of their capacities and potentials.

3. Recognition of what their previous roles were and what their new roles are or can become.

4. Determination of the routines and activities they want to and can carry on.

5. Decision regarding amount and type of remunerative employment, if any.

Inquiries may or may not be detailed and formalized, but some type of analysis is possible and desirable by and for many of the elderly.

The elderly, like every other age group, have common and particular needs. The Institute of Gerontology of the State University of Iowa enumerates the "needs and drives" of older persons. They are relevant to individual and social planning for use of leisure time. They include the following needs:

1. To render some socially beneficial service.

2. To be considered a part of the community.

3. To occupy increased leisure hours in satisfying ways.

4. To enjoy normal companionships.

5. For recognition of an individual.

6. For opportunity for self-expression and a sense of achievement.

7. For health protection and care.

8. For suitable mental stimulation.

9. For suitable living arrangements and family relationships.

10. For spiritual satisfactions.

All of these hopes are not achievable by all elderly people. Society offers assistance in this realization. Of course, many older people find their own ways of fulfilling a modicum of these needs.

There are many classifications of types of leisure-time activities and programs which are not the focus of this introduction. Some of them are discussed in the body of this book. Suffice to say here that leisure-time activities may be oriented to people, to things, to self. What the good leisure life is for any given individual is a variable. Leisure in retirement is an end, has a life of its own, and is not a subordinate to work.

Those whose function it is to help retired older persons enjoy and benefit from their leisure realize that capacities, interests, opportunities, have to be brought into congruence. Utilization of retirement leisure usually requires a constellation of adjustments, not just a single one as to reduced income or change of residence. Only if offerings meet with the desires and capacities of the individual will he enjoy and benefit from them. Meaningful leisure programs must satisfy the greatly differing desires of the elderly for peace and quiet, for activity and variety, for service to others and for self-satisfactions.

V. How Do the Roles of Older People in Retirement Differ from Those of Their Work Lives?

A role is defined to mean a collection of behavior patterns associated with status or position and which can be identified and given a name such as the following:

1. Familial roles: husband, wife, brother, sister.
2. Parental roles: son, daughter, father, mother.
3. Occupational roles: white or blue collar worker, banker, merchant, professor.
4. Professional roles: lawyer, judge, doctor, surgeon, pharmacist.
5. Political roles: governor, town board chairman, voter.
6. Religious roles: clergyman, bishop, parishioner, chorister.
7. Friendship roles: confidante, companion, "pal."

Behavior patterns in role performance are largely determined by the environment and by the culture. This is true in the performance both of the generalized or major roles and of the particularized or minor roles. To illustrate: The expected behavior of a professor is different from that of a farmer or plumber or carpenter. Although no two professors perform their functions or play their roles identically, there are societal expectations about their behavior. Society assigns a normalcy of behavior or a set of rules which steer the activities of the various roles. Before retirement the most important roles of most persons are dominated by the work ethic and by the family.

Every individual also performs particularized roles in varieties of situations. For example, a particular husband may perform also as a particular employee in a particular plant and as a particular member of the city council and of his particular church. Sometimes these roles, major and minor, do not mesh and when this happens, conflict situations are likely to result.

Linked with role performance is position or status. A doctor, a professor, a bank clerk, or an elevator operator do not occupy the same position or status in society. The respect, rewards, honors, rights, and responsibilities assigned those performing these roles, or assumed by them, vary. Their roles as men who work and earn with the corresponding statuses or positions are not the same as those of men not working and not earning. Elderly persons usually have changed generalized roles and corresponding statuses when they retire from their occupational activities. As retired persons, they may have what have been dubbed "roleless roles."

Gerontological literature points out that both situational changes, such as loss of employment and assured income, and changes in roles and status, such as unemployed old men with only the memory of status, affect adjustments. Attitudes toward retirement influence the retired person's image of leisure, quite as much as the fact of retirement. Some older people anticipate the role of retired persons. Others deplore and resent it and find life formless and uncertain.

Role flexibility is desirable for retired older persons, but shapeless and undefined behavior or "roleless roles" are not.

VI. *What Is a Social Group? What Roles May Its Members Play in the Group?*

Leisure-time activities of elderly people may be characterized by isolated or solitary activities such as watching football games on TV or by listening to stereo records or by reading or knitting or gardening. They may occur in masses, as attendance at a World's Fair or watching a parade or participating in a large choral event. They may be in small groups, such as in a committee to organize something or in a discussion or activity group, or in a purely sociability group.

In one sense, a group is any aggregate of individuals from two people to a crowd. The social group of this book is a small number of people—four, eight, ten, twenty, aware of each other, who have common interests, and who do things together. The members may come together primarily for sociability because they like each other and want to be together; or because they have common interests; or because of a combination of both. Leaders of these social groups are interested in all motivations.

Whatever the motivations for coming together, leaders learn to observe conditions and relationships such as follow:

1. The origin of the group.
2. Size and composition.
3. Selection process.
4. Elimination and exclusion process.
5. Means of determination of goals.
6. Definition of goals.
7. Structure, including location of authority and power and utilization of sanctions.
8. Communication network of pairs, isolates, triads, constellations.
9. Methods of selecting and content of program.
10. Tensions, conflicts, resolutions.
11. Acceptance and rejection of insiders and outsiders.
12. *Esprit de corps,* the "we" feeling.

Observation of such conditions enables leaders to adapt programs and to facilitate cooperative relationships. This book emphasizes the desirability of careful observation of these types of situations and offers innumerable suggestions for achieving rapport and satisfactions.

Leaders and members of social groups have had the experience of sitting out deadly, dull unproductive sessions characterized by lack of preparation, choppy and irrelevant activities, indifference, bickering. On the other hand, they have had the exciting experience of participating in lively, stimulating challenging activities and of enjoying associations with congenial and resourceful people. This is to say that the dynamics of groups vary. Leaders attempt to understand motivations, roles, relationships, and to serve as a resource and stimulant for activities. They observe the con-

scious and unconscious assumption of roles. Some of those roles
are constructive for the group and some are not. Among the roles
often observed are

idea man
clarifier
mediator
parliamentarian
democratic leader
understanding and encouraging confidante
sponger
chronic complainer, whiner, griper
joker, the fool, attention getter
pinch hitter
"big boss," dictator, strutter, "braggadocio"
"Pollyanna"
dour and depressing "killjoy," "scrooge"

These roles and the position of those performing them have
their effects upon group pleasures, accomplishments, and cohesion.

Every sizeable institution housing the aged has one or more
disorganized and disoriented individuals. Unless the condition is
physically caused and is recent, those people often have been
among the incompetents and inadequates of society. Their family and work lives may have been characterized by irregularity, in-
competence, unproductiveness, misery.

Such a person is Mr. White, a former urban resident who in-
termittently received public assistance and earned laborer's wages.
His wife, long deceased, was a miserable housekeeper and incom-
petent mother of their five children who are dispersed around
the country and who themselves are incompetents and completely
disinterested in their father. This man is garrulous, a chronic
complainer, an obstreperous and troublesome member of the institutional family and of a social group interested in cards. His
condition is due primarily to limited intelligence, inadequate
training and education. His life history has been one of failure
and unhappiness for himself and his family. It continues into
old age and the pattern becomes more pronounced. It is not necessarily one of disorientation due to physical deterioration, but
one of disorganization manifested over a long span of time.

The staff of the institution and leaders of groups can sometimes find resources for helping people in these latter two classifications. The partially dependent person can even be helped to want to be a good resident, contributor, beneficiary. The contributions of the third type to his fellow man and to his own satisfactions are expected to be limited. Staff can sometimes make minor contributions to the happiness and socialization of these individuals and thus contribute to the larger group.

There are many conscious ways that the leader can fulfill his enabling functions. Since the text extensively points up these skills, I shall mention only a few.

1. Careful preparation for a group session.
   a. Attention to physical arrangements.
   b. Obtaining information about each individual.
   c. Preparation of essential materials.
   d. Tentatively preparing a plan or focus or agenda.
   e. Preparing oneself to respond with patience, but also with resourcefulness.
2. Beginning and maintaining group meetings.
   a. Helping the chairman, if there is one, get started.
   b. Allowance of time to get down to program.
   c. Sensitivity to individual responses.
   d. Introductions and explanations.
   e. Following or interrupting an agenda or order of activities.
3. Helping to obtain and maintain amicable relations.
   a. Encouragement or participation by suggestions and adaptations.
   b. Assuring equality of attention.
   c. Waiting out long-winded members.
   d. Diverting long-winded members.
   e. Expressions of appreciation.
   f. Acceptance of resistance, hostilities.
   g. Laying down limits.
   h. Repetition.
   i. Picking up clues.

Writers on group dynamics interested in the socializing of individuals stress the importance of simultanious understanding of group relationships and the conscious use of techniques to help the group move toward its defined tasks and goals. This book stresses both.

VII. What Relationships and Types of Role Performance Do Group Leaders Hope to Stimulate and Facilitate?

Nothing in our universe is more complex than human behavior and interpersonal relationships. How obvious and how true! We can get to the moon and make atomic bombs, but we do not seem able to prevent war, riots, angry and disruptive dissent, demoralizing personal problems, and social disorganization. Keen perception, sympathetic objectivity, controlled emotions and behavior are assets of the leader working with retired persons. In a small and limited situation, he attempts to apply the principles, policies, and techniques of the social sciences, especially sociology, psychology, and social psychology. These he combines with common sense and down-to-earth behavior.

The residents of county homes are physically handicapped, and an appreciable percentage have personality and emotional problems. This book describes types of institutional adjustments necessary for the physically and psychologically handicapped.

One classification of types of aged persons, both in and out of institutions, and based upon personality characteristics follows:

1. The independent person with good self-images who is self-reliant in making decisions, and in regulating the routine of his life. Such a person has made good adjustments throughout his life.

2. The partially dependent person who relies largely on beneficial environmental conditions for his stability. Such a person has needed and sometimes had supportive resources to help him keep his head above water.

3. The "anomic" or more or less disorganized and even disoriented individual who through his life has been unable to use himself and his environment to achieve maturity and social adjustments.

Elsewhere, this book provides illustrations of these types of behavior. County home residents in the first classification are those who play such roles as idea or resource man, listener, pinch hitter, integrator, democratic leader, conciliator, stabilizer, mediator, initiator, and implementor of activities. These people are great resources in congregate living. The resident with multiple sclerosis and wheelchair locomotion, who organizes a library for residents, receives visitors, dispenses daily newspapers, inspires cancer bandage groups, is such a person.

Residents with characteristics in the second classification may be active disrupters or passive nonparticipators. If and as long as conditions meet their demands, they may be minor irritants in institutional living and in small leisure-time groups. Such a person may be like Mr. Mueller, a widowed, unproductive tenant farmer with a serious heart condition which restricts his movements.

He constantly complains about food, too much or too little heat, employee inefficiency; he attends a carpentry club where he putters and produces little, but where he does generate irritation which results in avoidance of his company.

It is a fact that most social groups in county homes have conciliatory, peaceful, resourceful, cooperative members and also those exhibiting varying degrees of antagonistic, unloveable, uncooperative, disruptive behavior. The leader attempts to learn how and when the particular roles are performed, what kinds of situations encourage, discourage, precipitate the desirable or undesirable behavior, what are the interactions resulting from the roles being played, and what are the constellations of cooperation or resistance including pairs and various other associations.

VIII. How Do and Can Local, State, and Federal Governments and Private and Voluntary Resources Assume Responsibility for Meeting the Multiple Needs of the Aging?

It is an assumption of this book that the provision of congregate housing and recreational outlets is an aspect of community responsibility for the aging. Many other resources are needed and are or should be available. This introduction draws the reader's attention to the necessity of community planning, public and private financing, and adequate and competent administration if the complex of problems of the aging are to be realized, confronted, and met. Increase in public understanding and acceptance of the challenge of doing something are responsibilities of all of us.

The primary responsibility for satisfactory aging rests with the

individuals themselves and their families. Undoubtedly, more retired elderly persons will find it possible to define useful and satisfying roles as more planning prior to retirement occurs and as
social attitudes about retirement change. Modified attitudes plus
the provision of many kinds of resources for medical care, rea-
sonably priced respectable housing, above-the-minimum level of
income, recreational outlets, community service opportunities,
and perhaps even for remunerative work are essential for maximum satisfactions in retirement.

The affluence of the American economy makes possible the
present provision of many social services including those for the
aging and will provide many more, as there is public demand for
them. Many resources are provided by the tax dollars and come
from the Federal, State, and local governments, singly and together. Momentum for assumption of responsibility of the Federal Government for the economic security of the aging came
with the depression of the 1930's and the Social Security Act of
1935. A compulsory insurance scheme financed by employee, em-
ployer, and the tax dollar for retirement and for death of old
persons sixty-five and over was an innovation in that year. Benefits are received as a matter of "right." The scheme has been expanded over the years to include hospital and medical insurance
for the aged and for disability insurance. Millions of people
now receive most of their income from this source. Old Age and
Survivors (OASDI) scheme will continue to expand in coverage,
in size of benefits and contributions.

The Social Security Act provides also for federal grants to the
states for Old Age Assistance, a plan requiring a "means test."
Where OAA existed prior to this time it had been a niggardly
program financed by the states and localities. Despite the fact
that the Federal Government set up this scheme to increase the
economic security of the aging, the coverage and amounts of
grants in many states are below the poverty line as it has been
variously defined by governmental agencies. There is presently extensive discussion of 100 percent federal financing of public assistance. Present proposals for the introduction of a guaranteed
minimum income for families with children is an aspect of
changing attitudes toward public responsibility for persons with
economic insecurity.

There are many additional federal services designed to aid the aging. I shall refer to only a few.

The Bureau of Labor Statistics and the Woman's Bureau, both in the Department of Labor, carry on research activities and some other minor programs for the benefit of the aging. The Department of the Treasury has extended aid to the aged in the form of tax benefits. A considerable portion of the activities of the Veterans' Administration are awarded elderly veterans and their families.

A number of units of the Public Health Service concentrate upon the problems of the aging. They include the Chronic Disease Program, the Center of Aging Research, the Gerontological Branch, and the Section on Aging. The Public Health Service through its Bureau of State Services administers a number of programs of studies and demonstrations. These are designed to induce states to set up laboratories, clinics, and hospitals which are required to implement research findings. No direct patient service is involved. All these activities of the Public Health Service are within the Department of Health, Education and Welfare. So too is the Hill-Burton program, administered by the Bureau of Medical Services. It has extended aid to private, nonprofit, and public bodies which are willing to create facilities for the care of those suffering from prolonged illness.

The area of housing for the aged holds promise for growth. Encouragement of the purchasing of homes by older persons, the financing of rental homes for them, and the more ready availability of public low-rent housing are developing programs.

The National Government has set standards for institutional care in both the health and welfare fields. Although there is variation between states and localities in the standards accepted, there is improvement in medical and domiciliary care of the aged.

A special staff on aging has been set up in the Department of Health, Education and Welfare. It serves as the focal spot at the national level for crystallizing of activities going on in the various branches of the National Government and in the states. It provides consultative and informational services to states and communities.

This staff has had much to do with implementing the White

House Conference on Aging Act which provided for the first of such conferences in 1961. The second was held in 1971. These conferences are not dissimilar in purpose to the well-known White House Conferences on Children and Youth.[2]

These are a few of the types of services and agencies provided by the Federal Government. States, too, carry on activities, some stimulated and partially financed in Washington. For example, the State of Wisconsin has a Division on the Aging within the Department of Health and Social Services. It administers both federal and state funds for local programs for the aging.

Localities vary in their public and private programs. Telephone services, Meals-on-wheels, Friendly Visitors, chauffeuring, recreation centers, foster grandparents are among the types of activities which are organized locally and which derive their resources from various pocketbooks. Community planning by chests and councils, by public and private voluntary health, recreation, and welfare agencies, by church groups, by organizations of the aging themselves are all involved in obtaining more and better services for the aging.

Particularized programs supported by special interest groups contribute to the welfare of the aging. Many of these groups, like the National Retired Teachers Association (NRTA) have important political purposes. Without pressure, progress in legislation and in the provision of resources will be slower and more halting than is desirable or necessary.

Some leaders of groups in institutions where the aging population live will uncover interest in organized social action and will encourage and stimulate concern both in the institution and in the community.

IX. What Generalizations, Propositions, or Principles Regarding Aging Processes and Conditions Can Be Derived from This Chapter?

The following list serves to sum up the material presented.

1. "You can't teach an old dog new tricks" and "You're never

---

[2] Cottrell, Fred: Governmental functions and politics of age. In Tibbitts, Clark (Ed.): *Handbook of Social Gerontology*. Chicago, University of Chicago, 1960, pp. 624-654.

too old to learn." Both of these seemingly contradictory proverbs contain elements of truth. Learning when and how they apply requires careful observation and diagnosis and thoughtful planning.

2. Stereotypes of retired elderly persons are common. Pricking the balloon of the stereotype will help to create new images by and of the aging. Among the stereotypes are the inevitability of decreased status and of unhappy changed roles; unavoidable diminution in opportunities for rich daily lives; the certainty of fatalistic attitudes toward death. There is no single desirable pattern of behavior for the aging. Cautious generalizations about aging patterns of behavior and situations affecting them are legitimate but not stereotyping.

3. Roles in retirement may be different from those performed in the work life. They need not be inferior, feared, resisted, ambiguous, or formless.

4. Society and individuals need to prepare for the period of retirement and aging. Acceptance of certain phenomena and rejection of others will help movement from the work to the retirement period.

5. Youth can be helped to like and to appreciate older people and to prepare for their own aging.

6. Age and experience, economic resources and cultural opportunities affect the type and range of interests of all persons and of course, this is especially true of retired older people.

7. How an individual internalizes his experiences influences his externalized behavior.

8. Little or no apparent participation does not necessarily mean there is none. Participation is of various types and degrees. Its seeming or actual absence may be due to illness, inexperience, embarrassment, ignorance, unfamiliarity with language, and so on.

9. Individualization of every member of a social group by a leader is a prelude to the growth of the members, to the development of *esprit de corps,* and wise programming.

10. Group activities may be elementary or advanced, simple or complex, single or multiple in type, fixed and static, or progressive, therapeutic, or recreational.

11. The greater the group leader's inner security about activity skills and human relationships, the more he will be able to tolerate indifference and even hostility.

12. Too easy and quick generalizations and diagnoses of members of the group will often result in cutting off interests and contributions of shy, uncertain, and inexperienced individuals.

13. Lack of leader knowledge of specialized program activities need not preclude their inclusion in program planning. Experts are often available.

14. Lack of knowledge and understanding about the causation and meaning of particular behavior does not imply a do-nothing attitude on the leader's part. Experts are often available.

15. Awareness, imagination, resourcefulness, empathy are perhaps the most desirable and needed characteristics of leaders of social groups.

16. There are routine, dreary, and even menial aspects of all jobs, including group leadership. Willingness to perform them and to share their performance with group members will often facilitate growth in the quality of relationships.

17. Staff and residents of county homes have much to contribute to community understanding of the problems of the aging including health, economic conditions, social adjustments. Without knowledge and understanding, the public will be slow to meet complex problems.

18. Participation in organization for social change and for social action is a function of work with the aging.

19. The basic role of the group leader in recreational activities with the aging is that of enabler.

X. *What Are a Few Major Bibliographical Resources for Study of the Aging?*

See the Appendix for the answers to this question.

This chapter points out that many of the principles and theories about the aging discussed here and in the body of the book may also be appropriately applied to any segment of society. However, there are characteristics of the aging which are different from those of the infant or the adolescent. That there are differences at various stages of individual and social development is understood. Deciphering what they are will enable those working with the aging to apply principles specific to this population.

In conclusion, leaders of social groups composed of the aging will endeavor to achieve knowledge about people including themselves, about the society and culture in which the aging live and have lived, about programs and the process of programming, and about what skills to apply, when, and how.

PART II

DEVELOPING COMPREHENSIVE CLUB PROGRAMS

Viewpoints on Old Age

Observations of Staff Regarding Philosophy and Theory
  What Motivations and Inducements Are Employed?
  Isolation
  What Can They Achieve?

Thumbnail Sketches of Types of Patients
  General
  Heightened Fantasy Life
  Senescence
  Physically Handicapped

Values of the Club and Adaptive Activities

VIEWPOINTS ON OLD AGE

VIEWPOINTS of Greek and Roman thinkers regarding the aged do not vary essentially from modern thinking. The oldster was often considered odd, someone to be shunned and pitied. Aristotle describes the aged as people having little left, although Plato calls his old age "profound repose and freedom from love and other passions." Plato and Cicero felt that needs met successfully during younger years could be expected to continue satisfactorily in later life. Ulysses offered therapy to an old man: "Warm baths, good food, soft sleep and generous wine."

Change in life style has come in recent years with industrialization, urbanization, and increased longevity through medical science. It is still true, however, that in many parts of the world, life expectancy is only twenty or thirty years.

Youth has always been a preferred age in Western-European civilization. We seem to revere Hollywood youth and beauty, admire speed, achievement, and production, pride ourselves on personal success, and in progressive attitudes. Advertising focuses on youth, cautiously avoiding such references to old age as might offend or damage an image which up-and-coming Americans want to preserve.

In many parts of the world, however, old age is highly regarded, the ultimate triumph of life. The Turkish mother-in-law is in charge of the household, a total and unquestioned ruler regarding each detail of its management; the daughter-in-law has nothing to say until she herself becomes a mother-in-law.

A Japanese father maintains absolute authority over his full-grown son.

People in the Philippines and in Southeast Asia proudly point out that they have no nursing homes; they take care of their own aged and infirm! Indeed, it is a joy to visit such a family, where an elegant seventy-five-year-old matriarch, editor of a professional magazine and a former university professor, lives with her son, his wife, their two grown daughters, a grandson-in-law and a

29

great grandchild seven months old, thriving in love and happiness together.

Many of these societies take care of their own, if able, but when their aged and infirm relatives get sick, they may die unattended because the nursing home care such as we have in this country is not provided.

Some scientists infer that adjustment in aging can be managed by those who are no longer bothered by keeping up, who no longer feel threatened by youth and strength, who no longer think of themselves as competent middle agers, but just as what they are— or should be—well-balanced oldsters.

Study of reaction to stress of the older person shows that he is often unable to involve himself, that possessions and friends become irreplaceable and their loss more keen. The aged often show increased, even exaggerated interest in religion and life after death. Emotional problems are due to basic threats to health and security, which lead to anxiety. Adapting techniques to avoid fear through social groups can help limit overconcern about small pieces of life. For instance, given a chance to identify with younger people, the oldster may find the future has some hope.

Social groups invite good interpersonal relationships and offer the opportunity for a tapering off of activities commensurate with physical vigor. Joining a group as basic family ties are relinquished helps in recovery from stress and illness and becomes a vital aspect of living.

A county home nurse observes as follows:

> The process of aging takes place from the time of conception on through life; changes in life are the results of the process of aging, structural changes, disturbances in functions, chemical changes, accumulating of fat in blood vessels, hardening of the arteries as well as heredity which plays a part in aging.
>
> Social activities as well as nutritional factors, also affect the life span; and even educational factors influence long life. People vary in these changes. Why does it affect one and not others? Perhaps it's psychological. There's a retardation of cells, and one doesn't heal as fast; there's a decline of metabolism rate which slows down oxygen to the brain, heart, etc., and affects elasticity of tissues, slows muscles, and nerve reactions aren't the same.
>
> Vision fails and connective tissues are impaired, all organs get smaller. Loss of cell growth causes a decline in ability of tissue repair and

may result in arthritis. Organs slowing down turn into high blood pressure, liver damage, and may bring on pernicious anemia. Organs throw off toxic conditions to the body which aren't eliminated and complications and illnesses result.

A weight increase is common—3 percent is pathological obesity. The vitamin count decreases and there is a cardiovascular change. The heart, the only organ that doesn't get smaller, usually gets larger: there's a pigmentation of tissue growth, and all this brings out heart murmurs.

Something like these changes has happened to most of the residents. How are people affected in aging and how do they react? Their children may be busily involved with their own lives. Residents in nursing homes want someone to talk to and they say, "Nobody's doing a thing for me!"

Social groups prevent their members being inactive. The doctor pinned those hips so they would be able to walk out of the room, down the hall to the social club. Because deterioration happens to their minds, they must have some outside activity besides three meals a day. We avoid loss of memory and confusion through socializing.

OBSERVATIONS OF STAFF REGARDING PHILOSOPHY AND THEORY

(Certified Occupational Therapy Assistant, COTA.) My work is exhausting physically, but it's hardest seeing the frustration and discouragement among residents and lack of cooperation among staff. But I enjoy it because the residents need me—if it weren't for them I would be leaving. I work with the employees who believe in the program, support it and even give leadership themselves; but many employees are not rehabilitation minded.

(Recreation Therapist.) Recreation is an end in itself and a tool for achieving other socially desirable goals. It can bring the withdrawn resident out of his shell. As an example, maybe a person cannot make it by himself, but pairing him with a good player to form a team, enables him to share in the fruits of victory. Hopefully, from this the resident's attention may become focused on more wholesome trains of thought. Even the antagonist will respond favorably to a diversified program or social club if the therapist can administer to different physical, intellectual and personality levels.

All of us need some sort of constructive outlet for pent-up energies and anxieties that mount up through the day: the personnel manager who goes out to the golf course after work to smack the golf ball; the assembly line worker who comes home and after supper reads; the executive who looks forward to evening woodworking in his basement.

Likewise, the resident needs the socially accepted emotional outlet of throwing darts or hitting a croquet ball, spading a garden plot or debating at a club meeting.

(Professor of Recreation.) We can measure a person's stature by what he does, the work we do being the broadest indication of what we are. Residents no longer work; they have been retired one way or the other, relieved of responsibility, relieved of authority and productivity. Things have happened in terms of their personal family life: once they were in charge of a family, now their children say, "Dad, you do such and such," giving the command.

There's probably been a financial problem, no longer an income, or a steadily deteriorating process. They've lost their verve. Bed and board is provided, and no longer are they cast out.

We build lovely Homes and congratulate ourselves on what we're doing, but our residents are not living. Living means higher goals, as in a social club.

One needs this, the esteem of his fellow man. There is no one here who hasn't lost some self-esteem, and it's pretty uncomfortable. One of the major ways we seek esteem is in work, what we show through the way we dress, the way we talk, the way we interact and the way we relate.

And one of the ways to shatter esteem is to lose identity. Hopefully, a social club gives each resident identity.

(Occupational Therapist, OT.) Possibly, the greatest problem for the aging person is the emotional adjustment to a new way of life. This change may or may not involve increasing disability. The aging process, like the growing process, always involves physical change. We would not think of allowing youth to undergo their physical changes without attention to the emotional adjustment necessitated by it.

So also with the aging; emotional adjustment must go hand in hand with changing physical conditions. The latter years of life are a time of retirement from work to lesser activity. Most important for the resident of the nursing home is the change from family life to institutional life.

The social club must help the individual to stabilize or steady his emotional feelings while he makes the transition from one way of life to another.

Obviously, activities which link family life to institutional life will make the adjustment process easier; birthday parties, dinner clubs, coffees, teas, the social club, are a homey touch in the institutional atmosphere. Work assignments, through the clubs, make the adjustment to a life of decreasing activity, less shocking.

The social club is a desirable method for stabilizing emotions. Avocational activities such as art, needlecraft, workshop, ceramics and so on, fill and replace the hours spent in former vocational pursuits.

Another problem facing residents of the county home is integration into a different type of social unit. . . . If adjustment is difficult, there is an emotional tension, and the feeling of not being needed or wanted increases.

Entrance into the nursing home life means the resident is too feeble or too ill to care for himself. Ensuing emotional problems again can block speedy social integration. In general the aged are not as attuned to change as a younger individual might be. The adjustment to many of the emotional problems of the Home can be speeded up by social integration.

The individual must be helped to adjust himself to the new group environment, and not expect the environment to be 100 percent adjusted to his personal way of life.

All activities that take the individual out of the four walls of his room will help in the understanding and acceptance of the institutional society there. Work activity in the clubs in the form of setting tables, sorting linen, serving food, and so on, are good if the individual is physically able. Activities linked to family life such as anniversaries, singalongs, religious services and dances help make the transition easier. Box socials, travel night, and games move the individual to leave his room and join the group.

(OT.) "Remotivation: work with the wounded areas of an ill mind." A patient's greatest concern is what is to be, now that he no longer has the same obligations and responsibilities as formerly. He knows his role may not be a happy one.

The patient is not merely a patient: he's a man with a special make-up, an entire human being. He's fearful and he's looking for health. Treat the individual as a heart failure or some other physical failure, and the individual is lost. We look on the individual as a whole person, and what he's made up of.

If he's motivated, he can adjust. Any impairment plays a large part in his psyche. His performance system if disrupted means he loses his ability to communicate, which will have an effect on his output. He may do much to injure himself.

His behavior pattern is disruptive: sociologically, biologically, psychologically. One of the most important values in activities is that individuals are involved. If they're always given in to, they're just going to sit back.

What Motivations and Inducements Are Employed?

These are some of the ways: reason, find a basis of interest, set the time and place, score him, give him special consideration and interest, challenge him, engage him in work, coax and wheedle, cajole, incite his curiosity, stimulate him with music, feed him, assign him the function of a greeter in the group, prod him with a chance in a drawing, invite his best friend (or ask his friend to invite him), find his interests, urge him to assist others who need him, press him to some responsibility, send him a written invitation, provoke his spirit of achievement, goad rivalry, inspire, elevate, and uplift him, amuse him, find in what he excels, give encouragement, offer to take him there, cheer him, compliment him, surprise him, boost his morale, tickle his humor.

An activity aide (AA) listed these steps for motivating residents as leaders:

1. Assign residents a job where they can be useful within their capabilities.

2. Let them know you're depending on them.

3. Let them teach one another: they're much more apt to try harder with a resident showing them how.

4. The activity aide should participate less and less.

5. Appoint a likeable resident for a leader who will work to his capacity.

    a. Assign reporters for each floor.

    b. Discuss the last issue of the Home paper. What did they like? Dislike? What shall be put in its place?

    c. Have two residents appointed, one an assistant: let the leader suggest somebody. Residents recruit.

6. Residents, just like all the rest of society, are proud of any technique for which they're given special training.

7. They should be asked to assist in something familiar to them and they learn from there on. Every Friday there's a resident conference as well as in-between conferences with problems.

8. One has to get to know the residents.

9. To develop a big group, start with a small, selective one.

(OT.) Sometimes our oldsters are opposed to card playing and dice because their religions forbade such activities. Because of this background, some of the geriatric patients at the Home and hospital don't want to play and one must have something else immediately to offer them in activity. One of the first ways of improving the atmosphere is just to sit and chat, then form little social groups doing it.

(Social Worker.) Socialization! We're concerned about the involvement of participants: what the residents have in common, their interests and former activity.

They have many different levels of participation: at the bottom level of activity is the person doing something alone. This first stage when people work on a project, all in the same room but not converging, does not necessarily stimulate socialization.

A step above is when an individual is doing something in a team relationship, maybe loom activity where two people may work together, which calls on two who have to get together on a design. A lot of socialization takes place emotionally and socially. The more alive mentally, emotionally and socially he is, the more alive he will be physically. Life will have more meaning and purposefulness. Even if he ends up in a whale of a big argument, it's stimulating, and there are ways of resolving disagreements.

A third stage is to be able to work with a team of several members. If two people have difficulty, five people will have five times as much. Thinking up ideas and getting others' viewpoints, is emotionally stimulating and provocative. Even if the feeling is a little anger, emotions need to be exercised.

A step above that is a small group of people getting together to plan something: to arrive at some decisions together; all the activity has to be mental and emotional. A committee comes together to decide on something in a high level of human intercourse. The ultimate step is when the group comes together to plan something for others, making plans which are going to affect others, which doesn't happen if they're all doing individual crafts.

The poor leader says, "It's so much easier to do it yourself." Some of the best doers aren't always the best teachers. This raises the level of the activity toward socializing. It's not the money or the project he produces: The purpose is to keep the members functioning to their highest capacity, way above doing a craft by himself.

Examine the craft he's doing to see if it can't be turned into a partner activity. Friendships form this way; some are much slower in making friends than others: perhaps find partners by drawing lots.

To come together in a larger group, four or five, is still a higher level, with residents who have to have a reason, some purpose in doing this, a problem, a routine. Perhaps the problem in the Home is how people can be informed as to a better way of delivering the mail. Possibly four or five people are involved in a problem-solving decision. Form a committee for doing something for others. The goal is the working together, which goes on in the planning.

Any program the members can plan is a better program than the one the activity aide has planned for him.

(Professor of Recreation.) Older people are sensitive to the fact that they are adults and should be treated as such, not as children. In recreation we must be sure that the program which we conduct for the older person is an adult program. It may be necessary to approach the older person much as a child might be approached, but it cannot be the same, for the older person is an adult, a peer of the leader.

In addition, he must be helped to understand that after periods of stress whether the stress is work, treatment or interpersonal relationships he needs relaxation that brings him many kinds of satisfactions.

The social group in the nursing home provides the resident with the opportunity to choose. In this program someone does something *with him* rather than *to him*. If there is no recreation program, the resident has medical treatment, boredom and little else. The social group provides activities that are non-self-centered, that help to build morale and well-being, and thus give him a better perspective, and a greater potential for responding to treatment. In the social group, the patient satisfies his need to belong; to achieve and be recognized.

This is a time when he is a person!

(Doctor.) The important thing is someone in the family who cares, but sometimes there isn't that person. Maybe just an exchange of information is important, such as a club gives. We would die if we didn't have someone to talk to. This can be a problem in an institution where staff is more than busy. Talk about the cheerful things: if you know these folks, you will find things to talk about. What did they do when they were younger? Where did they live? What were they like? What buildings are now gone? Who's married to whom? See that they get from one place to another, have a meeting to look forward to, a responsibility.

How is the patient able to transfer from bed to chair, to the social club room? How does he get about? Stand? Walk? Can he function sitting in a wheelchair, to the alternative of lying in bed? Can he dress his upper limbs, wash? How functional are the bladder and bowels? Does he feed himself? Is he oriented, confused, alert, cooperative, motivated? Does he have a sense of security, motivated to others, adjusted to life? Can he communicate in a club?

(Professor in Adult Education.) People act and respond the way we expect them to. If we feel the resident won't respond by participating in the social group, he won't. But, he will begin to take more and more responsibility as he begins to feel more important in the club. These are most important expressions: "Thank you," "If you please," "I like you," "What do *you* think?"

What is the program for? The felt needs or the unfelt needs? What "bugs" him now? When we who are in charge decide the program and define his real but unfelt needs, one may miss the boat.

One must program in the area of the resident's own felt needs and problems, then help him to discover new needs, purposes, goals, objectives.

And one doesn't move him in one fell-swoop!

If the resident finds he has to change to something new and different, it may be uncomfortable and threatening to him. There are forces that keep us the way we are. There are also driving forces that make us move and forces that keep us where we are. One of the things that drives us is pain.

Being dissatisfied, upset, or pained will cause us to begin to seek. Before any learning can take place, the resident has to want something. A driving force is a feeling of dissatisfaction with the way things are.

A good way to decrease the threat of change which the patient fears, is to talk it over. It isn't quite such an unknown then, and the change is likely to cause less turmoil.

One should make people feel wanted and needed, doing something for someone else. "If I'm not there, I'm going to be missed." One helps him discover his unique contributions to the good of the club, which is important to everyone still functioning mentally.

If one sees the resident only as a chair-sitter, chances are he'll feel that way and will never be anything else. Deep down, does one really feel he can change? What happens to the helper? "I feel good helping him: what will happen if I cure him?"

Why is it he doesn't want to participate? One has to get at the reason. Keep open to investigation. He may really want us to prove that someone cares. Maybe he really wants to do nothing. "This is what retirement means," he says.

The helper must develop a sense of awareness, a thought process that looks beyond the appearance. If we promise more than we can deliver, after a few times of broken promises, he won't try again. . . .

(AA.) Many of our geriatric patients have never known play, only work, work, work. If a person was born back in the 1890's, there weren't any playgrounds and children didn't always learn how to play. These older people didn't have our 37½ hour work week; they worked ten to fourteen hours a day. In puritan terminology, work was good, and play was evil.

Among our resident-leaders, one takes attendance, issues supplies, another runs the commissary; we have committees operating on the Co-op, the Supper Club, realities orientation, a resident handyman, cleanup committees.

We study the residents' nature and readiness in looking for leaders.

(Registered Nurse, RN.) In helping people plan social activities, the aim of the leader is to find out what the something is that each person can do well enough to be proud of, regardless of handicap or age.

Without pride of achievement and the satisfaction of creativity, life in a Home becomes tragically tarnished.

So leadership is one of the most important single factors in a successful social club. Leadership that is patient and friendly can unearth talents and stimulate skills.

Patience, understanding, and imagination frequently can build up confidence of the reluctant individual to the point where he ends up running the whole show.

(Medical Social Worker.) For many aging, passivity, self-pity or bitterness can have filled the void caused by the removal of a familiar job or release from the task of raising a family. By showing them that age isn't the worst thing that can happen to them, and that the ability to do something for themselves and others is not measured by years, we increase their feeling of usefulness.

A person can lose identity and status in the family group or community. This fact stresses the necessity for having everyone included in some activities: those in wheelchairs and bed as well as the healthy and vigorous ones. To bring them as much personal contentment as possible is frequently accomplished through social clubs which provide opportunity for creativity and achievement.

Isolation

(COTA.) When they sold her house she gave up, just like smothering a fire; a couple minutes and then she starts wandering again.

Residents often feel isolated even if they're in a room with someone else or in a room full of people, still they feel alone. We found they enjoyed tape recorders at the club meetings, playing back concerts given in the community.

(AA.) Stroke victims can speak words with their eyes. If they can point, they could be included in the activity which means a great deal to them. But it's possible for us to be too helpful. Let them live as fully as they can. The happiest people are those who touch the greatest number of points.

(Speech Therapist.) You can help residents with speech, hearing or vision problems to keep in touch through a social club. Sometimes it's hard to tell whether a person is saying "Help, help, help" or "Hello, hello, hello." What the person is saying is not as important as the fact that he or she is talking and trying to communicate. Somehow make him active with the group.

(RN.) Listening to radio or television constantly will wear people down. If all the TV sets are turned off when the club activities are going on, there is no reason for residents to stay behind. For the person who asks to go to the bathroom each time he arrives in the activity room, ask him to wait two minutes while you run an errand. Wait three minutes and see whether he hasn't become interested in the activities by then.

The behavior of confused residents often seems childish. You must be careful not to talk down to them. Praise them, but not as you would a six-year-old with an "A" on his report card. The tone of your voice is important. Even when a confused person doesn't get all your words, he can pick out the wrong inflection in your voice.

Frequently, residents will withdraw and say "no" to activities. But, after they get started, they enjoy it. A very withdrawn person wasn't going to the recreation room. She didn't want to go she kept insisting, but after she came back, she said, "It was real nice!" and told what songs were sung and how one of the residents danced. Now she's easier for us in nursing care.

(Administrator.) We try to develop socialization for residents. Bingo we find has little challenge, but can be good for regressed people. For more active people who could be given more of a challenge, it does very little. If the social club is therapeutic, we ought to ask, what is the goal? The patient should graduate from physiotherapy to an activity program.

Isolation is the lowest rung on the ladder, socializing the highest.

(AA.) If they choose not to take part in an activity, this is their prerogative. The first couple days they're in the Home they could like the leisure; but theirs is a forced leisure. They have nothing else to do, perhaps for the rest of their lives. That puts leisure in a different light. My job is to encourage them to participate in some self-satisfying activities, like joining a club in the Home. Just to care that they exist is something important to them; just to care enough to plan that club meeting, is important.

What Can They Achieve?

Communication, gregariousness, friendliness, fellowship and companionship, awareness of a commonwealth in the Home, courtesy and consideration for others, respect for community life, knowledge, good social usage, service, security, correct democratic procedures, fewer frustrations and pressures arising from infirmities, approval, belonging as part of a circle, special recognition and status as club officer or committeeman, a code of ethics, the satisfaction of righting wrongs, new social adjustment through appreciation for others, self-assurance and adequacy, improved hand motion! And fun!

THUMBNAIL SKETCHES OF TYPES OF PATIENTS

General

Before drawing up a blueprint in developing a comprehensive club program, the oldster must be introduced, studied, and understood.

Age is a time of life, the measure of our days. "The days of our years," the Bible says.

It is a time of maturity, of adulthood and adultness. It's a full growth, an age of seniority, of eldership, a deanship—yes, and a time of deprivations.

The resident may have some or many of the thumbmarks of oldness: senescence, an incurable disease, a slow decline on a downward slope, forgetfulness, delusions, bitterness, proneness to crying or quarreling, infirmities.

On the other hand, he may show only mellowness, tolerance, generosity, brightness, good cheer, and contentment.

In nursing homes, one is more likely to find the resident who may weep when one shakes hands. Another resident, without legs, sitting on his bed with prophylaxis nearby, may greet visitors gaily.

Heightened Fantasy Life, Senescence

Many a young girl thinks of herself as the daughter of the President of the United States, enjoying the fantasy of what the details of her life would be like, a daydream that can occur to her hourly, making her less glamourous life more pleasurable. All of us fantasize more or less. Many of us are constantly imagining what it would be like if. . . . Thus we're carried away to an unreal world, if only for a few moments. Residents do, too.

Sometimes residents are confused or illogical, which can be characteristic of senescence.

A double amputee who sat in her wheelchair demanded to have her shoes on the floor where her feet would be. The nurse said she insisted on seeing shoes there, wanted them tied and untied, polished, and kept in good repair.

When he came into the room of an aged resident in a county home and saw several bouquets of artificial flowers, the visitor, by way of starting a conversation, said, "Well, you have the right kind of flowers: you don't have to water them!"

The resident said, "Yes, my daughter brought me these flowers and she told me not to water them. But I watered them and they lasted *three weeks!*" A finger stuck into each vase confirmed what she had done!

In a Home where a resident was told she was not logical, she said, "Well, I never was one for joining lodges!"

An oldster, caught alone for a half hour in an elevator which stalled halfway between floors, was the concern of staff in the Home. Through the crack in the elevator door they tried to reassure her, asking if she was all right. Unconcerned, she affirmed that she was; but "I wish someone would give me a chair to sit down," she said. Afterward, when they asked why she hadn't sat down on the floor, she explained that she was afraid if she sat on the floor, she wouldn't be able to get up again. But she somehow hadn't realized the situation in which she might well have felt frantic.

Senescent patients may be convinced someone in the next room is being raped at night or that they haven't been fed for three days, or that they're being robbed of some belongings in their room. Convinced of it themselves, they often succeed in convincing gullible visitors of these delusions.

Often pathetically, a senescent resident asks the visitor to take him home to Fennimore or to some early homesite. An eighty-seven-year-old left the Home unnoticed, walking along the highway as a hitchhiker, and directed the driver who picked her up to take her to an industrial plant in the next town where she demanded her stocks in that company.

Many times oldsters find it painful to accept others occupying the house they loved, where so many years of living is still real to them. No one knew Mrs. Martin had a key to her former home or that she could leave the county home and walk downtown by herself; but she found the street and walked to the house that was once hers, now sold and occupied by a stranger. She unlocked the old familiar front door and entered, demanding to know what these people were doing here, ordering them to leave, while they in astonishment asked who *she* was!

Sometimes, when asked if they know where they are, residents name the village where they lived as young people; or a woman gives her maiden name instead of her married name, or thinks Cleveland is President, or cannot identify the year or season, much less the day of the week or the time of day.

Sometimes, they cry out for their mothers or weep for the people who need them at home!

Women often cuddle and sing lullabies to a baby doll, making the attachment a love object from which they will not be separated.

A Type of Response Technique for Reality Orientation

Twenty 8″ × 10″ cards, each labeled in large crayoned letters, are used by an OT in reality orientation with a circle of senescent patients, who don't know who they are or where they are.

The OT says, "Who is Minnie Brown?" and holds up the card with her name. Maybe she doesn't recognize it, but others in the circle of six may point her out, *"That's* Minnie Brown," and the OT pins on the card or with a string puts the card around her neck, repeating the procedure with each person in the circle.

Then the OT says, "What is *my* name?" at the same time holding up the card with her name. She asks each resident separately by standing in front of him with the card to repeat the name, looking at the card.

Next she asks, "Where are we?" showing the patient the card which reads "Golden Age Manor" and asks her to read it or reads it for her, asking her to repeat it, "Golden Age Manor."

Other questions include the following: What year is it? 19—. What season? and she lists on the card the four seasons for her to pick out the correct one. What month? It is December, but the patient says "July," and is told to look at the snow outside the window and to repeat the correct month after her. What day of the week is it? The OT again holds up a card, this one reading Tuesday. What is the date? What country is this? Who is President? What state is this? Who is governor? What county is this? What city?

No opinions or discussion is attempted. No questions go into the past; all are geared to the present. When it is apparent that these questions are too elementary, the OT asks more difficult ones regarding only the present, for example, What is the name of your nurse today? Your room number? The daily paper in this city? What did you have for breakfast?

Having the card there which they read, both seeing and hearing the answer, is a help in learning.

The method is of no use unless used daily, for instance setting aside half an hour each morning to work with six disoriented people. Good results are often shown after a few consistent sessions are followed through at the same time and place, with the same OT or other worker, and the same cards used with little variation.

Residents are told at the end of the half hour to bring something tomorrow to show and tell the group, and a woman in the group remembers to bring a bracelet which she shows and comments on.

An aphasic who had sat mumbling unrelentlessly, "dadadada-dada," was quiet and was in contact, although he couldn't speak.

Progressing, residents soon roll dice (instead of putting the dice in their mouths) in a game of coverall, even surprising the leader by being able to add the two numbers. They guess what's in the box, tell what they see in the picture in the magazine, put a wooden puzzle together; even if confused, they braid calico strips or yarn, or roll the strips into a ball, instead of pounding their table shrieking in desperation and frustration, as they once did.

Eventually, they may be brought down to the club to take some useful part there, either in preparing materials for meetings, singing, joining a group at a table game.

Physically Handicapped

There is a great cross section of physical disabilities in county homes, as probably in all nursing homes. In Wisconsin county homes, there live the uncle of a former governor, the father of a senator, several former ministers, doctors, dentists, librarians, and nurses, and other professional people, as well as illiterates. An aged gentleman in one county home receives mail correctly addressed, "Mr.," "Dr.," "Atty.," "Rev.," and "Col."

Among them too, are poets, authors, inventors, as well as the uneducated hired hands and roustabouts.

Indeed, a great composite representation of the country!

The most severely handicapped are sometimes giants in courage!

Blind, deaf, and mute, a county home resident makes dolls, a phenomenon since she has never seen a doll. She sews, threading the needle by putting the needle and thread in her mouth; no one knows how.

She wears a "Bell glove" on her left hand, a letter of the alphabet printed on each joint inside her fingers. She spells out words by pointing to each letter on the glove and her "conversationalist" spells out words to her, again touching the letters on the glove.

The new manager in the Home was astounded when he and his wife, enjoying a walk one evening on the grounds of the Home, were met by the blind deaf-mute who "recognized" his presence. She touched his arm and pointed above them to his apartment under which they were standing, then smilingly pointed to him. Another kind of Helen Keller! Someone had "told" her the news of the new manager's arrival and the location of his apartment and she was aware of the exact spot where they stood. He never ceased to marvel at what had happened in this mysterious communication!

The writer watched a fifty-year-old CP patient, born with no use of her arms, pick up a needle from the floor with the bare toes of her left foot, and thread it with the toes of her right foot. She laboriously and incredibly threaded the needle with her feet! She could pick up a pencil with her toes and write her name.

The visitor, not understanding what the patient was saying, put her hand on the patient's forehead and found it wet with perspiration from the effort she was making. What a resolute, undaunted invincibility!

Another CP patient, born without use of his arms or legs, invented a band to go around his head, a small stick attached on the front, with which he strikes the keys of the typewriter by bowing his head and hitting each key. He uses an electric typewriter, moving the carriage to the next line by the touch of the button and in this way types his poetry.

Once the writer watched him painting, a paintbrush taking the place of the stick, and the paper cup with poster paint attached to his wheelchair arm. Someone had drawn the outline of an enormous flower in black lines on a large paper on the table before him. He was filling in the flower with color, a decoration for the walls of a recreation room, the setting for a monthly dance.

With the stick device, he has put together a two-hundred-fifty-piece jigsaw puzzle. One at a time, he turns the pages of a magazine. What a plucky titan, overcoming the "impossible"!

A man paints, though paralyzed except for a few muscles in two fingers and some shoulder muscles, legs strapped to the wheelchair, his hands in wrist-to-palm braces. He began with pen and ink drawings of tigers in various jungle settings.

Awarded third prize in a state newspaper contest for one of his drawings, he was given some instruction by a local artist who came to the Home to help him work in oils. He now does portraits of the doctor, the doctor's wife and children, working from snapshots. He also excels in floral bouquet paintings, for which he gets $75. He plays pool from a wheelchair, this man who "likes to kid and tease."

So it would seem one ought not to give up on these people!

To quote Thomas Jefferson, mastermind in blueprints of governments: "A mind always employed is always happy. This is the true secret, the grand recipe for felicity. The idle are the only wretched."

VALUES OF THE CLUB AND ADAPTIVE ACTIVITIES

WHAT COULD BE VALUES OF THE CLUB TO THE ADMINISTRATION? Residents do less complaining, disputation, self-pitying, and weeping, and actually need less drugs and medicine if they are involved in something to live for, convinced they can still be useful and are still needed. Residents, through constructive activity, require less costly care.

WHAT COULD BE VALUES OF THE CLUB TO THE HANDICAPPED RESIDENT? The leader finds what the resident can do and plans programs accordingly.

1. Activities that help the handicapped resident function physically. *The resident who has the use of only one hand* can make seed pictures, roll dice, work on puzzles, paint, draw and color, embroider, keep scores and play cards, type, fringe, work with clay and plasticine, glaze pottery, count out (markers for guessing, brochures, material for games in the club), read, cook, pour tea, serve as receptionist, do copper tooling on plaques, paste (scrapbooks, greeting cards), conduct paper and pencil games, take care of library shelves and magazine racks, serve as a club officer. What other ideas can the residents add?

Semiambulatory or wheelchair residents can take part in wheelchair square dancing; water plants; take care of aquariums; feed the birds; fold napkins; arrange flowers; prepare club games; sew on name tags; mend; tie flies; do carpentry; sand furniture; work on assembly kits; carve and whittle; tear discarded sheets for bandages; gimp lacing (moccasins, prepared wallets, comb cases, link belts); play cards, Chinese checkers, shuffleboard, darts, ring toss, horseshoes; bowl, and serve on committees or as a club officer. What other ideas?

The *visually handicapped* fray luncheon mats and napkins, do freeform ceramics, work on tile, make tapes in recordings, sand and stain wood, make pomanders, work on hobby looms, tear rags for rugs, knit washcloths, take part in special games, type, fold *Readers' Digest* into decorations (see Appendix), braid, play a familiar musical instruments, snip nylon or dacron for stuffing, polish and wax, sort buttons, sing, play in the rhythm band, do oral quizzes, serve as club president or on certain club committees. What else can be added?

The *hard-of-hearing*. The leader can find the deaf impossible to reach in the social setting of a club because they don't hear and they simply walk out. Sometimes these lonely and isolated people must work alone, but they should never be ignored. Suitable activities could be found for them while the rest of the club members are socializing.

They can weave, play table games, do handiwork, knit, crochet, tat, make seasonal decorations, sew on name tags, make paper flowers (or any of the above crafts), play dice games, guess what's in the box, walk and escort others, deliver the mail, paint outdoor furniture, build birdhouses or feeders, make children's educational toys, refinish and repair toys, make whistles, cane, weave willow baskets, garden, edit and write, prepare material for club meetings, take care of club correspondence.

Senescents play simple roll-the-dice games (help-your-neighbor, coverall), guess the card (red or black), sing, tear paper for paper-mache, toss beanbags, play beachball, toss Turkish towels to one another, rope rings or horseshoes, walk, picnic, braid, wind yarn or cord into a ball. Others?

Aphasics can play dice games (chuck-a-luck) or often any table game they knew before their aphasia, toss an object, sing, take part in any of the above games or crafts depending on their other abilities. An aphasic can enjoy attending the club meetings; even though he does not speak, he can hear and understand what is said and can often take part.

2. Activities that help the handicapped resident do more for others. *In the Home.* Read to others, visit, play games with roombound or bed patients, escort others, prepare crafts and games for others, write letters, give manicures, brush hair, distribute hymnals, help with bingo games, serve on cleanup committees, greet new residents and adopt them, distribute the newsletter, do hand laundry for those unable.

In the community. Make puppets, aprons, cushions for Headstart; give holiday parties for children; mount crossword puzzles on cards for book cart distribution; repair wooden toys; make puzzles, tops, and educational toys.

WHAT FACILITIES ARE AVAILABLE, FEASIBLE, DESIRABLE? The proper facilities are important.

1. Large room, properly heated and ventilated (with nearby toilets) accessible area for wheelchair square dancing, club meetings, resident council, discussion groups, sing-a-longs, talent shows.

2. Large room with wheelchair-high tables. Play table games, make layettes and dresses for needy children, cut out quilting blocks, make lap robes, fold bandages, tear discarded sheets for bandages and roll them, cut out new dresses for themselves, play bingo and bunco, conduct mixed card parties, and so on.

3. Large room with wheelchair-high tables and $100 in equipment and supplies (could reach fifty residents daily in a Service Club or Pin Money Club). Scissors, sewing basket supplies, water colors and brushes, poster paint, tile, Elmer's glue, construction paper, frame loom, copper tooling kits, carpentry kits, leather kits, lace doilies, tin foil, cards and dice, knitting needles, crochet hooks and cotton, six subscriptions to *Weekly Reader* and *Good Old Days*, goldfish, scrapbooks, beachball, rubber horseshoes, portable bowling game, simple manicure sets (no scissors), cards and dice, anagrams, Flinch, Old Maid, Chinese checkers, stamped embroidery projects, cord, balloons, and so forth.

Acceptable items at no cost (often donated through families, employees, or volunteers): clean rags and sheets, cardboard, Talking Books (free except for return postage), free movie film, discarded hats, artificial flowers, greeting cards, magazines for folding decorations, scrap lumber, discarded nylons, beanbags and homemade beanbag board, used table games, costumes, donated make-up kits.

4. **Large room and $200.** Viewmaster or second-hand slide projector, slides for discussion groups, small kiln, greenware and equipment, hibachi, shuffleboard equipment, second-hand pool table, small aquarium.

5. **Large room and $300.** Second-hand 16-mm movie projector (free films are available and are useful in discussions).

6. **Large room with sink, stove, refrigerator, tables, sufficient and suitable pots and pans for cooking.** A cooking class uses quick mixes and ingredients for fondue, candy making, popcorn popping, frosting holiday cookies, making their own birthday cakes, making cookies to sell at cost in the Home.

7. **A Home with paved walks.** Bird watchers, outside games, ball toss, Nature Study Club. Paved areas: table games, picnics, cookouts, circle games, relays, horseracing games, resident parades and talent shows.

8. **A Home with a suitable room for carpentry and $170.** Basic carpentry equipment—sander, Demel saw with a guard, work table, vices, T square, hammer, screwdriver; steel wool, caning material (only if residents are already proficient); a work table and lamp for former engraver, watch repairman, craftsman.

The program ideas of this book are designed primarily to help residents function socially, but also to develop satisfying skills and interests.

PART III

HOW TO LEAD A CLUB

The Leader
  Do's and Don'ts for the Leader
  How to Listen
  Interviewing the Residents (Patients)

Before the First Meeting

The First Meeting
  Ways of Opening Club Meetings
  Procedures
  Program Brochure
  Ways of "Beefing Up" Resident Participation
  Other Ways of Later "Beefing Up" Club Attendance
  A Type of Discussion Technique

Records

Teaching Report
  Comments of a Resident Leader

THE LEADER

We assume that every club needs a leader.

It is not necessary for that leader to be male or to be an authority on the topics discussed in the club; he often asks the questions and learns from residents. It is not necessary for him to be an expert on carpentry or any of the specialities or skills suggested for club projects. No one can be an authority on everything, nor is it advisable. The club is based on the notion of sharing experiences and resources.

The leader is there to see that the club grows and flourishes, that the group works as smoothly as possible, to help it with new interests, to direct it in meeting happily and on schedule, to provide recreation materials and equipment along with resource material for study, and to assign more and more responsibility to individuals as they are able.

In small but important ways, the club draws on the knowledge and experience of its members. Suppose no one knows the answer in the discussion group, or in the quizzes and games, or on the field trip! Life is full of unanswered questions, some of which are never solved! It may help residents relax and feel close to the leader who says, "I don't know. Who knows? Who'll report on it next time?" If he must, the leader looks it up himself before the next meeting.

The tactful leader hands a club member the printed quiz asking him to conduct the activity with the group, instead of posing as the all-knowing authority, an attitude which immediately humiliates the residents and builds up a wall between the leader and them.

The wise leader uses few prizes; people in hospitals and Homes should not be "put on the spot" in competition since they are no longer equally capable. With much more satisfaction, they may occasionally enjoy drawing for prizes and playing games of chance.

The resourceful leader does not overlook the use of free films

51

or short articles obtained from almost any college or community publication, to stimulate interest and discussion. Some agencies have generous libraries of documentary films available for the asking: oil companies, American Red Cross, the army, professional sport leagues, travel agencies, public libraries and universities.

There are many more sources than those given in the appendices, but those listed have been recommended by county home activity personnel. Many federal departments, like the Department of Agriculture or State Departments of Natural Resources, supply fine slides, records, and exhibits, as well as short films.

Do's and Don'ts for the Leader

Do's

1. Be friendly, be a good listener.
2. See that policies and rules of the Home are observed.
3. Make your appearances interesting—see if they notice you're wearing your spectacles upside down, a jacket on backward, a flag in your hair because it's the Fourth of July.
4. Be prompt in starting the program and finish on time.
5. Withhold all criticism of the Home, unless they have constructive criticisms to make.
6. Act within good taste.
7. Cooperate with other departments in the Home.
8. Support and defend each resident member.
9. Refer all requests to the proper department in the Home.
10. Maintain poise in case of seizures, illness, and accidents.
11. Maintain a sense of humor.
12. Maintain proper respect toward each resident.
13. Maintain proper reaction to residents' wants and needs.
14. Serve as moderator, teacher, friend.
15. Act sincerely.
16. Always notify nurse on duty of residents escorted to the club and taken from the ward.
17. Group discussion with residents should be of a general nature, with nothing personal or embarrassing asked; be tactful.
18. Encourage residents who do not seem to be actively participating; however, don't be insistent.
19. Before the meeting, see that committees have performed

their work; see that assignments are going smoothly. Direct duties to others, when necessary and possible.

20. Act between the Home and community when local resources can offer trips, exchange club meetings or friends, provide information and materials for club use.

Don'ts

1. Don't start with an activity which is too difficult for the group to do physically or which they don't understand.

2. Avoid making announcements in a large group without a mike; avoid giving club members close work which requires good eyesight or moving and reacting quickly.

3. Never make promises that can't be kept.

4. Don't argue, talk too much, or insist on having the last word; wait for residents to respond, and urge them to dominate the club, not you.

5. Don't allow residents to dwell on their illnesses.

6. Don't give all the attention to one or a chosen few.

7. Don't discuss residents or staff in critical ways.

8. Don't set meeting time and dates which conflict with schedules on the ward, since the care of the residents is of first consideration.

9. Don't make newspaper appeals for supplies, equipment, or volunteers for the Home or hospital without the permission of the administrator.

10. Don't be impatient with residents' mistakes or lack of initiative and motivation.

11. Don't use a patronizing tone or attitude nor speak to residents as if they were children.

12. Don't let the new member feel ill at ease, but introduce him to the other members.

13. Don't try to hurry residents; learn to work at their speed.

14. Don't emphasize controversial differences, such as religion and politics. Discussion material on these subjects as suggested in social club programs is introduced with caution!

These do's and don'ts are derived from common sense and experience but also reflect an appreciation of principles and theories regarding human behavior and association.

How to Listen

Often, more than anything else, the resident needs a good listener; how can one develop a good social club program without knowing the resident and how can one get to know him without listening?

The following "Ten Commandments for Good Listening"[3] can be applied:

1. *Stop talking!* You cannot listen if you are talking. Polonius, in *Hamlet,* said, "Give every man thine ear but few thy voice."

2. *Put the talker at ease.* Help him feel that he is free to talk.

3. *Show him that you want to listen.* Look and act interested. Do not read your mail while he talks. Listen to understand rather than reply.

4. *Remove distractions.* Don't doodle, tap, or shuffle papers. Will it be quieter if you shut the door?

5. *Empathize with him.* Try to put yourself in his place so that you can understand his point of view.

6. *Be patient.* Allow plenty of time. Do not interrupt him. Don't start for the door or walk away while he is talking.

7. *Hold your temper.* An angry man gets the wrong meaning from words.

8. *Go easy on argument and criticism.* This puts him on the defensive. He may "clam up" or get angry. Do not argue, for "even if you win, you lose."

9. *Ask questions.* This encourages him and shows that you are listening. Also, it helps to develop points further.

10. *Stop talking!* This is first and last because all other commandments depend on it. You can't do a good listening job while you are talking. Nature gave man two ears but only one tongue, a gentle hint that he should listen more than he talks.

Interviewing the Residents (Patients)

Interviewing for various purposes goes on continuously in hospitals and Homes. The group leader conducts interviews to make the club most valuable to the resident.

[3] From Davis, Keith: *Human Relations at Work.* 1967. Used with permission of McGraw-Hill Book Company.

The interviewer extends his hand but lets the resident squeeze it: it is often too painful for arthritics to be touched. They introduce themselves if they are not acquainted.

The interviewer avoids asking how the patient is; instead, he can say "It's nice to see you." Easy questions and comments follow, admiring what the patient is wearing, commenting on what he is reading, pictures of the family on the dresser, a fancy bedspread, an antique watch, a view from the window, and so forth.

The interviewer can assess the resident's sight, hearing, difficulty in speaking, use of one or both hands, or whether or not he's ambulatory if a walker or wheelchair is in evidence. He can decide whether or not he could join a club with his particular physical disabilities. From the conversation, he learns whether or not the patient is alert, delusional, fearful, or vigorous and active.

The interviewer can decide on the type of club the individual could enjoy by asking other questions. Probably, the resident won't know what the interviewer is talking about if he asks about hobbies, but he responds to such questions as does he speak another language, where did he live, what was his work, does he play cards or other table games, does he like movies, did he belong to any clubs, has he traveled, does he like gardening or singing, does he do carpentry, did he have a pet, does he like sports?

The interviewer may observe that there are many Norwegians in the Home, so he feels a Norwegian Club would be feasible and worthwhile. There are some residents with time on their hands who are capable, so he concludes that a Service Club would be easy to start; or there are numbers of idle, lonely men and the first need could be to start a Men's or Old-Timers Club.

Wisely, he does not ask if they would like to join a club, because too often he knows what the answer would be. Probably, he selects a few friendly, easy to reach residents who can hear and begins with this nucleus as a committee to talk over plans and decide on a few things before inviting large numbers into the group.

A list is made of residents who agree to come to the meeting and arrangements are made to escort wheelchair residents to reach the meeting on time. More able residents can be assigned to this task.

BEFORE THE FIRST MEETING

The leader will want to read all the activities described in the book under the club headings in order to select from the resources suggested. Perhaps he will find something appropriately seasonal in the club material, activities residents will be sure to like doing, checking on resources available. Seasonal activities must be culled from the materials, since they do not appear in a sequential order.

If the game or activity is new, the leader will want to try it with a few residents first, not only to help the leader and resident master it, but to make helpers out of some of the residents.

A good way of discovering people's aptitudes and physical abilities is to assign each to a duty in advance of the first meeting. Someone will register each arrival at the door, make name identification tags which they pin on those attending; someone will arrange the chairs—a crescent shape may be a good way of starting if residents must read the leader's lips. Other residents can be asked in advance to help at the elevators, distribute ashtrays, songsheets, materials, and supplies.

This gives the leader an opportunity of getting to know what the resident is able to do.

THE FIRST MEETING

Everyone is introduced. Pinning on a name tag is a help.

A song is sung, or clapped to. Roll can be taken by special responses such as naming a flower, giving the month in which the individual was born and so on.

The following suggestions could be considered for discussion: The group may consider whether they would like having a study club or some other interest club, or a social club. They can decide on a name for the club or feel that this should be tabled. The list of clubs described in this book could be suggested and discussed.

They could contribute aims and goals and determine how long the meetings should last, whether or not roll is taken, what committees were to be appointed, whether or not a business meeting is important.

They decide as to the size of the club and how new members

will be invited to join. They give opinions on adopting service projects in the Home: visiting the roombound, assisting staff, escorting, working with those less able, or taking on community projects.

Residents could be asked each time to assume some responsibility for part of the next program. What will the program be? A roster could be made of names and duties.

With resident help and through Chamber of Commerce and local newspapers, lists can be made of community agencies, local citizens, or clubs for demonstrations, tours, exhibits, talks, and discussions in the future.

If no one seems suitable as chairman, probably no one should be elected or appointed. Without electing officers, the most qualified members first serve on committees. Temporary officers can be appointed by the leader if he feels he knows the group well enough. Officers must be as dependable and efficient as possible, for the success of the club could rely on them. Responsibilities in club duties can be a growth experience for residents.

Ways of Opening Club Meetings

There are several approaches to opening the meeting.

1. When residents arrive, the leader furnishes some music and asks members to guess the song title or dance or keep time to the music.

2. He has a surprise visitor greet them.

3. He announces a new book or magazine for their use.

4. He announces winners in a recent tournament or lists the patients (from the nurses' office) who are now doing more for themselves: using a hand, getting out of their rooms, dressing by themselves, writing their own letters.

5. He announces a birthday, anniversary, employee's arrival or departure, volunteer recognition, and suggests ways residents could take part in the planning of a tea or party.

6. He reads a short piece of news, amusing or of special interest.

7. He passes around harmonicas, tonettes, combs for individual musicians to perform for the group.

8. He passes around a surprise or conducts a grab bag.

9. He directs a few simple exercises to music.

10. He contacts everyone with a guessing game: guess what time my watch says, what color my thumbnail is painted (green), how much I paid for my glasses, the picture pasted at the bottom of this paper bag, where I've hidden the thimble (in my hair), the unusual bird that so-and-so saw this morning, who the next person will be coming in the door, what the menu (temperature, census) was a year ago today.

He announces the winner at the end of the meeting.

11. He gives out bow ties and hair ribbons when members arrive. He sets up card tables in the middle of the room with materials for making paper bow ties in various colors of crepe paper (scissors, wire or tape to wind at the center). Volunteers and the leader start making these items to pin on residents, who can also be asked to help when they arrive.

12. He shows and perhaps presents residents with pictures of themselves.

13. He has a surprise cup of coffee or a glass of Kool-Aid®, cookie, or mint, not as the come-on but as an occasional treat.

Later, when the club is established, refreshments are not served or favors delivered to people who can leave their rooms but who refuse to come to meetings.

A successful club begins its meetings on time. Business meetings are well organized and kept short. Members take turns as club officers and committeemen, as far as they're able.

Procedures

Simple Outline for Conducting a Club Meeting

The outline below is a helpful form to follow.

1. The meeting of the ———— Club please come to order. (Roll call by secretary and responses by members.)

2. Will the secretary please read the minutes of the last meeting? You have heard the minutes, are there any corrections? If not, they stand approved as read. (Use gavel.) (Presentation of new members, if any.)

3. Is there any old business to come before the club?

4. Is there any new business to come before the club?

5. Will the treasurer please read his report? Are there any corrections? If not, it is approved as read. (Use gavel.)

6. Will the chairman of the ———— Committee read his report? You have heard the report. Are there any corrections? Any discussions? If not, it stands approved as read. (Use gavel.)

7. The Program Committee will now present the program for this evening. After the program, the meeting is turned back to the president, chairman, or leader.

8. A motion for adjournment is now in order. (Use gavel.)

How to Make a Motion

After someone makes a motion, the leader or chairman says, "Will someone please second that motion?" After the motion has been seconded, the leader or president says, "A motion was made by ———— and seconded by ———— that ————. Is there any discussion on the motion? Are you ready for this question? All in favor, please signify by saying "Aye," opposed "No." Announce the result. (Use gavel.)

When a member wishes to speak, he should address the chairman as "Mr. Chairman" or the president as "Mrs. President." The member must be recognized by the chairman or the president before he may proceed with his remarks.

Program Brochure

A program brochure for the year can be drawn up after the club has become established. Mimeographed and stapled, ready to be distributed to each member, it could include the creed, club song, calendar of events (with names of hostesses and project leaders), a list of advisors involved in the club leadership, a page for community phone numbers needed in club work, and other items of interest.

Of course, some clubs will not want such formal organization.

Ways of "Beefing Up" Resident Participation (in the Club as Well as Outside Club Meetings)

An aim of the leader is to penetrate the withdrawal pattern into which many residents retreat. Frequently, he asks the resident for opinions and suggestions, no matter how minor. The leader uses any help the resident offers and adopts his ideas if possible, thus demonstrating that he can be a constructive assistant.

The leader offers program varieties in each meeting for handicapped people so they can participate whether blind, in wheelchairs, or mute. Even though the deaf are often unable to socialize, there can be a table or area where they work at something by themselves during the business meetings and discussion time.

As individuals show abilities, the leader assigns them duties, such as greeters; MC's introducing people on the program or new members; a song leader or discussion leader; publicity agent through bulletin boards and PA systems; recorder of birthdays; someone responsible for contacting absentees; a correspondent writing news of the program for the Home or city newspapers; an assistant finding pages in the songbook for those unable; server of refreshments; writer of get-well cards and thank-you notes; distributor and collector of materials such as paper and pencils.

Other Ways of Later "Beefing Up" Club Attendance

Several possibilities exist, and are described below.

1. Teenage hostesses make room to room visits, urging attendance. Or, before the club meeting, hostesses with slips of paper get as many signatures as possible of residents with blue eyes, those under a certain age, people getting mail today, all plumbers (or any skill or profession), people who can swim. One category is taken and the list read at the meeting.

2. Before the meeting, a decorated cart publicizing the meeting is taken into the wards or into the rooms, containing something to examine which somehow amuses or attracts attention.

3. A resident in costume wearing a poster-announcement goes into each room, personally inviting patients.

4. On a pleasant day, the leader announces the meeting place on the lawn or patio.

5. He announces that someone will read palms; that someone will report on an exhibit at the county fair, community fall festival, or local church bazaar; that a local "golden age" group will be there to join them; that a tape recording will be made of their voices; that there will be a drawing and surprise giveaway, such as a newly decorated hat; that they can watch an artist sketch;

that a new greeting card or a flower will be given those attending; that someone will sing a song, do a trick.

6. He announces that mail will be distributed at the end of the meeting; that someone there will later repair their shoes, give haircuts, and so on; that someone after the meeting will type a letter for them.

7. He announces that they are needed, perhaps on a project for a needy child.

8. He makes announcements on the public address system as reminders.

9. He asks residents to wear something "old-fashioned" or self-designed.

It is safe to say that if there is activity, residents will want to be included; if acquaintances are having fun, no one wants to be omitted.

A Type of Discussion Technique

Residents need a kind of *caring urgency* from their leaders, leaders who will keep working in their conviction of being able to do more. With feelings of success, they will start to realize they can be responsible people, not just conformists.

When a resident begins to depend on memory rather than on thinking for himself, he fails to find identity in the world and his place in it.

Ways should be adapted to involve leaders with individual residents, as this Home directs:

> One method used is that of the group meeting once a day or at least three times a week. The leader gets his class in a circle or crescent, as he prefers, for a discussion of something of interest to them, something happening in the Home or a news event such as a local corn roast or a personal topic like making friends. In a warm and interested but uncritical way, he urges residents to think, to talk together and to listen to each other.
>
> For instance, the leader can describe a situation: "You're locked out of your house in a blizzard; it's getting dark and colder. What would you do?"
>
> The residents start exploring this probability. "I would call a neighbor." "Suppose you didn't have one." "I would turn on the porch light." "Suppose no one can see this." "I'd turn it on and off now and

then." "What precautions would you take against frostbite?" "I'd sweep the snow to keep warm." "Beat on a tin can." "Try to break a window." "Crawl in a shed."

Residents begin to think about this realistically; the leader is talking about things that demand their reasoning. Significantly, they go from one question to the next, thinking things out.

The shy resident sometimes becomes a leader in the discussion, while the resident who led at the start might be less talkative and begin to speak more thoughtfully.

Some Homes have found oldsters becoming more social, more confident, less destructive and in better contact. Sometimes residents so absorbed in fantasy or so buried inside themselves they were mute, speak up for the first time in this type of discussion.

We can begin to feel, "This works: I'm really improving with these residents. Basically, it's a matter of liking them and wanting to help, not a matter of spending more money, but of spending time and accomplishing response.

"We must be willing to provide the kind of Homes to help them live in," one of them says. "If we don't do this, we are going to be paying heavily for the failures: the regressed, the weepers, the senescent."

RECORDS (THREE TYPES)

There are three types of records to be kept.

1. Club leaders should keep a record of the club and if possible an individual record of each member. Since there will probably be no stenographer, dictaphone, or tape recorders available, records will be handwritten. They should be simple and easy to keep.

Every club should have a record form, whether printed or not. The outline may not necessarily be as complete as the one which follows, perhaps a 6" × 8" card for each member:

Name:	Age:
Religion:	Sex:
Skill and interests:	Occupation:
Running narrative:	

5-6-72 Today she engaged in activity for the first time: she sang a song by herself.

2. A list of all residents' names is typed down the left-hand column of a long sheet of paper; 20 vertical lines are drawn, the date at the top of each line. A check mark shows each resident in

attendance, or each resident reached in his room by efforts of club members through room visits, reading and writing letters for others, remembrances, refreshments served those unable to attend.

3. Another type of record could help the leader assess himself, again with a chart of club members' names.[4]

The club meeting helped them be more independent.

They learned a new skill.

They made new friends.

They understood themselves better.

They taught one another.

The activities gave them more self-assurance.

They made acquaintances in the community.

The program was directed to residents' interests.

It helped them feel they belonged to a group.

It helped give them something to look forward to.

It held their interest.

It helped develop feelings of self-worth.

A new interest, game, stunt, hobby was introduced.

The activities were the choice of the residents.

The leader will want to check to see if each member took part in some way and determine what he can be given next time. He will be sure that at this meeting, planning was done for the next meeting. Residents will be taught to be reliable, to remember.

He will work toward community involvement with the group.

TEACHING REPORT: A NARRATIVE ON THE FIRST TWO SESSIONS OF A SOCIAL GROUP

Place: ——— County Home
Group Leader: Miss ———, Social Service Department

Date: June 14, 19—

Goals:
    The purpose of this group is to help members spend their leisure hours more constructively through activities and discussions instead of sitting and rocking, and to develop a sense of identity and belonging

---

[4] Permission granted to use material from *Senior Age Clubs, A Guideline of Creative Group Activity for the Older Citizen,* Jerome Kaplan, editor-in-chief of *The Gerontologist.*

which they lack. Before the group was formed, I announced its purpose in their terms: "plan and do things together," strictly a social group.

Group Composition:

Members have similar alertness, intellectual ability and physical conditions and walk alone or with walkers.

Process of Group Formation:

Around 9 A.M. ———— (a summer employee in the OT department who has volunteered to help recruit group members) and I began to visit each room asking the prospective members to come to a group meeting. Previously I went around to become acquainted with the residents, and at the time I talked individually about the formation of a social group, an idea which many of the residents liked. By 9:20 about fourteen members gathered in the west lounge of the second floor. Mrs. ———— asked me about the purpose of this group and I answered, "This is a social group and we want to plan and do things together." She said, "Good!"

I asked the members whether they would like to elect a president and a secretary by popular vote. When they all agreed to do so, I distributed the pieces of paper for ballots. When I handed out the paper, many of the members said they wanted Mrs. ———— as their president.

Mrs. ———— was elected as president with nine votes out of fourteen, seemed to be pleased and thanked the group. Later I asked her to help elect a secretary, which she did willingly, handing out the pieces of paper and gathering the ballots.

Mrs. ———— suggested that they orally nominate the candidates for secretary and then vote. Members also agreed to this, nominating ———— and ———— as candidates. Mrs. ———— was elected with seven votes. Mrs. ———— getting only four votes, seemed to be uncomfortable and said that she did not want to be elected because she had many things to do.

Mrs. ———— became very hostile and refused to vote. She said that there is no one that she wanted to vote for; angry because no one nominated her, she cast a blank ballot. Except for this incident, the election was a gay activity. After the election, we discussed having a name for this group. One member suggested the name should be something like the "Happy-go-lucky" club, and everyone laughed at this jolly name.

It was nearly 10 A.M. at which time some of the members were to take a bath so we decided to think of the name at the next meeting, June 16, and adjourned.

After the group was dismissed, some of the members remained and asked ———— to play some hymns for them and we all sang together for about ten minutes. Later I congratulated Mrs. ———, the president, and Mrs. ———, the secretary, for their elections. They seemed happy and said they thought the group was going to be fun.

Mrs. ——— mentioned, "Some of the members will not come regularly but most of them will come and enjoy the group meeting."

Club Meeting
Date: June 16, 19—

Group Process:

When I entered the west lounge of the second floor at 3 P.M. most of the members were sitting and waiting for me. It was 89 degrees, humid and hot, with no breeze at all; everyone seemed tired and sleepy.

I reminded the group that we were going to discuss a name we wanted for our group and asked them to give as many names as possible so that members could choose the best one. "Happy-go-lucky," "Pleasant Club," "Golden Bees Club," and the "Talking Bees" were given. One member named one that sounded just "dandy." Everyone smiled at this comment, Mrs. ——— suggesting that the name should be voted on by raising hands to which all the members agreed.

The "Golden Bees Club" was selected as the name of the group.

Then I suggested that since we do not know each other very well, it would be very helpful if each one introduced herself and told where she was born, the school she attended, her work before coming here, etc.

——— asked me to start, so I spelled my name, told what schools I attended and how I had come to know about the ——— County Home, Forest Lawn. One member asked me whether I remembered the war and where my parents and I were during the war, etc. I explained I remembered only too well; a machine gun bullet had missed me by about 20′. They were interested in what I said and asked many questions about the war.

Mrs. ——— sat next to me and I asked her to tell her story. She gave the full story about schools she attended, activities she liked most, teachers she was fond of, how she met her first husband and how many dates they had. It took her nearly ten minutes to finish her story. The third was Mrs. ———, who did the same thing and took nearly ten minutes too. But this time the rest of the group members got irritated about the fact that these two members took so much time.

I did not intervene but waited until some members exerted group pressure to make the stories short.

After Mrs. ——— suggested that we make the self-introductions shorter, everyone agreed, saying that they would not be able to finish before supper if everyone spent ten minutes on their story.

Mrs. ——— said she would like to know more about other countries. Mrs. ——— and others agreed to this and asked me to bring some pictures of foreign countries. I promised them I would bring some pictures to the next club meeting. Just before the meeting adjourned, Mrs. ——— casually mentioned how Miss ——— bothered her. With this signal, almost all of the members then started to illustrate how she behaved and bothered them. Two or more of the members expressed utter hostility toward her, and the conversation became very lively.

I waited for a while, not wanting them to develop a habit of gossiping with others during the group meeting, but I did not want to close a means of channeling bottled-up hostilities. After a while I called their attention to the matter that there could be all kinds of people in the large institutions like this county home and it might not be practical to expect everyone to be nice around here. I also pointed out the fact that all of the members present here have lived happily with their families until they came to the Home, but ——— had lived in this institution ever since she was 16 years of age and she really did not have a chance to live a normal family life.

They agreed, saying, "That is true!" They became thoughtfully quiet. Mrs. ——— said, "I guess we have to learn to live with all kinds of people." Some of them sighed, agreeing, "I guess so."

When we adjourned the meeting, almost everyone said that it was sticky, a hot afternoon, and they were very tired.

Mrs. ———, the president, asked me who would arrange for food for picnics if they would decide to go on a picnic. I said I did not know exactly but added that this might be a matter to take up with either Mrs. ——— or Mrs. ———, that if we planned a half-day picnic, we might not need to take lunch with us. For refreshments, we also have to talk with (charge nurse or superintendent). The members agreed.

COMMENTS OF A RESIDENT LEADER

While we were cutting off overalls and hemming them for the men on the farm, we talked about forming the Merrymakers Club. We started it with just six residents who decided to meet regularly for some fun. Now we have thirty-five, most of them in wheelchairs, but they look forward to it. It's been the central point of social life in the Home, getting to know one another, where we would just have stayed in our rooms or gone our own separate ways before!

But we couldn't have done it without an activity aide! We started with the $7 we got for a rug. The memorials given to the club by friends are wonderful! We bought all the card tables, the organ, piano, clock, flag, birdbath, and now we're talking about building a patio, winterized so we can keep a pool table there.

We started singing; our activity aide was a singer; we had a piano which we didn't use because it was so out of tune.

Gradually we attracted more people. We always met evenings, 6-7:30 P.M. We started by electing officers right away; they elected me president and another secretary-treasurer who had had church experience in that office. We call roll so people will learn one another's names.

We plan the program and always try to have something different, riddles and stunts and games we made up. We always have "guess-what's-in-the-box" and even confused people have done it for so many times, they guess too. We plan games everyone can play.

We begin by singing the club song I made up; I used to make up rhymes about people who were new which was fun. We have discussions and vote from the floor. Our activity aide helps settle any problems we have in the club.

We residents plan programs, decide on refreshments and often spend the afternoons making sandwiches or doing other preparations for the evening meeting.

We play a game with numbers adding up to 7 (6 and 1, 2 and 5, 3 and 4). One through six is numbered on each of the tile blocks on the floor. Two dice are rolled and are scored if one or both stop on the clock, adding up the right combination to make 7.

Our newest project is Rolling Wheels, helping thirteen hundred retarded children and adults in getting wheelchairs by contributing used postage stamps for us to sell.

What I like to see in our Home is the spirit of unity, people pleased to help; thirty-five attend out of sixty-five in the Home. We visit those in their rooms who can't attend.

We composed a song: (Tune: *Ach du Lieber Augustin*).

I.

We are the Pleasant Acres Merry Makers, Merry Makers.
We live at Pleasant Acres, our group is OK.
We play games and sing songs
And have fun that's not wrong.
We try to help each other, be happy each day.

II.

The more we get together, together, together
The more we get together the happier we'll be.
For your friends are my friends
And my friends are your friends,
The more we get together the happier we'll be.

III.

The more we work together, together, together
The more we work together the happier we'll be.
For your club is my club
And my club is your club,
The more we work together the happier we'll be.

PART IV

SAMPLE PROGRAMS

Old-Timers Club

Homemakers Club

Automobile Club

Men's Club

Travel Club

Hobby Club

Garden Club

Fin and Feather Club

Nature Club

OLD-TIMERS CLUB

Let me grow lovely, growing old—
So many fine things do:
Laces and ivory and gold,
And silks need not be new;
And there is healing in old trees,
Old streets a glamour hold;
Why may not I, as well as these,
Grow lovely growing old?

—Submitted

Goals

Every leader must be resourceful in finding and using program ideas. Essential is his ability to relate patiently and with understanding and adaptability. The following records emphasize the programming processes. This book does not attempt extensively to discuss group processes including individualization, relationships, roles, indigenous leadership, professional leadership, and so on.

This club record describes activities as an attempt at helping oldsters find and maintain their identity, socialize, get out of their rooms, and do more than sit in wheelchairs facing the front door of the Home lobby.

The program comprises mostly games and suggestions for discussion, often listing questions in some detail since this type of resource seems needed by most leaders. Out of this variety of activities, perhaps the few most successful might be used again and again, but something new as a surprise or novelty ought occasionally to be introduced as stimulation.

Motivation Techniques (May Be Applicable to All Clubs)

Several approaches can be used.

1. Say please and thank you, smile, be a pleasant, courteous leader.

2. Outline the program.

71

3. Advertise the program with posters, announce programs after meals and fifteen minutes before start.

4. Try jesting, serve as a sparring partner.

5. Give the resident responsibilities: watching the elevators, distributing or preparing something, picking up after activities.

6. Invite a relative (mother-son or father-daughter) for a special activity.

First Meeting

See "The First Meeting" in Part III, "How to Lead a Club."

OLD-FASHIONED CLOTHES may be nearly forgotten. Residents are found who remember when women wore heavy stiff corsets with steel stays and corset covers instead of brassieres; black stockings and high-laced or buttoned black shoes; two or three petticoats— full at the bottom, tied at the waistline, and trimmed at the edge with embroidery; padding in their hair called "rats"; dresses with high-neck collars, usually with ruching; long dresses with bustles.

Club members continue, discussing advantages and disadvantages in types of clothing, propriety, taking each item of clothing and telling how it has changed. What differences are there in the materials?

Second Meeting

SLATE GAME is like the TV "Matching Game."
Equipment. "Magic slates" purchased at the dime store, one for each player (usually six)—the slate a cardboard type with a plastic paper sheet which lifts up to erase; prize.
Procedure.

1. The team members are numbered by counting off, wherever residents happen to sit, three on a team, two teams; 1, 3, and 5 are on one team; 2, 4, 6 on the other.

2. A slate is given each person.

3. The leader asks a question, something that could be answered correctly with several answers (one question for each game).

    a. What is found in a lady's handbag?

    b. What is found in a little boy's pocket?

    c. What is open on Sunday?

d. Name an animal which can be identified by sound.

e. Name something learned in school.

f. What is served for breakfast?

4. Players write the answer, whatever they think of first, on the slate.

5. Like the TV game, if only two people write the same answer, there is no score; if all answers match, the score is doubled. (Or another way of scoring: if two people match, they get ten for a score. If the whole team matches, they get twenty points.)

6. The paper is torn off and they're ready for the next question.

7. A prize is given at the end of the afternoon for the highest team scored.

"Residents play it twice a week without getting tired of it. Sometimes we repeat the question to see if they get a similar answer. We make up our own questions to keep it new and interesting," an activity aide explains.

TOPICS TO TALK ABOUT. What's his favorite vegetable? color? person? place? What's the warmest place he knows? the coldest? prettiest?

The members decide on a secret friend for whom they'd like to make a May basket; a committee is appointed to collect the material necessary for next week's meeting.

Third Meeting

A MAY BASKET FOR A FRIEND'S DOORKNOB is constructed.

Equipment. Round paper doily and piece of aluminum foil (saucer size or dinner-plate size); scissors; colored toothpick; wad of wet cotton; ribbon; flowers.

Procedure.

1. The aluminum foil is cut the same size and shape as the doily. The doily is laid over the foil; the foil shows through the lace.

2. The double-thickness is rolled to form a cone, the overlapping edges fastened with a colored toothpick or sturdy flower stem (woven into the lacy openings).

3. The foil is twisted to a sharp point at the bottom so the moisture won't leak out.

4. The wad of cotton in the bottom of the cone keeps the flowers moist.

5. A piece of ribbon is tied to the top of the cone, leaving a loop large enough to slip over the doorknob.

SYMBOLS AND AMERICAN MONEY. "The Story of the Indian and the Nickel" is read. About 1911, there was a little circus known as Miller Brothers 101 Ranch. Among its attractions was an old Indian known as Chief Iron Tail, of the Sioux tribe whose home was in Oklahoma. Also on exhibition was a jet-black, beautiful live buffalo.

In late 1913, the government wanted to honor the American Indian and chose as their model Chief Iron Tail and put his face on the nickel. On the reverse side of the coin was Black Diamond, the buffalo. One seldom sees a buffalo nickel today, for they are avidly collected.

What other symbols appear on American money; on foreign coins? How many can be named?

ADS FOR THE CORNER GROCERY (1920) are read. What items and their costs are recalled?

Anger's Noodles—2/9¢	Lard—19¢
Best Head Rice—8¢	Large Lima Beans—2 lb/21¢
Del Monte Sauce—2/15¢	Coffee—24¢/lb
Toilet Soap—5¢	Libby's Deviled Ham—5¢/can
Washing Powder—2/5¢	Verybest Creamery Butter—47¢
Sugar—2 lb/15¢	Cloverland's Milk—10¢/qt
Largest Bread—5¢ loaf	

Were some of these products better than they are now? Why? What has made costs rise? Are grocery items more varied now? How has their packaging changed? Delivery?

Residents are each asked to bring a spool prepared for spool knitting as described in the next meeting.

Fourth Meeting

SPOOL KNITTING (makes a knitted cord).
Materials. Use a large spool in which are four brads equal distances from each other and extending ⅜″ to ½″ from spool; twine, yarn, or rug warp.

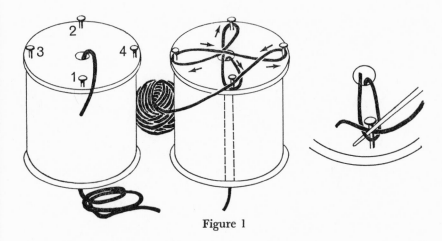

Figure 1

Procedure. Wind twine or yarn as follows:

1. Stick end through spool leaving several inches hanging down.

2. Loop around peg No. 1 then across hole around peg No. 2, then around No. 3 and No. 4.

3. Hold spool and yarn in left hand; pass yarn around peg No. 1; use small knitting needle to pull lower loop over top loop, dropping it off needle into hole.

4. Repeat counterclockwise for other pegs. Occasionally pull lower thread slightly to bring knitted cord down through hole.

5. When cord is long enough, take last loop off peg No. 1, put it on peg No. 3. Take bottom loop off No. 3 and repeat until one loop remains. Cut yarn, draw end through last loop and pull tightly. Different colors can be added by tying ends of yarn together and tucking the knot into the center of the cord.

The knitted cord can be used for drawstrings, can be sewed together as in rug making, be used for table mats, doll rugs, potholders, coin purses (using two round mats and a zipper), or can be braided into belts.

Using five nails instead of four, wind alternate nails until each has a loop of yarn around it, which makes a different weave of cord.

For hands that cannot handle a spool, use a 3" square of soft wood with a round hole ½" in the exact center; use five nails.

When knitting on a larger spool, the edges of the square can be placed on the edges of two books, or nailed on two pieces of wood to hold it off the table, leaving room for the cord underneath.

A TRIP is planned: An excursion to a local scenic chapel, a tour through the woolen mills or a Boy Scout camp, whatever the locale offers of interest to the members.

"SPONSOR A CHILD TO CAMP" a local brochure admonishes. Camps for mentally retarded children or underprivileged children sometimes charge $50 for one child for one week. If the members are looking for projects to which to direct money from craft sales, the camps will provide information.

Members are asked next time to bring dictionaries, paper, and pencil.

Fifth Meeting

POETRY CONTESTS are "set-up." Here, by way of illustration, is how one started:

> A notice read: The first Old-Timers Poetry Contest will be held this month for the members of the club. The reading and judging of the poems entered will be on (date). All poems must be original and about something pertaining to senior citizens. The poems must be placed in a box designated for them. You must have your name and room number with the poem.
>
> Try your luck at writing; who knows, you might be the winner and be a poet! Don't say you can't until you try!

Paper and pencil can be distributed, dictionaries made available, subjects discussed, and ideas jotted down at the meeting.

To prime the poets, the following couplets can be drawn from a hat. Members add rhyming lines as county home residents did:

> I am a happy member of the Happy Hour here
> And when we get together there's no time to shed a tear.

> We aim to make hearts happy by saying first a prayer
> And when we sing a song, there is no thought of care.

> We drew some pumpkin faces that smiled at us so sweet
> And when we wore them on our head, we smiled; it was a treat.

Our names have all been written and pinned onto our dress
So when we get together no one will need to guess.

Some of us read about stories we were asked to tell.
I know mine was about a snow storm—
That part I remember well.

There are so many patients who need a cheery word
That Merry Makers members perhaps have heard. . . .

Helpless and lonely some people go through life
In this world where there is war and strife.

For some of these people who are unhappy here,
Our Leisure Time Club gives them a word of cheer.

A ROUND DANCE is walked through. Volunteers (and ambulatory residents) can do the walking, wheelchair patients the clapping and singing.

Captain Jinks

Single circle facing in—hands joined. No partners needed.
  A. I'm Captain Jinks of the Horse Marines
  I feed my horse on corn and beans (stamp feet eight times)
  I sometimes live beyond my means
  For that's the style in the Army (stamp feet eight times)
  B. Captain Jinks came home last night (stick left foot out)
  Pass your partner by the right
  Swing the next with all your might (stick right foot out)
  For that's the style in the Army (pass partner and go to the next)
Repeat.

Sixth Meeting

RINGTOSS. A cardboard or rope ring is tossed onto somebody's foot, three times out of four for a prize.

THE HIGHEST CARD is drawn. Winner may choose a song to be sung by the group.

CATCH-IT-AND-SCORE.
1. Residents form lines.

2. Two players bounce or toss a ball to one another, counting to see who continues longest.

3. When one of them misses, the ball goes to the next in line. A member-scorekeeper counts the bounces.

Seventh Meeting

THE PAPER TREE is decorated (relay). Outlines of Christmas trees are drawn on two large pieces of wrapping paper and pinned on a curtain or wall. Blindfolded members form two teams. They are given paper ornaments with masking tape at the backs of each piece to stick on the paper tree.

Each team is lined up in front of its tree. Proceeding in relay, one player at a time from each team is led to the tree outline to decorate it.

The team getting the most decorations inside the outline wins. The paper trees can be used as a wall embellishment for the season.

A CHRISTMAS STOCKING is filled (relay). Two or more red stockings are hung at one end of the room, one for each team. Each member is given a spoon and three apples. The apples must be picked up off the table with the spoon, carried to the stocking and dropped in. (Or, one spoon could be used by each team, contestants handing the spoon to the next in line after placing the apples in the stockings.) The hand holding the spoon is the only one used: the free hand must be held behind the back at all times. The first team to fill the stocking is the winner.

GOOD FRIENDS are described. Each individual characterizes his best friend, the most pleasant visitor he's had here, or someone he's known before. Each lists qualities he likes best in a friend. He relates a happy day he's had with a friend.

Can everyone tell of a dog who's been a good friend? How did he prove himself?

Committees are appointed to work on the props for the next meeting (see below).

Eighth Meeting

SNAPSHOTS. A huge picture is painted with figures of two people, perhaps a man and a woman in old-fashioned clothes, and the faces are holes cut out the size of a human face. A high school art class can do this painting.

This was depicted in a Home newsletter:

> At the picture-taking booth, we took a trip into memory lane. A huge picture was painted with the faces cut out of a young girl and her beau, dressed in the clothes of yesteryear. The painting was put on a frame so that we could stand or sit behind it, put our faces through the holes allowed, and have our pictures taken with our family or with one another. Even some of our nurses got in on the pictures. It was fun to pose as in the days when we were young.

A local photographer can volunteer, or the leader, with a little camera and flashbulb, can do a first-rate job.

Ninth Meeting

OLD-TIMERS CABIN is a game of chance all patients can do. The outline of a cabin is drawn on a paper, 14" × 20", and tacked on cardboard or square Bristol board. Each resident is given a brown paper log and asked to sign the log.

The log cabin frame is passed around the circle and each member places his log in the frame, wherever he chooses. Hidden on the back of the cabin is a secret mark placed there previously.

The resident whose log is closest to this mark is the winner.

STOVEPIPE HAT is a target. A black stovepipe hat is made from construction paper and corrugated paper; or, a man's old-fashioned silk hat is used. The hat is placed upside down about 3' beyond the resident's reach as he tries to toss beanbags into the hat, getting two out of three for a candy kiss.

Residents are asked to come up with a funny story next time.

Tenth Meeting

EARLY PIONEER COMPETITION. Points are given for the funniest story, longest beard, broadest handspan, best shot (hitting a mark on the floor with a rope ring, or a designated mark with a sling-shot).

26—A COUNTER GAME. The player selects any number from one to six before he begins to cast the dice. He then throws ten dice thirteen times. If his number appears twenty-six or more times, he wins; if it appears fewer than twenty-six, he loses.

Players can be given checks or tokens that can be cashed for punch, cigarettes, or candy.

Eleventh Meeting

TRAY FAVORS.

Equipment. Paper punch, construction paper, colored yarn, seasonal candy, pattern.

Procedure. Members make favors of small boxes of construction paper, punching holes at the edges, lacing up each side with yarn.

Then bows are tied at the top and paper-strip handles are pasted on the sides. Someone fills the boxes with candy for bed patients (who are not on diets).

THEY ARE GUESTS AT AN ATHLETIC EVENT. Volunteers get permission from the charge nurse to take interested and able members to a local game; volunteers furnish cars and sit with residents during the performance, whatever the competition.

Croquet, horseshoes, and darts can be played outside during good weather, or pool or shuffleboard inside in inclement weather.

CARDS can be the most popular entertainment of all. An assortment of cards are at the tables from which residents choose their game for the afternoon. Traveling trophies can be awarded, the single prize going from table to table as the winner is announced there.

MEN'S FASHIONS are discussed. The following revelations are those of a male resident:

> Some people call the present goings-on in men's fashions an evolution, others think of it as a revolution; but whatever you choose to call it, our red-blooded American male is certainly taking on crazy dandified airs in a hurry.
>
> Incidentally, the last time I was in town I saw a man that wore powdered hair, lipstick, rouge, rings on his fingers, silk stockings, fitted coat and other fripperies. I have read over $4,000,000,000 worth of grooming aids such as colognes, after shave preparation, powders, facial creams and hair sprays is spent each year. I will say that our American men are sure slipping.
>
> I am a man of eighty-eight years and have never used any of the above makeup. All that is women's stuff. When I was a young man in

my teens and twenties, if we had used these cosmetics, we would be the laughing stock of the country. Back in those days there was only one divorce to twenty now. I think this is due to the fact that men back in those days were all man and complete masters of their homes. Today men are too soft, too easily led by outsiders, both men and women. . . .

What comments do residents have? What were some of the old-fashioned fripperies? Are men vain at heart? What are modern women's fripperies? Are they similar?

Residents MOUNT OLD-FASHIONED CUTOUTS on the walls and windows with masking tape—decorations typical of the season.

Each member is asked to bring an Easter anecdote, or something seasonal, to tell at the next meeting.

Thirteenth Meeting

THE CLAP GAME. One person leaves the room while another hides a favor or a well-wrapped candy or seasonal item. The resident who has left the room returns to hunt for the treasure.

The rest of the players clap loudly if the hunter is near the prize, softly if he is going away from it until he finds it.

EASTER CHIT-CHAT. Do they remember Easter pets? Hats? Parties? Trips or spring vacations with the children? Special church services? Young animals on the farm?

The following excerpt from a Home newsletter is read:

> Our discussion group brought out some interesting facts unknown to most of us. Talking about Palm Sunday, we learned that in days of yore, pussy willows were used in place of the now-popular palm branches. In those days the ladies wore new hats to church, but the men and boys wore big boots with copper toes, which could be purchased for $1.00. Many traveled to church by oxen team; the driver walked beside the team, calling out "haw" and "gee" (meaning turn right and left, or stop and go).
>
> Easter eggs were colored with whatever was in the home. Some boiled onion skins with the eggs which gave a red color. Others boiled fresh sprouted rye that gave a green color.

Can residents add to these ideas?

Residents are asked next time to bring several "white elephants" for an auction.

Fourteenth Meeting

A FUN AUCTION is adapted to the Home and its residents. This is what happened in one Home:

> At the fun auction one member suggested they prepare as many articles as possible for the event.
>
> Everyone cooperated and there was a big box full when the auction began. We were given fifteen kernels of corn apiece to be used for money. Some members were reckless bidders and bid all their "money" on one article as the activity aide held it up and gave a clue as to what it was and if for a man or lady.
>
> Others got two or three articles by bidding smaller amounts when others were out of cash. Some of the articles were jewelry, cosmetics, soap (the clue for which was "If you've got it, use me to check it, don't spread it!"), apples, gum, cookies, candy, "handies," penny, needle, safety pin, button, etc. So everyone of the thirty-three residents received at least one and some two or three items; over forty articles were "sold."
>
> A member gave a reading, another read an Easter prayer, another told some jokes. Radishes in the mystery box were prepared by ———— and guessed by ————.

Fifteenth Meeting

LOOKING BACK A YEAR (five years) can be a sentimental accounting. Members list new residents, deceased, and other changes in this time in the Home.

NUT CRACKING is an old-timers' pastime. Nuts in the shell, nutcrackers, large stones, and hammers make this a possibility for a club activity.

Conundrums are given by each member for others to guess.

Residents are asked to bring a picture, news clipping, or postcard to brag about for the next meeting.

Sixteenth Meeting

AN OLD-TIMERS' BRAG BOARD (bulletin board) is mounted low enough so wheelchair patients can read it; residents mount pictures of acquaintances and relatives of whom they are proud and to whom they want to call attention.

Regarding theirs, a resident writes:

There have been several interesting pictures on our Brag Board recently. A picture of the depot in Schleisingerville would have caused raised eyebrows had the article not explained that this was taken in the town we now call "Slinger," certainly easier to pronounce and to spell!

―――― supplied us with an old picture of the toll gate that was located at Oklahoma Avenue and Janesville Plank Road. While several of us were looking at these items, he mentioned that there had once been a plank road between Cedarburg and Thiensville.

A PICNIC at an old landmark is scheduled perhaps between club meetings. Residents discuss how to get there, where to go, day and time; if food or refreshments are to be planned, a responsible committee is appointed.

A Home newsletter runs this item:

A tour of Pioneer Village was taken with two volunteers driving the residents to the village where they were impressed with the restored buildings and the many implements on display, used years ago. A picnic lunch prepared by the staff at the Home was eaten in the Hawthorne Hills Country Club. Before returning home, they drove past the covered bridge and saw where the new one was built.

Club members are asked who would like to attend a Senior Citizens meeting in the city. Are there residents who will volunteer to entertain at such a meeting?

Seventeenth Meeting

ATTENDING SENIOR CITIZEN MEETINGS is arranged. Ambulatory people attend meetings at a local Senior Citizens Center, where they are entertained, or play bingo, sheepshead, and euchre. Often, they take part as the entertainers, giving recitations, reading a skit they've rehearsed, playing on the musical saw, doing a card trick, or reading a seasonal poem.

Eighteenth Meeting

POOL TOURNAMENT (MEN).

Procedure. Prior to the date set for the tourney to get under way, informal and practice matches are played in a double elimination tourney to determine abilities and best pairing. Entries are split into two sections so that outstanding players do not meet to begin with.

In the first-round matches of each section, players when paired play 8 ball to speed up play. In later matches, players decide among themselves the type of pool game they would like to play: rotation, cribbage, or 15 ball with the rule that a player must win two out of three games to advance.

In a double elimination tourney, each man plays at least two matches. A player defeated in his first-round pairing is matched again in a consolation bracket. Spectators enjoy these tourneys if contestants are posted and the games publicized with some fanfare. Sometimes, a sports film caps a memorable evening, or prizes are awarded at the annual awards party.

OLD-FASHIONED TEA PARTY (WOMEN). Reading tea leaves is an agreeable amusement. Most people enjoy hearing their fortune, all in fun. Someone in a gypsy dress with head scarf and earrings and with a flair and a little self-confidence, may pose as a convincing fortune teller at a tea party. She tells only what is pleasant and will cause no concern.

After the tea is drunk, the cup drained and turned over, tea leaves are examined by the fortune-teller and a lengthy fortune told. Placing the cup upside down on the saucer, she tells a fortune, asking each person to concentrate on a wish.

With good imagination, she proceeds:

1. The handle of the cup is south. The area nearest the handle indicates the topic of concern.

2. Tiny dots are journeys in the direction in which they point.

3. Sticks are people; a curved stick is a stranger appearing.

4. The bottom of the cup is the future; the rim, the present.

5. The most controlling events are concentrated around the handle of the cup; a number, an initial, a hand—success in a skill; a foot—travel; a round piece—money. In each case, those of most importance are nearest the handle. The wish is fulfilled in proximity to the handle.

From the tea leaves the following symbols may be read into the fortune:

Acorn: health
Anchor: success in love or business
Arrow: disquieting news possibly by letter
Basket: present of additional possessions
Bat: mysterious omen

Bouquet: loyal friends and happy marriage
Car: long journey
Castle: good fortune, inheritance
Chain: wedding, if unbroken
Circle: money or gifts
Clouds: an appointment
Cloverleaf: good fortune
Cross: one, good fortune; several, honor after misadventure
Crown: fulfilled ambition
Cup: opportunity
Dagger: sharp wits
Drops of moisture: tears
Ear: gossip
Eye: solution of problem
Fan: love of admiration
Ferns: steadfast love
Fish: news from abroad
Flag: warning of danger
Flower: passing pleasure or temporary happiness
Gate: opportunity
Hat: good luck
Heart: if distinct, future happiness
House: marriage
Ivy: patient friends
Key: problems solved
Ladder: influence
Lamp: business success
Lighthouse: security
Mask: end of love affair
Moon: great honors; luck in traveling
Mushroom: many friends
Necklace: presents
Numbers: friends, honors, gifts, days, years; position and surrounding symbols influence meaning
Padlock: a surprise
Pagoda: foreign travels
Pyramid: honor, wealth, fame
Question mark: indecision

Quill: legal document
Ring: happiness
Scales: legal proceedings
Scissors: quick decision
Shoes: enterprise
Spade: fortune
Spider: inheritance
Star: good luck, deserved recognition
Sun: good luck
Table: consultations
Tent: many travels
Tree: good health
Triangle: fortunate meeting with friends or with strangers
Trumpet: entertainment
Turtle: wealth, luxury
Umbrella: grumbling
Wasp: gossip
Windmill: success

Nineteenth Meeting

GOOD LUCK. Each tells his luckiest year and why. Where was he? Why was it different than other years? Does he believe in luck? In superstition? What superstitions? Walking under a ladder? Friday the 13th? Does he remember any superstitions his parents had? What are some good ways of influencing one's fate? Are there incidents in his life which have proven this? Does he know people who have determined their own fate in bettering their lives? Are there people here in the Home who have?

WHAT ARE THE ODDS? How good are they at guessing odds in the following situations?

1. When a coin is flipped ten times and a head comes up ten times in succession, what would they say the odds are for a head on the eleventh throw? (Even.)

2. What are the odds on the first roll of the dice against rolling a 7? (5 to 1.) rolling 11? (17 to 1.) rolling double numbers? (35 to 1.)

Twentieth Meeting

PREDICTIONS IN THE TOURNAMENT (HOCKEY, FOOTBALL, BASKET-BALL). Each interested resident is given a sheet on which he writes in his guesses as to season's winners and submits the sheet before the first game is played. Winners are those who make perfect predictions announced at the end of the tournament (see Men's Club Tournaments).

A SURVEY by a local radio station was made in a Home.

1. What are the most pressing problems for you as senior citizens?
2. If you were writing and producing these programs for people of all ages to see, what would you say about senior citizens?
3. Do you feel the state legislature is sensitive to the needs of senior citizens? If not, why?
4. How do you feel about retirement? What are the good and bad aspects of being retired?
5. Would you like full or part-time employment?
6. Do younger and middle-aged people understand senior citizens?
7. Other comments.

Can residents interview people in the Home and send the results to the local radio station, the Commission on Aging, the Senior Citizens Club, or other interested groups?

GAMES. A topic for discussion: Can they explain how the following games are played? (Draw up a set of rules for one.) Fencing; archery; rifle shooting; tournament; horse racing; cricket, tennis (lawn, table, deck); squash; Ping-Pong®; trap bat and ball; battledore and shuttlecock; badminton; pall-mall; croquet; golf; curling; hockey; basketball; soccer; football; rugby; polo; tent-pegging; greasy pole; quoits; throwing the hammer; putting the weight; tossing the caber; leapfrog; tug-of-war; blindman's buff; hide-and-seek; baseball; lacrosse; billiards; pool; bagatelle; skittles; ninepins.

What others?

Twenty-first Meeting

MOVIES (DOCUMENTARY FILMS). (See Appendix.) When a particular OT shows free movies from the county library, documentaries for instance, she shows part of the film. Then she stops it so that residents can talk about it, asking questions to encourage discussion and encouraging thoughts on subjects connected with the film topic.

The leader who chooses such a program can say before the film is shown, "What do you know about this state (or this subject, country, mineral, fruit, person, and so on)? Listen and watch, and then tell us; we're going to ask questions at the end of the film."

What is its value? Where is it found? Has the resident experience or information to comment on? What is its use, size, color? If it's a product, what steps are taken to market it?

Twenty-second Meeting

HOW HAS THE COMMUNITY CHANGED? This is a topic to develop discussion. A newsletter column is submitted and read aloud to a group around a table. The following illustrates the types of questions which can be asked (extract from a Home newsletter):

> Do you remember way back when Gentry Bros. Dog and Pony Show exhibited on the Old Hay Market lot, now a parking lot?
>
> When we annually held a street fair on Barstow Street with shows of all nature, and, even a midway?
>
> When we would get up after midnight, and go down to the Omaha Depot to see the Ringling Bros. Circus train come in, and watch the unloading of the elephants, and see covered wagons from which fierce lions roared?
>
> When we would gather on the banks of the Chippewa River near the Milwaukee Railroad bridge and watch the lumberjacks at log-rolling, as they competed for prizes on the 4th of July?
>
> When we would listen to the old German band, as it made the rounds of the taverns and tooted away, all of a summer's day?
>
> When after a show at the Grand Opera House, we would hurry to the Jim Charles Chop House on Eau Claire Street, and enjoy a midnight snack?
>
> When we would go to Don Smith's Ice Cream Parlor on North Barstow, for a cooling refreshment?

Any reader with some "Way Back When" to contribute can drop it in any of the newspaper boxes on the wards, for publication.

Residents are asked to bring a tall tale for the next meeting.

GEMS are discussed. They describe gems they felt attached to.

What's the difference between diadem, tiara, pendant, locket? Between a bracelet, anklet, armlet, chain, brooch, torque?

What other ornaments can be named? (Cosmetics, manicures, beading, embroidery, lace, gimp, fringe, trimming, tassels, star, rosettes, bows, feathers.)

What jewels can be named? (Diamond, brilliant, aquamarine, alexandrite, cat's-eye, emerald, jasper, bloodstone, agate, onyx, garnet, lapis lazuli, opal, chrysolite, sapphirine, ruby, topaz, turquois, amethyst, moonstone, pearl, coral.)

Can they tell the origin of some of them? Value? Can each name the gem for his birth month?

Twenty-third Meeting

TALL TALES are recounted or invented. Members volunteer to read aloud stories from a county home Liars' Club as in the following instances:

I'll tell of a time I lived near Current River. On a Sunday morning there was a fire at a Port Arthur building. I had to walk half a mile to catch a ride on the streetcar. The streetcar never did come, as it couldn't cross the firehoses. While I stood waiting and watching the fire, it was so gol-darned cold that the flames froze as they came out of the windows. Firemen had to get blowtorches from Port William to unthaw the flames before they could put the fire out.

* * *

On a beautiful October day, my wife and I went moose hunting. She was low on meat for the family table, and coaxed me to go out near the Current River to hunt. Only having two shells left, I hesitated to go, but knew we needed meat, so away we went. After we followed a trail through the woods, my wife soon spotted a big bear. About the same time I saw a bull moose a bit farther down the trail.

Wondering which one to shoot, my wife said, "Oh, shoot the bear, 'cause you can always 'shoot the bull'!"

* * *

It gets so cold here in the winter that we have to put heaters under the cows to milk them.

* * *

That's nothing. It gets so hot back home that we have to feed the hens ice so they won't lay hardboiled eggs.

They continue.

THEY RETELL THE GREAT MAIL ROBBERIES. Have some of them been postal clerks, rural mailmen, ridden horseback in remote parts of the country to deliver the mail? Has anyone seen a mail robbery or some other crime? What were some famous plots in these crimes?

A resident authors this account:

The first robbery of the airmail that I recall occurred when Albert Sidney Burleson was Postmaster General. He proposed to prove that airmail was feasible, so he withdrew a package of currency which I was told was valued at $40,000. He selected an aviator to make a trial trip with the package. The aviator went up with it and never came down.

The nearest I ever came to being in a train robbery was one night when we were stopped at Mankato Junction and told that the sheriff and forty men would board the train at Mankato to frustrate a train robbery. The freight, coming toward Mankato and two hours late, had run into a pile of ties which had been placed on the track to wreck our train, and the Brown gang was expected to loot the wreckage. We disobeyed the orders of the sheriff and did not put our lights out for we had a lot of mail to deliver at destination.

But the Brown gang had taken alarm when the way freight scattered the ties on the track and had left for parts unknown. Afterwards, I asked special agent Risinger if they ever caught the Brown gang. He told me that they were all doing time with no parole or pardon permitted. The Brown gang was an aggregation of desperadoes who terrorized settlers and farmers.

Later when I was on the day train we stopped at Waseca to exchange mails and a man climbed up on the side of the car into the doorway and asked how to get to a certain town in Iowa. I recognized Roy Gardner, who was a notorious mail car robber. He made the brag that he had never shot an unarmed man. I was armed with a Detective .45 caliber gat which weighed eleven pounds, and I was careful not to make any false moves for that would have been very foolish. I told Gardner he would have to backtrack to Owatonna and take the Rock Island which went through his destination. I never saw or heard of him again and I often wonder if they caught him like the Brown gang.

There was a postal inspector who went bad and organized a mob to rob the Milwaukee Train 57, which carried the Trans-Pacific registered mails. That plot failed and Fahey was apprehended.

There was a local train on the Illinois Central which we called Chi and Carbondale Train 31. It was a local and operated from Chicago to Champaign. It delivered all of the registered mail as far as Champaign. There were two clerks on that run and a gang tried to rob the train. One of the clerks, who were armed with new Colts and Smith & Wessons, opened fire and badly wounded one of the bandits. They escaped. The Chicago banks gave these clerks $1,000 but the postal hierarchy soaked them with a lot of demerits because they claimed these clerks had a door open.

When I went into the mail cars, it was advertised that only one railway postal clerk in a thousand went wrong. But the figure for post office clerks was higher. As the politicians downgraded our mail car service, things got so bad that peepholes in the ceilings of the stationary facilities were incorporated in the plans, and thievery became an ordinary hazard. Some of this was due to the low wage policy of the hierarchy. Some of it was political. I once had a letter from General Superintendent saying that Congress had passed a law which required that he pay me for my many ideas and inventions, but that they had not appropriated any money so he couldn't pay me.

Residents are asked to bring a New Year's Resolution next time.

Twenty-fourth Meeting

A NEW YEAR'S RESOLUTION is formulated by members, then drawn from a hat and read aloud.

1. I will read aloud, listen, visit with a bed patient each day.

2. I'm going to walk (compliment my enemies, and so on) daily.

3. I will eat less (if this is what the doctor recommends).

4. I will personally greet each new member, as they are admitted to the Home.

5. I will keep up with my diary.

6. I will volunteer to work on a committee.

7. I will write a new friend.

8. I will tell a joke every day.

9. I'm going to do something about a physical fitness program.

10. I'm going to read or visit with —————.

11. I'm not going to find fault with my lot.

12. Next time I'm angry, I'm going to count to ten.

13. I'm through procrastinating.

14. I'm not going to say something unpleasant about the Home, ever.

15. I'm not going to interrupt (push ahead in line, exaggerate).

16. I'm not going to gossip (scream, shout).
17. I'm going to make someone happy each day.

TRADITIONAL ANNIVERSARIES. How many can they name?

1st paper	13th lace
2nd cotton	14th ivory
3rd leather	15th crystal
4th fruits, flowers	20th china
5th wood	25th silver
6th sugar, candy	30th pearl
7th wool, copper	35th coral
8th bronze, pottery	40th ruby
9th pottery, willow	45th sapphire
10th tin, aluminum	50th gold
11th steel	55th emerald
12th silk, linen	75th diamond

GOODBYES are said; old-timers like to shake hands. At the end of each meeting, members form a circle. They choose the resident nearest the door to begin inside the circle, shaking hands with the person to his right. Then the next and the next until he has shaken hands with all and has said goodbye to all. As he finishes with the last person in the circle, he goes out of the room.

After the first person shakes hands with the person at his right, that person falls into line behind and follows him in shaking hands with the remaining members. The third person in turn falls in behind the second and so on until there is no one left in the circle. All have shaken hands and said goodbye and started out the door.

TO READ ALOUD

Books obtained from the local library or state traveling library (don't read so long that listeners tire).

Chase, Mary Ellen: *The Lovely Ambition*   Fiction
The parson's daughter narrates the family story which also gives a picture of a Maine village.

Davenport, Owen: *The Wax Foundation*   Fiction
A romance, much ado, and a wry look at philanthropy combine to make an amusing story.

Dermout, Maria: *Yesterday* Fiction
A gentle lady in her sixties looks back upon her childhood on
the magic Dutch islands and brings enchantment to the reader
who appreciates fine writing.

Duerrenmatt, Friedrich: *Traps* Fiction
The impact of this tale follows upon a game in which an ex-
judge and his cronies frequently match wits.

Erdman, Loula Grace: *Many a Voyage* Fiction
Edmund and Fanny Ross lived in Milwaukee before moving
to Kansas in 1854. The courage of Mr. Ross is a matter of record, but the significance of being his wife is imaginatively por-
trayed in this novel.

Forbes, Kathryn: *Mamma's Bank Account* 822
Refreshing episodes in the life of a Norwegian family living
in San Francisco.

Maule, Hamilton: *Jeremy Todd* Fiction
Jeremy Todd, who was ten years old when his grandfather
died, had to learn how to live all over again in this tender and
humorous story of life with grandmother.

HOMEMAKERS CLUB

Introduction

Who are the Homemakers? Women—wives, mothers, or spin-
sters—who love keeping house and may enjoy a cooking class,
sewing, knitting, crocheting, tatting, or discussing old familiar
customs and ways of life in the households where they once
reigned.

In nursing home situations, women more than men seem to socialize well. This is probably because they've been used to pleasant get-togethers, munching sandwiches, and giving committee reports in Veterans of Foreign War Auxiliaries, Gold Star Mothers,
the Ladies Aid, the Dorcas Society, Lionettes, or Zontas. Perhaps
the flavor of life they miss most in moving into a nursing home
or hospital is the social life of a club: the chatter, buzzing, and
laughter that goes on in women's gatherings; the greetings, the
fussing, the gossip and news, the warmth of a kiss or clasp of
hands, a waist encircled. . . .

And the old friends, how sad to have lost so many! And with what longing they want new friends!

In several nursing homes, Homemakers Clubs under the county home demonstration agent have come in monthly or bimonthly to organize and sponsor a Homemakers Club. Perhaps a telephone call to one of them (there can be as many as sixty-three clubs in a single county) asking for Homemaker sponsorship, can bring leadership for monthly meetings in the Home club. These can be like the programs of the community groups or projects adapted or original.

One should insist that the club is a residents' club, with resident officers and committees responsible for the programs. The community Homemakers present are a resource and stimulant, forming a bridge between the Home and the community! Some county home Homemakers Club members pay twenty-five cents in state dues per month as all statewide club members do, print a program for the year, and visit and exchange ideas with other neighboring county clubs.

Homemakers' Creed

We, the Homemakers of Wisconsin, believe in the sanctity of the home, the cradle of character . . . blessed by motherly devotion and guarded by fatherly protection.

We pledge ourselves:

—to work for the preservation and improvement of home and community life;

—to strive for healthier minds and bodies, and better living;

—to promote the welfare of our boys and girls, the nation's greatest asset;

—to be true to God and country and of lasting service to our Home and community.

—*Homemakers Bulletin*
Sauk County, Wisconsin

Homemakers' Prayer

Dear God, give us the grace to see
The blessings which have come from thee;
Give us the strength to do our duty

To see in everything some beauty;
Teach us that love and cheerful giving,
Tolerance and decent living,
Make of our home a place sublime,
Where there's no room for hate or crime,
A place where good friends gather 'round,
Where laughter, mirth and cheer abound,
Not selfish thoughts nor worldly greed,
Let this, Dear Master, be our creed.

—Homemakers Bulletin
St. Croix County, Wisconsin

Sample Club Developments

The Homemakers meet monthly; a meeting includes a speaker; forty-two residents sing, give roll call response, decide on bus trips for alternate Tuesdays (going to the historical museum, to the airport, to outdoor picnics, visiting new workshops for the handicapped, skiing events). Club dues are 5¢ per month.

Twenty residents are in a Homemakers Club, with local club members from all over the county attending. Three residents in turn attend their local club meetings in the community. A blind resident is president and the vice-president, secretary, treasurer (all residents) conduct each business meeting.

Our women enjoy these get-togethers more than any activity in the Home, making friends with the sixty-three county Homemaker Clubs assigned turns at attending our meetings, reporting on local clubs, encouraging more residents to join, pointing out projects they can do for others, finding pleasant ways residents can take part in county meetings or bringing the community to the Home.

Fifteen to eighteen residents meet monthly at the Home with the Homemaker volunteers to decorate the doors for special holidays, to frost fruitcakes and make Swiss fondue (cheese and dry bread, or marshmallows and chocolate). Volunteers bring a door prize to each meeting.

Can the community Homemakers Club and the prospective Home members talk over these and other plans which make a club possible? Can they list worthwhile activities approved by the Home and of interest to residents, and can they meet financial limitations?

First Meeting

See "The First Meeting" in Part III, "How to Lead a Club."

GUESS, PICK A NUMBER, OR OBSERVE. To aid in giving conversation a focal point, to "break the ice" and produce a relaxed, informal atmosphere necessary for the success of a meeting, do the following:

1. They guess how many red circles on this dress, bingo counters in a small bottle, the identity of something hidden.

2. They pick a number, stake a claim in the lost gold mine, guess the number of fish in the fish pond, the location of buried treasure in the picture. (The X on the back of the picture previously placed there, determines the winning guesses.)

3. They observe the contents of a tray. They look for thirty seconds and then name the items with the tray covered.

4. They consider a teasing question: Is a dollar bill shorter than a postal card? They exchange conundrums; guess the name of the record being played.

They TALK ABOUT PEOPLE.
1. The person who lived in the county the longest.
2. The woman remembering the year of her first wood stove.
3. The woman who lived on the largest farm.
4. The woman who's been here the longest.
5. The woman with the most living relatives.
6. The youngest grandmother.
7. Mother of the most children.
Residents suggest others.

Each brings a Thanksgiving anecdote to tell, a poem to read, or picture to show at the next meeting.

Second Meeting

RECALLING A THANKSGIVING I WILL NEVER FORGET, a volunteer leader gave this account:

A turkey for Thanksgiving is a tradition in most American families. We had never had one until the year I was nine. My sister and her husband wrote they were coming to visit and would bring a big turkey.

Since I had never tasted that particular fowl, I was very excited at the prospect.

As the roasting turkey sent its delicious scent all over the house, my little-girl nose told me my tummy was feeling very empty. Sis had brought a huge box of chocolates along with the turkey. I now eyed that box with longing, and decided to find one with a caramel center. Choosing a square one which I felt sure was a caramel, I pressed my finger down hard on the center.

The chocolate coating cracked revealing a white cream center. Next I tried an oblong one, but that was maple cream. Proceeding to push in the tops of a dozen pieces, I met nothing but failure in my search for a caramel. It was then that I noticed how terrible that top layer of candy looked. I was bound to be scolded for ruining it.

What could I do but eat the evidence of my dastardly act?

As mother brought the big browned bird into the dining room, she called me to come to the table. My tummy was turning flip-flops by this time, but I went out and sat in my place. After the blessing was asked, my father cut off one of the immense drumsticks. Thinking to please his youngest child, he put it on my plate. At the sight of all that meat, I turned an odd shade of green and bolted for the door.

I was not able to eat anything the rest of the day. Everyone felt sorry for me and the comments went something like this: "Isn't it a shame that poor child couldn't eat even one mouthful of her Thanksgiving dinner?"

Later, my sis decided to pass around the box of candy. When she lifted the cover and saw all the empty spaces, she said, "Oh, this explains why our little sister couldn't eat her Thanksgiving dinner. Look at this box of candy!"

Other Thanksgiving stories are told.

BABY SHOES, a project to take back to their rooms, can be given as gifts. Purchased in a department store, felt shoes, ready to assemble, come packaged with necessary pieces and directions.

Shoe tops and soles have perforated edges and can be sewn together easily, providing a suitable project for the bed-bound, visually handicapped, and those with clumsy hands.

Third Meeting

FRINGED MAT AND NAPKINS to sell or give as gifts are easy to do. *Materials.* Indian head cotton or any other material which can be fringed; a sewing machine.

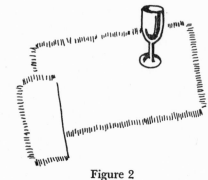

Figure 2

Procedure. The sighted resident can machine stitch; the visually handicapped can fringe. Cut the material 17" × 12" for the mats, 10" square for napkins.

1. Residents fringe mat ends ½"; top and bottom edge ¼" each.
2. Fringe napkins ⅜" on all four sides.
3. Machine stitch with small stitch around mat and napkins as close as possible to fringed edges.

Fourth Meeting

HALF APRON is an old, familiar craft.
Material. Skirt: two 20½" lengths of toweling full width of material; 1 waistband—width of material—4½" deep; 2 ties—width of material—3" deep; 1 pocket—5½" wide × 6¾" deep, border at top.

Figure 3

Procedure.

1. Resident seams together two skirt pieces along 20½" selvage from apron center. If material has border pattern, this will form a double border at skirt center and single border at each outer edge.

2. Turn up hem 1¼"; allow the ¼" for turn-in. Stitch.

3. Gather apron top to 14½", distributing fullness evenly.

4. Seam ties. Turn, press.

5. Fold waistband in half lengthwise.

6. Place wrong side of gathered edge of skirt and right side of waistband together matching center. Seam.

7. Turn waistband and top-stitch down on right side attaching ties at either end in same operation.

8. Turn down ½" hem at pocket top. Stitch.

9. Place pocket evenly 7" from bottom edge and 6" from side edge of apron. Stitch.

DAILY GAMES AND CRAFTS which members can help with in reaching the bed-bound and room-bound. An Annex, now opened to ambulatory residents, is visited from eight to ten every morning by the activity aide who brings materials for games and crafts: foam rubber, needles and thread, stuffing for animals, blocks to quilt, coloring, materials for matchstick crosses, paints for textile embroidery, and various bedside games. Residents come to the main building for monthly bunco and birthday parties directed by the residents' Homemakers Club.

Can residents be interested in taking projects to bed-bound patients' rooms, threading needles for them, keeping them encouraged and supplied with materials?

FRIGHTENING EXPERIENCES were told by residents and appear here as samples.

It was a cold night and I had put my baby's bed out by the heating stove. I undressed and put my clothes on a chair. My husband had been sick in bed for some time and when I was ready for bed, he asked me to light a cigarette for him. I struck a match by the stove and gave him the cigarette.

Shortly after I had fallen alseep, he awakened me and said he thought someone was coming into the room with a flashlight. I investigated and found that a spark from the match must have fallen on my clothes, as they were on fire, also, the window drapes. I picked up the chair and threw it outdoors. Then I took the dipper and pail of water and put out the fire on the drapes. I had been extremely tired when I went to bed, but didn't sleep the rest of the night.

* * *

As a younger woman, I peddled butter to different places in La Crosse.

One time I tied my horse up at the place where the Bodega is now located. I bought some tomato plants and put them in the buggy, and then went over to Doerflinger's to do some shopping. When I came back, my horse was gone. The bridle hung on the tying post and the tomato plants were sitting upright in the middle of the street.

People had gathered and a policeman was there. The policeman told me my horse had gotten into a fight with another horse and had pulled out of his bridle and run away, but that a man had caught him and had him tied up in a shed. My brother-in-law got my horse and loaned me his buggy to go home, as mine was pretty well damaged.

My horse was still nervous and scared and I had to hold the reins tight as I had a real fast ride home.

Could residents write their experiences for the local paper or Home newsletter?

Fifth Meeting

COOKING CLASS is a must in a Homemakers' Club.

Peanut Butter Cookies.

1 cup shortening—half butter	½ teaspoon salt
1 cup white sugar	1 cup brown sugar
1 cup peanut butter	2 eggs
2½ cups bread flour	2 teaspoons soda

Cream butter, sugar, and peanut butter. Add unbeaten eggs. Beat well. Add sifted flour, soda, and salt. Mix well. Form into balls the size of a walnut. Flatten with a fork. Bake for 15 minutes in 350-degree oven.

SEWING PROJECTS can be adapted from salvage materials. A Home accepted discarded felt skirts from the local high school drum and bugle corps to make decorative boots, Christmas tree aprons, stockings, or candy holders.

Other felt sewing projects might be pillows, napkin holders, and so forth, from simple patterns available from department stores.

A COLLECTION OF PAINTINGS, as well as a collection of plates from someone's home, has been exhibited on the walls of a particular Home dining room. Could some resident volunteer make inquiries on how it could be done for this Home?

There can be dozens of ideas members can be encouraged to introduce.

Sixth Meeting

AN INTERVIEW BROADCAST was set up after a superintendent inquired as to a club-breakfast radio show. Can one like the following be adapted?

> Every year a local radio personality does breakfast interviews with each club member, and broadcasts live from the Home. There are always many telephone calls to the superintendent after the show, telling him how "wonderful" it was.
>
> The residents love it because it's something different. We couldn't terminate the conversation with some of them during the hour-long program. The interviewer comments on what they're wearing or a piece of jewelry, and has no trouble getting them to reply. One woman remembered him from years ago when her father owned the Farmers' Store and so they began reminiscing.

Contacts could be made with local radio stations. As second-best, tape recordings could be made and played back.

A DRAWING CLASS FOR INTERESTED MEMBERS can be an experience of discovery. One Home committee speaks on their happy group:

> A gifted artist conducts a drawing class weekly. Between ten and twenty residents turn out to draw freehand pictures, which are put on display for all to enjoy. The favorite subjects are pretty flowers, horses, and other animals. (What else?) It's important for the volunteer and leader to accept all drawings without comment, good or bad, never judging them in any way or the residents will give up in frustration and discouragement.

CHRISTMASES OF LONG, LONG AGO. Discussion stimulates reminiscences, as a county home volunteer reports.

> Many residents remember their Christmases of long ago as happy occasions of family gatherings with many goodies for eating and simple gifts of homemade clothing and a toy or two.

My mother was born in 1879, the second youngest in a family of ten. I remember her description of Christmas in the 80's. My grandfather always locked the door at the bottom of the stairs which led to the children's bedrooms.

On Christmas morning, the boys and girls would line up behind that locked door, pressing against it and pleading to be let out to see their Christmas gifts. As Grandfather and Grandmother worked to fill the ten stockings with an orange in each toe, a few pieces of taffy candy and a five-cent toy, the excitement mounted and the children pressed hard against the first in line.

When the great moment arrived, Grandfather would turn the key and open the door. Like a stack of dominoes standing in line, the children burst out piling one on top of the other in their haste. Since they received little, each piece of candy and that wonderful orange were treasured for days after. The small china trinket or rubber ball were appreciated much more than the abundance of expensive toys most modern children receive at Christmas.

My husband's grandfather also came from a background of hardworking but humble people. He became a professional photographer when he grew up, and he kept a small china dog sitting on his desk. When asked about the little brown and white animal, Grandfather Dan would explain it was the only boughten toy he ever owned! His toys had all been handmade, but one Christmas he had received the little china dog as a gift and it was treasured as long as he lived. This little memento found its way to our home eventually, and I liked to see it on the shelf above our breakfast table.

It was a constant reminder to us to be grateful for our blessings.

Residents could recall childhood pranks, the happiest of holidays, a sentimental homemake gift, the most pleasureable of all moments at Christmas, or a big surprise!

Seventh Meeting

NAMING OBJECTS could be a new club opener. Residents divide in opposing teams facing one another. The captain on one side names a household item or anything from a definite class of objects, beginning with "A." Her opponent does the same and the game continues as long as players on the teams can name objects alternately.

When a player of one side fails to give a name with the required initial, that side loses a player to the other side. Then another letter is taken. The side with the most players is winner.

This stunt has no apparent purpose or relevance to the club, but could suggest other activities or stunts for socializing, either by the leader or member.

CONDUCTING A CONTEST, a leader reports the following:

A resident sponsored a contest which sounds simple but which was enjoyed:

Make a list of everything you can think of that can be worn on the foot. And it must start with the letter "S." A silver dollar to the one who turns in the longest list with all answers which can be checked in the dictionary. No foreign words are accepted. Give your entry to ————, along with your name and the date and time turned in. Contest closes Monday noon.

Residents can suggest some other idea for a contest that could be fun, e.g., guessing the date when the robins will hatch or the first strawberries will be served, or some old-fashioned stunt.

QUILTING. Residents piece material for a local church and the church society puts it together and ties the comforter; is there room to keep a quilting frame set up, the frame set high enough for wheelchair arms to go under?

Eighth Meeting

CROCHETED MOCCASINS (Size 5½). Members with good ideas who remember crocheting directions might like to try this.
Materials. Pennsylvania Dutch rug strips (narrow); needle—steel crochet hook—size 7.
Procedure. Foot: Use single stitch taking up back of stitch except where indicated. Chain 11 1 sc in second ch from hook. 1 sc in each stitch for seven stitches. 2 sc in last stitch. * Working along other side of chain—2 sc in first stitch, 1 sc in each stitch for seven stitches, 2 sc in last stitch. Repeat from * four times, adding

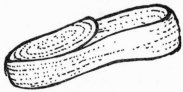

Figure 4

one extra stitch at either end between increases, keeping ends rounded in shape and ending with a slip stitch catching back and front of stitch below. Slip stitch back for three more stitches. Chain thirty-six stitches (this forms top around ankle). Fasten chain to opposite side of instep with slip stitch catching back and front of stitch below matching number of stitches from point of instep. Be careful that chain is not twisted before fastening. Working back on lower edge of chain make 1 sc in each stitch (without increasing) around chain and instep for four rows, ending with slip stitch. Fasten. Taking up both back and front of stitches work around entire top of slipper including instep with 1 sc, skipping one stitch on either side where instep joins side of slipper. Fasten.

Sole: Make a chain 2 inches less than size of foot. Work half double crochet (yarn around needle and through all 3 loops at once) over half of chain, work 1 sc on balance of sts. to within last st., work 2 sc in last st., continue around chain, work 2 sc in first st. on other side, 1 sc in each st. to where the half double crochet is on other side, work half double crochet on balance of chain working second half double crochet sts. at the increasing point. Continue to work round and round in same manner for three rows ending with a slip st. break yarn. Sew top to sole. Work 1 sc around entire top of slipper including instep.

Ninth Meeting

WASHCLOTH. Even a blind member could remember knitting simple washcloths, using large wooden needles.
Material. 1 hank washable cotton yarn, white; 1 pr. #6 knitting needles.
Procedure.
1. Cast on forty stitches.
2. Knit eight rows.
3. Pearl four rows for border.
4. Continue knitting forty-eight rows.
5. Repeat pearl border (4 rows).
6. Knit eight rows.
7. Cast off. (Washcloth should measure approximately 8¾" square.)

Figure 5

A sighted person could add the design stitch—duplicate stitch:

1. Thread tapestry needle; fasten on the wrong side of work.

2. * Insert needle in center of bottom of stitch to be covered and draw yard through to right side of work, then insert needle under the two strands of yarn at bottom of stitch above (as illustrated).

3. Draw yarn through; then insert needle in center of same stitch below and draw yarn through to wrong side of work.

4. Repeat from. *

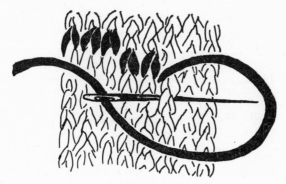

Figure 6

CHRISTMAS CRAFTS are made by the handicapped. Craft shop workers in one Home used the drawn threads pulled from luncheon cloth edges to form birds' nests in the Christmas trees. The luncheon cloths and napkins of Christmas poinsettia cotton prints or plain red and green, made by blind people, were sold or given as gifts.

For the retarded, the mentally infirm, or people with the use of one hand, a medallion project was described.

Equipment. Scissors; bright colored paper or Christmas cards (discarded); glue; cardboard; pipe steam cleaner; gold seal; small pieces of cardboard.

Procedure.

1. Many 3″ long slanting slivers of bright colored discarded cards are cut.

2. Glue is put on a cardboard circle, the size of a quarter.

3. The broad ends of the slivers are glued along the edge of the circle.

4. When a circle of slivers has been placed on the circle of glue, the process is repeated with a smaller cardboard circle of slivers pasted the same way and another layer of slivers is put on top of the circle.

5. A gold seal covers the unfinished center to complete it.

6. A pipe steam cleaner attached to the back converts it to a boutonniere, a party favor, or tray or planter decoration. A bunch of medallions of different pipe steam cleaner lengths becomes a bouquet.

Homemaker members could make these for boutonnieres for visitors or people receiving special honors in the Home, or perhaps find a place in the Home to decorate.

Tenth Meeting

SLIPPERS.

Material. 3 balls Mid Rose (slipper material and traveling case ribbon trim should match); steel crochet hook No. 2/0.

Gauge: 6 sc make 1 inch; 6 rows make 1 inch. (Directions are written for small size. Changes for medium and large sizes are in parentheses.)

Procedure. Sole: (Make 2) Starting at center, ch 30 (36-42).

1st rnd. 3 sc in 2nd ch from hook, sc in next 15 (18-21) ch, dc in next 12 (15-18) ch; make 7 dc in last ch (toe end); working

Figure 7

along opposite side of starting chain, make dc in next 12 (15-18) ch sc in next 15 (18-21) ch, 2 sc in same place as first 3 sc were made.

2nd rnd. Sc in each st. around, increasing across heel and toe as necessary to keep work flat—to inc 1 sc, make 2 sc in 1 sc. Repeat 2nd rnd. until 8 (8-9) rnds. have been completed. At end of last rnd., join and break off.

Uppers: Starting at back, ch 106 (122-146). Join with sl. st.

1st rnd. Sc in same place as sl. st. (Ch 3, skip 3 ch, sc in next ch) 7 (9-12) times; (ch 3, skip 2 ch, sc in next ch) 6 times; (ch 3, skip 1 ch, sc in next ch) 5 times; (ch 3, skip 2 ch, sc in next ch) 6 times; (ch 3, skip 3 ch, sc in next ch) 7 (9-12) times, ending with ch 1, skip 3 ch, half dc in first sc.

2nd rnd. * Ch 3, sc in next loop. Repeat from * around, ending with ch 1, half dc in top of half dc. Repeat 2nd rnd. until 5 rnds. have been completed.

6th rnd. Place marker at center loop of toe. * Ch 2, sc in next loop. Repeat from * to within 8th loop of marker (not counting the center loop) (ch 1, dc in next loop) 15 times. Complete other side as before.

7th rnd. 3 sc in each ch—2 loop, sc in each ch—1 sp around.

8th & 9th rnds. Sc in each sc around, decreasing 3 sc evenly across toe—to dec 1 sc, work off 2 sc as 1 sc.

10th rnd. Sc in each sc around. Join and break off. Sew two soles together. Sew upper to sole. Make another slipper the same way.

MAKING HOMEMADE SOAP, discussed in one Home, prompted tales of early days.

Bacon drippings, lard renderings, all waste fats in cooking were saved for the soap-making kettle. That usually hung suspended over a roaring fire outside the house, because "it stinks" to quote one of the club members discussing this remembrance from long ago. Members all recalled seeing the mixture when it had reached the proper consistency and it was a deep yellow color like naphtha soap. This was poured into a wooden framework or box which gave it shape. It was cut into bars when nearly hard and did most of the cleaning jobs around the home. We actually had in our possession the very recipe women used.

Most housewives saved the little pieces that remained after the bar of soap was almost gone; these were placed in a jar, a little warm water added and let stand. The resulting "jelly" was used in dishwashing.

One of our members laughed as she recalled the joy of most women when manufactured soap powders appeared in grocery stores.

"Why, I felt I had the world by the tail on a downhill drag when they invented Oxydol!"

Soap Making. Clean fat by bringing to a boil in an equal amount of water. Remove from heat and stir in 1 quart of water for each gallon of liquid. Cool. Remove cleaned fat from top when firm.

1 can lye
2½ pints cold water
6 pounds clean fat

Slowly add lye to cold water and stir until dissolved. Melt fat and let it cool. Pour lye solution into melted fat in a thin, steady stream with slow, even stirring. Continue slow stirring ten to twenty minutes until it looks like thick honey. Pour into wooden box, cover with old blanket or rug to retain heat. Let stand twenty-four hours. Remove and cut into bars.

Aging improves this soap.

The residents could discuss other WORK SAVERS. What is their favorite household invention: the flush toilet, vacuum cleaner, garbage disposal, dishwasher, clothes washer and dryer? Show of hands.

Eleventh Meeting

WHAT WOULD ONE FIND . . . ? Visiting a grocery store, what could one find in the dairy case? At the meat counter? Frozen foods? If one went to a roadside stand? In a hardware store?

A TOUR OF THE HOME KITCHEN. This is easily planned and directed by an employee, includes a detailed description of equipment, how it is operated, names of employees in this area, description of the uniforms, duties, service, job descriptions of residents assisting, and so forth.

Twelfth Meeting

FITTED TRAVELING CASE. This attractive white glazed chintz traveling case bound with shocking pink picot ribbon contains a knitted wash cloth and crocheted slippers both of which can be made by the blind.

Material. ¼ yd 36" white glazed chintz; ¼ yd 36" transparent plastic; 1 yd shocking pink picot ribbon ¾" wide (ribbon should match slippers).

Cut the following pieces: 1 8" × 22" white chintz strip for case; 1 8" × 18¾" transparent plastic strip (for lining); 1 8" × 5¼" transparent plastic (for pocket).

Directions. Allow ¼" for all seams and turned in raw edges.

1. Bind one 5¼" side of plastic pocket with ribbon, folding ribbon in half lengthwise over edge.

2. Place plastic pocket on plastic lining 13" from one end, ribbon edge toward 13" end. Clip in place.

3. Line 8" × 22" strip of chintz with plastic, placing glazed side of chintz and pocket side of plastic together. Match plastic and chintz at far end from plastic pocket. Stitch along 2 long sides. Turn.

4. Bind lined end of chintz strip with ribbon, folding ribbon

Figure 8

in half lengthwise over edge. Let ¼″ of ribbon extend beyond each side.

5. Fold bound end of strip up 5¾″ onto plastic lining. Turn in raw ribbon ends. Stitch either side to form plastic-lined chintz pocket.

6. At other end fold chintz that extends beyond lining 2¼″ down onto plastic lining. Turn in raw edges and stitch around 3 sides. This will form the closing flap of the case.

7. Bind edge of this flap with ribbon allowing ribbon to extend ¼″ beyond each side so it may be turned in for neat finish.

8. Fashion a tailored double loop tab for closing trim by making a loop 3″ deep. Over this make a second loop 1¾″ deep. Tack at top and fasten to inside of flap edge at center.

9. To close case fold twice. With tab at top and large chintz plastic lined pocket at bottom, fold case up on itself along large pocket's ribbon-bound edge. Fold flap down. Fasten with snap at flap center.

Thirteenth Meeting

Of DISCUSSIONS ON SUCH SUBJECTS AS OLD-TIME FARMING, a resident writes:

> Patients whose lives were spent on farms as homemakers had a discussion session on old-time farming. Those attending enjoyed this greatly as they were stimulated to reminisce. One resident reported that the people in her town were all farmers in the pioneering days. There were no telephones, radios or television then. I remember my uncle playing the violin or the bass for the barn dances and then there were cards and sleigh rides, neighborly visits and singing to the melodious old-time organ.
>
> The news was brought in to the cheese factory by farmers. They used lumber wagons, buggies, surreys hitched to a team or single, as the case may be.
>
> There was fishing in the nearby rivers and hunting. Sometimes they were even a little hungry. That's when a rabbit came in handy.
>
> Houses were heated with stoves, and I too, remember how cold it was upstairs when you crawled in the feathertick or corn husks with your wrapped brick or soapstone.
>
> Everyone did their own butchering and curing of meat, and there wasn't a farm without a smokehouse. They made their own butter and bread. And many is the casing I helped stuff with sausage, too. Root cellars underground were used for food storage.

Plowing was done by hand, the woman often following the horse; they also did their own horseshoeing. Houses were lit by oil lamps. And that's the old time farmer's wife and people were happy!

Residents could describe the farm kitchen: the dry sink, getting the pump primed, the pets brought up there, children studying there at night, the china patterns, the cooking ware, the names of the old cookstoves, what the ashes were used for, the water in the stove tank, how a meal was prepared, threshing day, butchering day, ironing and wash days, canning, social life in the kitchen at night, Saturday night baths, and so forth.

Fourteenth Meeting

MONOLOGUE. Her first marketing.

A resident could volunteer to read this aloud:

Enter a slight yellow-haired girl of about seventeen. She wears a large new wedding ring. She smiles sweetly at the clerk and shyly lisps:

What have you nice for two? Chops? No, I don't want chops. We had them all last week and one day while I was playing the piano they burn't themselves up and it smelled awful in the house the next day and my husband hasn't been real partial to chops since.

Porterhouse steak? That would be nice; give me one please, I don't want that long part. It's all fat and neither my husband or myself eat a bit of fat. I want that round thin part. Why can't I have it? It's the tail? Steaks don't have tails. No, I don't intend to have it if I can't have it with the tail.

How much does this chicken cost? It isn't a chicken—what is it? A duck? Well don't ducks look different when they are swimming. I think I would like a small chicken. About a pound and a quarter please. Why can't I get little chickens in winter? When we went into the country last week we ran over a little dounty teeny one with the car and I cried it looked so much like a baby—and my husband said—well I am trying to decide what I want, and I don't see why you should wait on the woman first. She just came in and I'm in an awful hurry.

Yes, I know what I want. I want a leg of lamb. Mother always said when in doubt choose lamb; you can send me a fat, I mean, a lean plump leg of lamb.

Five pounds! Good gracious no! We wouldn't eat that much in a week. My husband is a vegetarian anyway and only lets me eat meat because Mother told him I needed it and he believes—Well, haven't you any lamb with thinner legs?

Oh, dear, I wish I had gotten married in the summertime. A girl can get clothes heaps cheaper then and we could have stayed in the country with Mother and had lot of good things to eat, and—I know. Send me some beef, lean beef and we'll have beef stew and then I can go to the matinee, and leave it right on the stove cooking itself all the afternoon. Thank you. Goodbye.

What mistakes has each one made as a bride or new housekeeper?

AN HOUR OF TALK. Does working at a job make a woman lose interest in her home? How much time should she spend at home? Should a wife who is disinterested in housework do something else? Must a working woman neglect her family?
Or,
Should toy companies cease making toys connected with violence and aggression?
Or,
What do members understand "Women's Lib" to be? Will it last? Do they sympathize? At what age are women happiest? What economic status brings most happiness? How much independence does a woman really want? Can she actually compete with a man? How or how not? Does she really want to?

Fifteenth Meeting

FROG BEANBAG. Residents could make a gift for pediatric wards, a needy child, or a grandchild.
Materials. Two pieces of cloth 7″ × 6½″; needle and thread; beans, corn, or rice.
Procedure.
1. Trace the pattern.
2. Fold the material lengthwise and lay the pattern on the fold; pin and cut out two frog shapes.
3. Put right sides together and stitch or sew around the edge using a ¼″, leaving the "seat" open for putting in the beans.
4. Fill frog with about ¼ cup of small beans or rice.
5. Turn in the edges and overcast the bottom.
This is another project which could be started in the club and taken to the residents' rooms to finish.

HALLOWEEN PARTY! A member reports on Homemakers inviting men to a party!

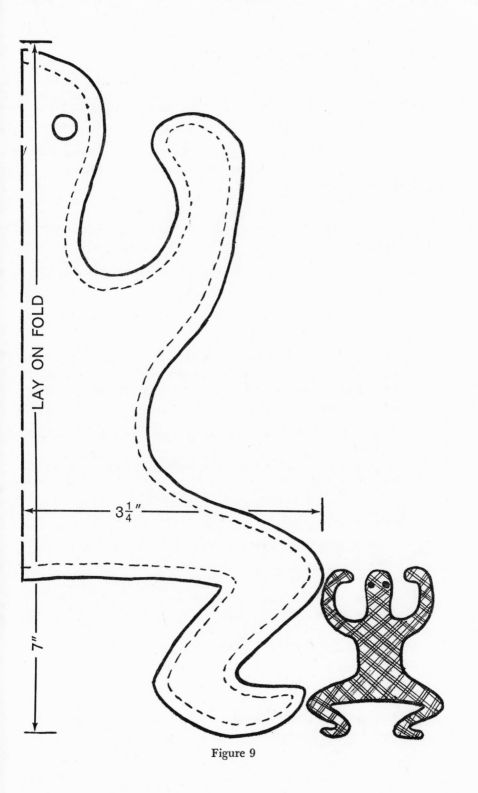

LAY ON FOLD

$3\frac{1}{4}$"

7"

Figure 9

On October 30 the Merry Makers meeting was held in the largest room in the building, the dining room, which can seat a hundred ambulatory residents. The fifteen tables were moved into the hall. A large crowd was expected to attend the Halloween masquerade ball. Over a dozen wheelchair patients were there and visitors lined three sides of the room. A short business meeting was called by the president and opened by the club song. Roll call was answered by over half of the residents in the Home.

A local orchestra arrived. The first masked dancer on the floor was one of our male residents dressed as a witch with a broom. One after another the residents and off-duty staff members appeared in carnival costumes.

It brought back many memories of happy times, especially to those who had received prizes when dressed as Little Red Riding Hood or as a gypsy or as Mrs. Claus with Santa.

———— guessed the long johns in the mystery box. Three residents decorated cookies for the evening meal in the dining room with their own original Halloween designs.

Could the club plan a seasonal party, perhaps for some other time of year, send invitations to friends or relatives, to other Home residents, or to another Home club? Could they publicize it, make decorations?

TALK-ABOUT-IT. Have they enjoyed shopping by mail? Will the teenagers of today make responsible citizens of tomorrow? Is there a difference in attitude toward work among young people?

Sixteenth Meeting

MAKING A CAKE, the biggest treat that could be devised!

Chocolate Cake Recipe. Sift together:

2 cups flour	¾ cup cocoa
1 cup sugar	2 tsp. baking soda
½ tsp. salt	

Grease and flour cake pan, either one 9″ × 14″, or two 8″ or 9″ layer pans. Heat oven to 350 degrees.

1 cup salad dressing (Miracle Whip is good)
1½ cup milk

Gradually add milk to salad dressing. Mix until smooth. Add 1 teaspoon vanilla. Fold dry ingredients into salad dressing mixture. Fold just until blended, like muffin batter. Do not overmix. Bake at 350 degrees.

COOKBOOKS, a yearly project with a Home auxiliary. An auxiliary published four hundred cookbooks selling for $1 each; residents made the covers and helped put the books together. The money cleared went for carpeting and drapes in the residents' visiting room. Residents in the ceramics class made lamps for the room.

Would residents like to help with a cookbook project? Are there other local contests or advertising gimmicks in which they could take part with the help of a volunteer? Can committees be assigned to work?

HOUSEHOLD HINTS can stimulate conversation which could be used in making up a notebook on do's and don'ts contributed by each member.

1. How to get out difficult stains.
2. First aid in the home.
3. Time savers.
4. Hints in good sanitation.
5. Hints in maintaining good health.
6. Economizing.

Seventeenth Meeting

MAXIMS are put on slips of paper which residents draw from a hat to read and comment upon, for example:

"Before beginning, prepare carefully."

"Life's a pleasant situation, let us take it as it comes."

"Learning makes a man fit company for himself."

"To do nothing is the way to be nothing."

"The glory is not in never failing, but in rising every time you fail."

"No one grows old by living, only by losing interest in life."

"Helping other people in their troubles leaves you little time to worry about your own."

"A good example is the best sermon."

"Most folks are about as happy as they make up their minds to be."

"Youth is not a time of life; it is a state of mind."

"Education makes people easy to lead, but difficult to drive; easy to govern, but impossible to enslave."

"It's very easy to forget what Christmas is all about. You bind it up with tinsel and let the spirit out."

SPRING HOUSECLEANING furnishes a subject for discussion. A Homemaker remembering, tells about it in the Home newsletter.

> I can remember back into the years when I was a child and Mom tore the entire house apart as she dug into every nook and corner every spring. Our modern housekeepers do not have the annual tussle with the living room rug! My Mom used to take hers out, stretch it across two clothes lines and then pound and whip the poor thing with a wire rug beater. This seemed to give her a great feeling of satisfaction. Perhaps the psychiatrists would say she got rid of her hostilities, but I'm sure that wasn't the case. She just got rid of the winter's dirt her old-time vacuum cleaner didn't suck out.

Is there such a thing as overdoing the cleaning bit? What are the extremes? Can there be any benefits in the exercise? Have some residents lived in log cabins with dirt floors or in other countries where housekeeping was far different? Should children be punished by giving them housework to do; could this make them always hate it?

Eighteenth Meeting

KISSING BALL, a Christmas mobile, can be a group project, each doing one step.

Materials. Discarded Christmas cards, wrapping, foil, or construction paper; stapler; pinking scissors; ribbon, pencil; paste; 3″ cardboard circle.

Procedure.

1. Cut the Christmas cards in twenty 3″ circles, using a cardboard circle pattern.

2. Make a cardboard triangle pattern in perfect proportion to fit on the circle pattern. Fold all the circles this shape. (To make a pattern for the triangle, fold a circle in half, then in half again. Fold the outer edge of the circle to touch the center; fold two more edges of the circle to touch the center to make a triangle shape. There will be three stand-up folds around the triangle.)

3. Staple or paste together twenty circles, ten in the middle

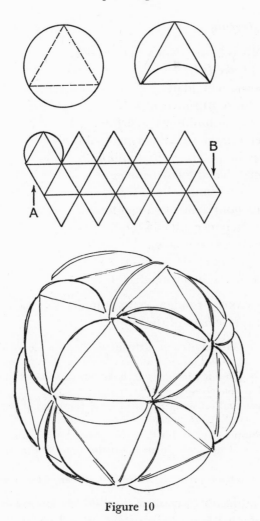

Figure 10

row, five in the top row, and five in the bottom row, flat on the table with the folds up. Paste or staple together the folds that stand back-to-back.

4. Paste or staple A and B, joining the ring of circles.

5. Paste or staple the circles at the top of the ball and those at the bottom of the ball, completing the sphere.

6. Staple or paste a ribbon on one fold to use for hanging the ball in a doorway, window, or on a chandelier.

Nineteenth Meeting

AN ORAL QUIZ is better than a written one.
What Kind of Cake Is It?
1. An appointment (date).
2. Upside down (turnover).
3. Used in grand buildings (marble).
4. The metal in the wedding ring (gold).
5. To wrap the wedding gift (ribbon).
6. An animal that absorbs (sponge).
7. Palm tree (coconut).
8. Heavenly nourishment (angel food).
9. Satan's sustenance (devil's food).
10. All the colors (rainbow).
11. A transparent cloth (chiffon).
12. From a root (gingerbread).

TO MAKE A CAKE, a resident can volunteer to read the following aloud for the amusement of the club:

> Light oven; get utensils and ingredients. Remove blocks and toy automobiles from table, grease pan, crack nuts. Measure two cups of flour; remove Johnnie's hands from flour; brush flour off him. Remeasure flour. Put flour, baking powder and salt in sifter.
>
> Get dustpan and brush up pieces of bowl Johnnie knocked on floor. Get another bowl. Wash Johnnie. Answer phone. Return to kitchen and find Johnnie. Remove his hands from bowl. Take up greased pan and find layer of nut-shells in it. Head for Johnnie who flees, knocking bowl off table.
>
> Wash kitchen floor, table, walls, dishes. Call baker. Lie down.

Was it this difficult to cook with children underfoot? How did people manage without baby-sitters? Residents tell a joke on themselves in cooking.

Twentieth Meeting

HANDCRAFTS FOR OLDSTERS. A volunteer comes to teach one of the following:
Handmade rugs—Turkish knot, punch and hook, braided, pompom.
Handwoven design in dishcloths.

Yarn animals.
Embroidery and needlework.
Stitchery wall hangings.
Paper crafts.
Carving animal caricatures.
Paper flowers and party decorations.
Candle making.
Modern felt handicraft.
Modernistic chip carving.
Etching small aluminum trays.
Huck towel weaving.
Stencilling on cloth—placemats, aprons, card table cloths, dish towels.
Reed crafts.
Painting—wooden boxes, spoon and fork, salt and peppers.

IMPROVISATIONS in the craft shop. Gold powder mixed with gloss varnish makes an inexpensive paint for crafts.

Carpet samples cut in squares and pasted on a burlap backing can be used for attractive throw rugs.

Popcorn is strung and hung outside for the birds, a nice way of disposing of part of the Christmas tree trimmings.

To serve refreshments, hostesses pass paper cups in a muffin tin instead of a tray, to avoid tipping.

To decorate "Italian" bottles, liquid solder is used to outline the design on the bottle surface; a "stained" glass paint colors the sections and is purchased in a kit from a craft company.

Cotter pins instead of nails for rake knitting are smoother and the yarn is hooked off more easily.

Twenty-first Meeting

VALENTINE FORMALS can "swing" successfully; this volunteer tells how.

> Residents nominated candidates for Valentine king and queen, the leader conducting the procedures of an election. A volunteer took care of the registration of voters. Pictures were on display identifying the candidates and a resident in the voting booth showed residents the procedure of voting by numbering, for candidate one, two or three. The majority of votes received determined the royalty.

The Valentine formal was held in the recreation room, gay with red and white streamers, Valentine hearts and cupids, bouquets of cut flowers and music from a volunteer band. The king and queen sat with their court in the front of the hall surrounded by flowers.

Ladies attending the party were dressed in varied colored formals donated, altered and pressed by volunteers, the men wearing white shirts and dark trousers or suits.

All available seats were filled along the sidelines with onlookers from the Home and visitors from the community. Many enjoyed dancing. The superintendent took pictures of the queen and king, their court and other groups. Punch and Valentine cookies were served.

Would the women like to invite men in the Home to a party? Could formals be collected? (Usually, the difficulty is in getting formals large enough, strapless bras large enough, and so on.) Could volunteers help? Perhaps, without the formals, a simpler party might be planned with the president of the club, a queen, or the people with perfect attendance given crowns as the club's sweethearts. Could they draw names for secret pals and send one another an unsigned Valentine which they've made?

VALENTINE CLUB MEETING in a Home is described:

Residents made Valentines with poems, puzzles or jokes written by hand and put in a Valentine box. Each guest was greeted with a red heart corsage to wear and made by the women in the Art Class.

The club president read the minutes of the last meeting; roll call was taken with each resident giving his birthdate. The earliest birthdates determined the man and woman present as King of Hearts and Queen of Hearts, crowned with Valentine crowns.

The story of St. Valentine's Day was read by a resident: it was an early Roman custom to give hearts and flowers; the first Valentine was written by a priest named Valentine in 270 A.D. to his jailer's blind daughter, who recovered her sight through his kindness.

The Valentine box was opened, verses read, and Valentines distributed by the club president; love songs were played by a resident on her echo harp with others joining in the singing.

Guessing the number of hearts in a jar was won by a resident who guessed three hundred candy hearts, the exact number.

With the next game planned by the committee, residents made words out of "Valentine," a resident with twenty-seven words taking first place. A Valentine gift of a lovely red wallet made by a resident was given to the wife of the superintendent.

Could these club ideas be adapted to a February club meeting?

Twenty-second Meeting

A BIG COUNTRY WEDDING. What goes into the planning? Residents compiled a list of procedures in the order of preparation for a country wedding.

1. Talk to a priest or minister to arrange the time and date.

2. Call different hall owners to arrange for time, price, hall capacity, guests to invite. Find out whether the supper club caters food or prepares their own. Plan menus with them, decide on drinks to be served.

3. Call different band leaders for available music and decide on a reasonable rate.

4. The groom asks his wedding attendants and the bride chooses the maid of honor.

5. The bride chooses the dress and bridesmaid's dresses. The bride assists her mother and perhaps her future mother-in-law in choosing hers.

6. Order flowers for the bride, groom, attendants, families, drivers and others.

7. Arrange for picture taking with photographer.

8. Pick out a ring for the groom, gifts for attendants and groom.

9. Pick out style of suit for male attendants of the party.

10. Arrange for drivers and passengers.

11. Contact organist and soloist.

12. Arrange the wording of the wedding ceremony.

13. Make sure to wear something old, something new, something borrowed and something blue.

14. Arrange for a rehearsal at the church.

15. "The day comes and everything goes as planned, maybe even better!"

Residents can discuss preparation procedures of long ago at the time of death, Golden Weddings, shivarees, or some special ethnic celebration.

Twenty-third Meeting

A MAKE-BELIEVE PICNIC requires nothing but imagination. For instance, in a discussion on planning a make-believe picnic, one of the members who had worked with Campfire Girls could discuss the cookouts and was helpful in an all-out club discussion.

"We got the potatoes all ready to bake and put right down on the coals." "How will we get there?" "My daughter will take as many as she can," laughing. "In the garage there are bicycles and motorcycles." "It's on the water: I'll take my boat." *"I'll* take *my* boat." "I'll be coming on cloud No. 9." "I'm coming in my wheelchair." "What games shall we play?" "Cards, hide and seek, bingo, pom-pom pull away, baseball, football (Florence will be the umpire), tag, sit down games, winkum, horseshoes, flying kites, paper plate toss."

During the summer, the talkative groups planned these picnics and imagined what each of them would bring: fried chicken, corn, sweet pickles, potato salad, beans, German salad, hard-boiled eggs, homemade biscuits, cookies, lemonade, and coffee. ("You can bake a batch of beans." "I won't come unless you have dessert: homemade apple pie and chocolate cake." "I'll bring a couple of apple pies." "How about cheese?" "And coffee?")

The COTA produced magazine pictures of a picnic basket, table, and red checked cloth. One of the residents wanted a picnic on the ground. They also discussed the modern picnic with the grill, bratwurst ("They make wonderful sandwiches"), cooking hamburgers outside, baked potatoes wrapped in foil ("Someone bring the charcoal." "Have it at my house and I'll bring the charcoal.") dixie cups, and ice cream bars.

Residents could surprise themselves with wild imaginations involving a picnic they won't actually have!

OR, A REAL COOKOUT with food furnished by the Home is possible. Successful cookouts are sometimes complete with a concertina and music to clap hands and sing to. They can be held in an area of cement or macadam on which to dance.

Even wheelchair residents can play bunco, beanbags, checkers, and cards. Others like lawn swings, horseshoes, a basketball hoop, or roulette wheels. Everyone enjoys the fortune telling, guessing booths, or shooting a popgun at a tin can on a fence.

Twenty-fourth Meeting

LEAF DESIGN, HOT PLATE MATS. Decorative hot plate mats are made from pottery shades of cotton yarn for the casual table setting. Best of all, they can be made by the blind crocheter.

Material.

	Quantity	Approx. Mat Size	Needle Size
Cotton yarn	1 skein	11¼″	steel 00
Rug yarn	2 skeins	11½″	steel 00
Heavy rug yarn, art. 235 (use to make largest of 3 mats)	2 skeins	15″	aluminum G or 6

Directions. Large Mat:

Ch 24, sc in 2nd st. from hook, 1 sc in each of the next 21 sts. of ch, 3 sc in next st. of ch, working on other side of ch work 1 sc in each of the next 20 sts., ch 3, turn.

2nd row. Working in front loop of st. only, 1 sc in each of the next 20 sc, 2 sc in next st., 3 sc in next sc, 2 sc in next st., 1 sc in each of the next 20 sc, ch 3, turn.

3rd row. Working in back loop of st. only, 1 sc in each of the next 23 sc, 3 sc in next sc, 1 sc in each of the next 21 sc, ch 3, turn.

4th row. Working in front loop of st. only, 1 sc in each of the next 21 sc, 2 sc in next sc, 3 sc in next sc, 2 sc in next sc, 1 sc in each of the next 21 sc, ch 3, turn.

5th row. Working in back loop of st. only, 1 sc in each of the next 24 sc, 3 sc in next sc, 1 sc in each of the next 21 sc, ch 3, turn. All the even numbered rows are worked in front loop of st. and all the odd numbered rows are worked in back loop only. Ch 3 to turn all rows.

6th row. 1 sc in each of the next 21 sc, 2 sc in next sc, 3 sc in next sc, 2 sc in next sc, 1 sc in each of the next 22 sc.

7th row. 1 sc in each of the next 25 sc, 3 sc in next sc, 1 sc in each of the next 22 sc.

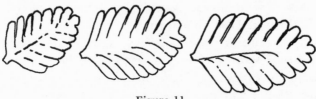

Figure 11

8th row. 1 sc in each of the next 23 sc, 2 sc in next sc, 3 sc in next sc, 2 sc in next sc, 1 sc in each of the next 23 sc.

9th row. 1 sc in each of the next 26 sc, 3 sc in next sc, 1 sc in each of the next 23 sc. 10th row—same as 8th row.

11th row. 1 sc in each of the next 26 sc, 3 sc in next sc, 1 sc in each of the next 24 sc.

12th row. 1 sc in each of the next 24 sc, 2 sc in next sc, 3 sc in next sc, 2 sc in next sc, 1 sc in each of the next 23 sc. Repeat last 2 rows 3 times.

19th row. 1 sc in each of the next 26 sc, 3 sc in next sc, 1 sc in each of the next 22 sc.

20th row. 1 sc in each of the next 23 sc, 3 sc in next sc, 1 sc in each of the next 22 sc.

21st row. 1 sc in each of the next 23 sc, 3 sc in next sc, 1 sc in each of the next 19 sc.

22nd row. 1 sc in each of the next 21 sc, ch 8 for stem, 1 sc in 2nd st. from hook, 1 sc in each of the next 6 sts. of ch, sc in same space as last sc worked of leaf, 1 sc in each of the next 18 sc, ch 3 turn, sl. st. in each of the next 3 sc, break yarn.

LEAF DESIGN, HOT PLATE MATS.

Directions. Small Mat:

Ch 14, sc in 2nd st. from hook, 1 sc in each of the next 11 sts. of ch, 3 sc in next st. of ch, working on other side of ch work 1 sc in each of the next 10 sts., ch 3, turn.

2nd row. Working in front loop of st. only, 1 sc in each of the next 10 sc, 2 sc in next st., 3 sc in next sc, 2 sc in next st., 1 sc in each of the next 10 sc, ch 3, turn.

3rd row. Working in back loop of st. only, 1 sc in each of the next 13 sc, 3 sc in next sc, 1 sc in each of the next 11 sc, ch 3, turn.

4th row. Working in front loop of st. only, 1 sc in each of the next 11 sc, 2 sc in next sc, 3 sc in next sc, 2 sc in next sc, 1 sc in each of the next 11 sc, ch 3, turn.

5th row. Working in back loop of st. only, 1 sc in each of the next 14 sc, 3 sc in next sc, 1 sc in each of the next 11 sc, ch 3 turn. All the even numbered rows are worked in front loop of st. and all the odd numbered rows are worked in back loop only. Ch 3 to turn all rows.

6th row. 1 sc in each of the next 11 sc, 2 sc in next sc, 3 sc in next sc, 2 sc in next sc, 1 sc in each of the next 12 sc.

7th row. 1 sc in each of the next 15 sc, 3 sc in next sc, 1 sc in each of the next 12 sc.

8th row. 1 sc in each of the next 13 sc, 2 sc in next sc, 3 sc in next sc, 2 sc in next sc, 1 sc in each of the next 13 sc.

9th row. 1 sc in each of the next 16 sc, 3 sc in next sc, 1 sc in each of the next 13 sc. 10th row—same as 8th row.

11th row. 1 sc in each of the next 16 sc, 3 sc in next sc, 1 sc in each of the next 14 sc.

12th row. 1 sc in each of the next 14 sc, 2 sc in next sc, 3 sc in next sc, 2 sc in next sc, 1 sc in each of the next 13 sc.

13th row. Repeat Row 11.

14th row. Repeat Row 12.

15th row. Repeat Row 11.

16th row. 1 sc in each of the next 14 sts., ch 5 for stem, 1 sc in 2nd st. from hook, 1 sc in each of the next 3 sts. of ch, sc in same space as last sc worked of leaf, 1 sc in each of the next 12 sc, ch 3, turn, sl. st. in each of the next 3 sc, break yarn.

TO READ ALOUD

Good Stories.

Henry, O.: *The Best of O. Henry One Hundred Stories*   829

Kyelgaard, James: *Lost Wagon*   822
  A story of emigrants on the Oregon trail.

Lane, Rose: *Let the Hurricane Roar*   Fiction
  A straightforward and exciting story of pioneer life.

Laughton, Charles: *Tell Me a Story*   808
  Sixty items good to read aloud to an audience of one or an audience of hundreds, chosen by a skilled storyteller.

Lawrence, Leland: *The Family Book of Best Loved Short Stories*   802

Leavitt, Robert: *The Chip on Grandma's Shoulder*   818

Malone, Ted: *Ted Malone's Favorite Stories*   818
  Stories about people, places, and things which have been favorites with the author's radio audience.

Moody, Ralph: *Little Britches*   818
  Appealing stories of family life on a ranch.

Papashvily, George: *Anything Can Happen*   Fiction
Story of a new American's first experience in this country.
West, Jessamyn: *Friendly Persuasion*   Fiction
Gently humorous sketches of a family of Quakers in Indiana
during the Civil War.
White, Helen Chappell: *This Is the Life*   Fiction
Stories of family life in a small town.
Humor.
Benchley, Robert: *Benchley Round-Up*   819
Collection of pieces by one of America's most genuine hu-
morists.
Day, Clarence: *Best of Clarence Day*   817
Contains "Life with Father" and other choice humor.
Golden, Harry: *Only in America*   811
Wit and whimsey, a love of people and learning characterize
these pieces by a newspaper editor.
Guareschi, Giovanni: *Little World of Don Camillo*   Fiction
Delightful story of a parish priest and his trials and tribula-
tions in dealing with his wayward flock.
Guareschi, Giovanni: *House that Nino Built*   858
"Read a chapter at a time; it should make for the gayety of
nations."
Of Dogs, Horses, and Other Animals.
Henderson, T.: *Circus Doctor*   92-H495
Reminiscences of the chief veterinarian of Ringling Brothers
and Barnum and Bailey circus.
Lorenz, Konrad: *King Soloman's Ring*   591
Delightful book about animal and human behavior.
Macauley, Thurston: *The Great Horse Omnibus*   808
A treasury of great horse stories from Homer to Hemingway.
Mowat, Farley: *Dog Who Wouldn't Be*   Fiction
A boy, a dog, a sense of humor, and a love of nature add up
to a grand tale.

AUTOMOBILE CLUB

Introduction

Automobile fanciers may not all be men, or drivers, or collectors of antique cars. Most people have some opinions to give on

cars: quality, performance, style, practicality, antique cars as an investment, cost, concern regarding roads and drivers, laws, sentiment, advertisements, and so forth.

Is this enough of a common interest to draw people together? Can such a group work with a local Hot Rod order? Can members share experiences in accidents, trips, first cars, teaching a potential driver?

Goals (for Residents)

Three main goals should be kept in mind.

1. To make good friends, share experiences.

2. Although not present-day drivers, to learn something about cars and driving.

3. To build a bridge between the community and the Home through this club.

Motivation Techniques (for Leader)

The following techniques are important:

1. Give individual invitations to participate.

2. Make introductions as icebreakers, especially with new admissions, volunteers, or visitors.

3. Learn residents' backgrounds and interests and use them in the activity.

4. Always be enthusiastic.

First Meeting

See "The First Meeting" in Part III, "How to Lead a Club."

SKILLS IN GIVING DIRECTIONS are tested. How good are they at giving directions? Residents ask one another how to give directions to strangers to get somewhere in the Home or somewhere in the city.

COURTESY IN DRIVING, a short course in human relations.
The six most important words: "I admit I made a mistake."
The five most important words: "You did a good job."
The four most important words: "What is your opinion?"
The three most important words: "If you please."
The two most important words: "Thank you."

The one most important word: "We."
The least important word: "I."
Similar word combinations have often been made; residents compose different ones for drivers.

GETTING ACQUAINTED. Before giving consideration to the special interests of the club, it might be wise to introduce this or some other similar game, even though it has nothing to do with autos.

Each resident is given a sheet of paper and pencil as he arrives. He writes his first and last name on the sheet vertically, one letter below the other.

Then he tries to locate among members present, those persons whose names have a letter also found in his name. He writes this name on the sheet, using a letter of his new friend's name:

A
M
O
JoSie Smith

J
O
Horatio Jones
N
S
O
N

Second Meeting

MY FAVORITE CAR locates a focal point of interest. A large poster, wheelchair height, is tacked to the wall. On the poster are the following headings to be filled in by residents: My Name, My Favorite Car, Present Value, Miles Per Gallon, Favorite Color, Size (weight, style), Manufacturer, Selling Points. . . .

AUTO SKETCH requires sketching pad and pencil.
Equipment. Paper slips with the following cars written on them are placed in a hat for drawing: Matador, Ford T-Bird, Fairlane, Mustang, Javelin, Hornet, Gremlin, Mercury, Gladiator, Lincoln,

Cyclone, Dart, Coronet, Demon, Colt, Barracuda, Duster, Satellite, Firebird, Tempest, Mark II, Crown.

Procedure.

1. The group is divided into two sides and a representative is chosen on each side.
2. One draws a slip from a hat, showing it to both representatives; it indicates the auto for which they will sketch a clue.
3. Each hurries to his group to sketch the clue, not actually drawing the picture of the car, and not using letters or numbers.
4. When the group correctly guesses the car through these sketches, they shout.
5. The winning side gives the answer first.

A TRIP could be taken to see new autos or to make a demonstration ride in a new car; residents could attend an auto race or an antique car show.

Third Meeting

AUTO RACE resembles a horseracing game, adapted here.
Equipment. Large butchers' paper marked off ten squares on side, twenty the length of the paper; checkers or markers; dice; several squares are marked "broken axle," "out of gas," "speeding ticket," "flat tire," and so on.

Procedure.

1. Players roll the dice in turn, moving the checker; they return to start when they land on one of the handicaps.
2. The player reaching the finish first, wins.

SIMILAR EXPERIENCES can offer further opportunity for getting acquainted. The signature (or if oral, names are given and introductions made) of someone who
1. Has never owned a car.   . . . .
2. Drove a car the greatest number of years ago. . . . .
3. Never had an accident.   . . . .
4. Never drove a car with an automatic shift.   . . . .
5. Never changed a tire.   . . . .

6. Drove a car most recently. . . . .
7. Had a car with a brass radiator. . . . .
8. Owned a garage (was a mechanic, sold cars). . . . .
9. Paid the least for a car. . . . .
10. Paid the most for a car. . . . .

A SINGALONG can be tried if some strong voices are present.

Pack Up Your Troubles

Pack up your troubles
In your tool kit bag
And drive, drive, drive.
While you've a new band aid to mend a tire,
Drive, boys, many a mile.
Fan belt fixed with dental floss
You may speed on in style, sooooo
Pack up your troubles
In your tool kit bag
And drive, drive, drive.

JUDGING MOTEL ACCOMMODATIONS and services, what would they consider? Can they name twenty regulations and standards? thirty? When it is open; location on highway; accessibility to restaurants; accommodations for children; pets, wheelchairs, accessibility to entertainment; comfort; soundproofing; tiled showers; cleanliness.

Fourth Meeting

An action game is made relevant in the Automobile Club.

TRIALS provide good competition for people in wheelchairs.
Equipment. From a piece of corrugated cardboard or wood 2′ square, 6″ squares are measured out. These squares are painted alternate colors. Scrap leather can be obtained at a shoe shop to make discs 2½″ in diameter. (Old rubber shoe heels can also be used.)

A set of five discs are painted the color of the odd squares, and another set of five in color of even squares.

Procedure.

1. Each player has five discs; pitching distance is about 6′.
2. If more than half of player's disc lands in the squares in his own color, he adds that number to his score.
3. If it is more than half in an opponent's color, he subtracts that amount from his score.
4. Players change colors every other round.
5. The person having the highest score at the end of the pre-determined number of trials is the winner.

Residents are asked to comment on this account of a wheel-chair traveler HITCHHIKING:

> A young man in Los Angeles who was confined to a wheelchair for most of his twenty-one years maneuvered onto the ramp of the Santa Ana Freeway and stretched his thumb for a ride. Nothing new for him, this is his seventh year of hitchhiking which has taken him across the country and into west Canada.
>
> "I feel sorry for people who say they never can get away anywhere," he said, crippled by meningitis when he was a baby. He went from New Orleans to California in three days. Another trip took him from Rhode Island to California and back in six weeks. He wears out one wheelchair a year. He carries with him a toothbrush, razor, mouthwash and soap. A change of clothes pads the seat of his chair. He wiggles onto the front seat, folds the wheelchair and puts it in the back.

Has anyone of them ever hitchhiked? Where? Any experiences in picking up hitchhikers?

FORM A WORD. A blackboard is used or each player is given a chart like the following. The letters may be selected in any manner.

The object of the game is to add as few letters as possible to form a word. Thus "car" in the first, "top" the second. In the fourth, it would cost two points if the word "very" were used. If no word can be thought of, a penalty of ten points is given.

No letters can be inserted between the two letters on the chart, no proper names or abbreviations used. The player with the lowest score wins.

1. A R = CAR, 1 point
2. O P = TOP, 1 point
3. O U = OUR, 1 point
4. V E
5. U R
6. N D
7. A M
8. R U
9. N T
10. Y P

Fifth Meeting

THE TICKING CLOCK they are asked to find. Before residents arrive, the leader hides a ticking clock. When the players enter, they all start looking for the clock. The one finding it hides it at the next meeting.

THINGS TO TALK ABOUT.

1. How many types of traffic accidents can be listed by the group (other moving objects, bicycle, pedestrian, train, parked car)?

2. What questions would the resident ask himself to avoid a collision with the car ahead? Factors to be considered: reaction distance, braking distance, total stopping distance. Are there vehicles in the roadway or on the shoulder? Are there marked or unmarked intersections? Is his turn signal on? Are his brake lights lit? Has he been drifting to the right or left preparing to turn? Are there parked cars, livestock? How much distance should one give for every ten miles of speed (one car length)?

3. In case of accident, what material should be collected immediately and delivered to the insurance company at once (name of insured, agency name, address and number, make of vehicle, identification number, name and address of driver, phone number, name and address of other driver or property owner and phone number, date and time of accident, place of accident, did police take a report, if so what city or county, was anyone injured—names and addresses, what happened)?

Sixth Meeting

OTHER TOPICS TO DISCUSS.

1. What car do they think has the best reputation?

2. Inventors, hot-rodders, and gas company engineers are putting together the auto they figure best meets the air pollution standards and gets 60 miles to a gallon. This is a car powered by a diesel engine. What are the best gas savers among the new cars? What is the latest to be said on cutting down noise pollution on cars?

3. Have they ever seen a getaway car leaving the scene of the crime? They discuss the circumstances.

4. Do they favor the law prohibiting liquor in cars? Would it be effective in decreasing the litter of bottles and tin cans on the highways and streets?

THEY CAN PLAN AN IMAGINARY FESTIVAL OF ANTIQUE CARS, horse-drawn carriages, old-fashioned bicycles and motorcycles, antique farm machinery, and other types of pioneer transportation.

What could be the incline of the hill climb regulations, rules on horse-drawn vehicle contests, vintage bicycle races, and fashion show standards in competition?

Could the source be the residents themselves who have attended such festivals?

A resident is asked to read "MA AND THE AUTO," an amusing verse by Edgar Guest (*Heap o' Living,* Reilly and Lee, 1916).

ROUTING A TRIP, residents describe the most scenic spot they know.

At the end of the meeting, each resident is given a road map of the state (available from a service station or through volunteers or employees). For the next meeting, he will mark the route for a (three-day, four-day) trip he would like to take.

1. For instance, he could start out from the county home, drive fifty miles to Madison for lunch, go on a tour of the capitol, drive through Maple Bluff and spend the afternoon in the Historical Museum. He could drive up to Baraboo before supper, find a motel, have supper, and go for a walk before retiring.

2. The second day he could see the Circus Museum in the morning, have a dinner at the Farm Kitchen, in the afternoon drive up to Wisconsin Rapids to visit old friends, drive to Holiday Inn at Stevens Point for supper and overnight.

3. The third day he could take 54 west to Black River State Forest, take 61 south to the Wisconsin River, continue to 53, have lunch with a grandson at Trempealeau, and drive down the Mississippi back to the county home.

Seventh Meeting

They DISCUSS THEIR PLANNED TRIPS.

NAME-THE-CAR RIDDLES.

1. Aged and fluid (Oldsmobile).
2. One who pats a boy (Patterson).
3. The North Star (Polara).
4. A kind of coffee (Maxwell).
5. Famous earl in English history (Essex).
6. Almost struts (Stutz).
7. A diplomat (Ambassador).
8. A weapon (Javelin) (Dart).
9. A bullfighter (Matador).
10. An insect (Hornet).
11. A semiprecious stone (Opel).
12. A pollutant (Mercury).
13. Pretty street (Fairlane).

Residents quiz others on these cars: Volkswagon, Cadillac, Plymouth, Chrysler, Fury, Barracuda, Valiant, Road Runner, Triumph, Fiat, Satellite, Saab, Toyota, Lincoln, Ford, Pontiac, Mustang, Jeep, Colt, Coronet, Imperial, Cougar, Cyclone, Maverick.

In teams, how many PARTS OF A CAR can residents list, without repetition? For instance, seated in two rows, each team names a part of a car, back and forth, until one team is "stumped."

RESIDENTS EACH BRING A JOKE ABOUT A CAR.

A motorist brought his car in for its 1,500 mile inspection.

"Is there anything the matter with it?" the service manager asked.

"Well, there's only one part of it that doesn't make a noise," the customer replied, "and that's the horn."

Eighth Meeting

In how many of the following VEHICLES have residents ridden? Describe them.

Coach, chariot, drag, landau, victoria, brougham, sulky, stage, omnibus, bus, cab, droshky, 4-wheel drive, dog cart, trap, gig, buggy, four-in-hand, random, tandem, touring car, racing car, side car, steam car, electric car, limousine, coupe, runabout, taxi, passenger train, freight, subway, luggage train, submarine, transport plane, flying boat, helicopter, balloon, blimp, parachute, gondola, junk, kayak, trackless trolley, cattle truck, sleeping car, club car, Pullman, observation car, pitchfork, ship, sail, man-of-war, merchant ship, liner, packet, whaler, collier, canoe, ice yacht, raft, rigger, sloop, cutter, clipper, ketch, barge, houseboat, fishing boat, trawler, greyhound, schooner, yawl, windjammer, paddle wheel, tug, launch, snowmobiles.

Can they name others?

"MAKES." Not more than six or eight at the most sit around one table. Each player has a deck of cards. Each player decides upon the "make" of a car he likes and calls himself this "make." Players try to remember the car of each player. When play begins, each one in turn turns over a card from his deck; this continues around the table until someone turns a card which is the top-turned card of someone else. Whoever can remember and name the other player's car first, wins the card from that person.

The game continues as long as practical and the player with the highest number of cards at the end is the winner.

At the next meeting, each member is asked to bring the picture of a car to be identified.

Ninth Meeting

A FILM ON AUTOS can be shown (see Appendix).

STUDY OF ANTIQUE CARS can mean a happy hour for those residents who have made a hobby of this classification. Pictures from a catalogue can be shown and discussed (see Appendix), or contributed pictures identified.

Tenth Meeting

BICYCLES OR "HOBBY HORSES" equipped with banana seats, monkey bars, speed shifts, and other gear are very modern remains of the first bike that "pushed" in the late 1700's. This subject introduces vehicles other than cars, and perhaps a new interest.

Can club members describe the best bicycle they ever had? The oldest they ever saw in a museum? A comic one used by clowns in a circus?

PHOTOGRAPHIC TOUR for camera enthusiasts can be imagined and planned at a meeting—a tour photographing cars or scenes from car windows.

LEASING CARS IN EUROPE. Cars can be leased for as little as twenty-five-day periods. With a lease, one gets a new car for a flat charge, full insurance, no licensed drivers' age limits, and no taxes to pay. Lease of a car for a six-week-period works out to a little more than $8 a day.

Members can comment on how they could use the car.

AWARD WINNERS are acclaimed. Group members are awarded who have never been arrested or paid a parking fine, who drove a car the greatest number of years, taught the most people to drive, or any other merits they may think of.

Residents next time team up for a debate, jotting down a few ideas in advance to argue as advocates.

Eleventh Meeting

A DEBATE can be just what everyone has been waiting for.
(1) What are pros and cons argument for being an automobile salesman?

Residents could present these points to begin:
Pros:
1. One meets a variety of people.
2. There is more freedom than with desk-bound jobs.

3. There's a possibility of better-than-average earnings. Compensation could include bonus plans and the use of a company car.

4. Surroundings are pleasant at new car dealerships.

5. A dealer can send a new salesperson to a manufacturer's school for special training; this training varies from a couple of days to several weeks. There are also general salesmenship courses in adult education classes.

Cons:

1. The successful salesperson is a self-starter who can't always keep regular hours because his (her) work is scheduled for the convenience of customers; this includes nights and weekends.

2. It is often necessary to change employers because one can't agree with the sales ethics of some dealers and used car sellers ("hi-balling" pressurers).

3. People sometimes resent haggling prices with prospects.

(2) Women can be good automobile salespersons.

Pros (they will be able to argue the cons!):

1. The idea can become quite interesting to women. The National Automobile Dealers Association (NADA) says there are "quite a few" women who deal in wheels—"it's not uncommon."

2. The rising number of women car owners and the influence of a wife's opinion in the purchase of a family car are two factors for being employed in sales.

3. One needn't be a mechanical whiz to learn enough about automobiles to answer questions of customers.

4. Many women have or can develop the ability to sell.

(3) Debate one make of car against the other.

AUTOMOBILE ADVERTISING. Is it helpful? Harmful? What is a favorite car ad? The one most offensive? Do they believe, as in *Hidden Persuaders* by Vance Packard (1957), that there is a hidden reason for selecting one of the cars advertised? Have they actually learned from an advertisement? Have they ever had the experience of finding automobile ads somewhat misrepresentative? How and when would they say that advertising cars is tasteful? What special gimmicks are there in persuasion?

Twelfth Meeting

CAR LITTER BAGS (to give to a friend) can be made at the club meeting.

Material. Lunch-size paper bags obtainable from grocery stores in packs of fifty for about ½ cent each; scissors; wrapping cord in 27″ lengths; paper punch; poster paint, crayons, or glue-ons.

Procedure.

1. Trim top of bag evenly.
2. Fold down bag top about ½″.
3. With paper punch, put two holes on one side of folded section of bag about 2″ apart.
4. Put end of cord (from outside in) through right-hand hole and pull through about 4″.
5. Wrap other end of cord clockwise all the way around bag and through left-hand hole, again leaving 4″ or 5″ section inside bag.
6. Cord will be double between holes.
7. Then run a line of glue around bag top and over cord and again fold down bag top about 1″, over cord.
8. Flatten bag, crease top edge and hold in place until glue dries.

This leaves a reinforced top and cord ends which are now tied together for hanging the bag on car door handle.

Bags decorated with poster paint or glue-ons can be refolded flat for decorating and distributing.

TALK SHOW. What is the solution for tearing down beautiful old landmarks to build macadam parking lots?

What tools does a modern mechanic need?

Are cars better today, or more poorly made, than the first ones?

Thirteenth Meeting

HOT RODS could be discussed by some young people who come to the Home to visit. How is a hot rod built? What are the merits of a Hot Rod Club? When were they started? Why have they become so popular? Can arrangements be made to attend a hot rod race, or inspect a hot rod at close range?

MILE A MINUTE is a guessing game. How long is a minute? Each stands, hands at sides. Exactly one minute from a given signal, they sit down (wheelchair patients may raise a hand). After everyone is down, those who sat down (or raised a hand) exactly at the end of the minute are named and applauded.

INVITE A LOCAL TRAFFIC OFFICER to come in for discussion about his work.

Fourteenth Meeting

RIDDLES FOR ANTIQUE CAR FANCIERS which stir recollections of ancient buggies:
1. Roosevelt's first name (Franklin).
2. To grind one's teeth (Nash).
3. The longest trip of all (Moon).
4. The Texas capital (Austin).
5. A river, one of our boundary lines (Rio).
6. A form of cooking and a skill (Studebaker).
7. A President assassinated (Lincoln).
8. A New York river (Hudson).
9. A cracker (Graham).
10. One color of human hair (Auburn).
11. To penetrate and an Indian weapon (Pierce Arrow).
12. A Spanish explorer (DeSoto).
13. A French explorer 1643-1687 (La Salle).
14. A chicken (Bantam).
15. The Latin word for land and an airborne craft (Terraplane).

HILL TRIAL is an action game relevant to climbs.
Equipment. As many sticks as there are players; a row of sticks for each row of players.
Procedure.
1. The sticks are laid in rows 12″ apart, like rungs on a ladder.
2. Players on each team line up and at a signal walk between the sticks; if their feet touch the sticks, they must start again. They walk up the row of sticks and back again to the next player who continues.
3. The row of players completing the procedure wins.

Fifteenth Meeting

SING-A-LONG needs a leader with a strong voice, or a musical instrument accompaniment.

When I Was Touring (to the tune of *When You're Smiling*)

> When I was touring, I was purring,
> Negot-i-a-ting machines around a curve,
> When I was touring, when I was touring,
> I circled the countryside assured.
> We saw this great land, my roadster and me,
> But now I'm grounded, an oldster, that's me.
> No more miling, but I'm smiling
> At each road map I see!

The Sidewalks of New York

East side, west side, all around the town,
Horns are tooting and there's polluting
And smog is darker brown.
We res-i-dents are safe here, safe from the hol—ocaust.
Hope the man-ufacturers *cap* the
Pu-trid car exhaust.

How D'ye Do?

> How d'ye do, Mister ———, How d'ye do?
> How d'ye do, Mister ———, How are you?
> Come to *our* club, if you can.
> You're part of our club plan.
> How d'ye do, Mister ———, How d'ye do?

DISCUSS the following:
Automobile transporters and drive-away companies.
Shock absorbers.
Speedometers.
Testing equipment.
Automobile trailers.
Rustproofing.
Repossessing service.
Toyota, Volvo, **MG**, Austin.

Armrests.

Vinyl roofs.

Carrier tops.

Transmission and engine exchange.

Wheel balancing.

Road service.

Exhaust system.

Night towing call.

Rebuilt transmissions.

From what countries do the following cars come?

Austin Healey	Morris	Datsun
Fiat	Alfa	Mercedes
Rover	Sunbeam	BMC
Jaguar	Peugeot	Porsche

Sixteenth Meeting

DISCUSS the following:

What is meant by frame straightening?

Car and truck rental and leasing?

Tire center?

Motor rebuilding and radiator shop?

Indoor showroom?

Bumper exchange—div. of allied plating?

Automobile carts?

Automobile clubs?

Crankshaft grinding?

Cylinder regrinding?

Foreign car garage (name as many cars as possible)?

WHO MAKES the following:

Fairlane	(Ford)
Sport Fury	(Plymouth)
Maverick	(Ford)
Barracuda	(Plymouth)
T-Bird	(Ford)
Valiant	(Plymouth)
Ambassador	(American Motors)
Duster	(Plymouth)

Mustang	(Ford)
Belvedere	(Plymouth)
Javelin	(American Motors)
Satellite	(Plymouth)
AMX	(American Motors)
Rebel	(American Motors)
Catalina	(Pontiac)
Hornet	(American Motors)
Grand Prix	(Pontiac)
Mercury	(Ford)
LeMans Sport	(Pontiac)
Jeep	(American Motors)
	(Kaiser Jeep Corp.)
Toyota	(Japan)
Executive	(Pontiac)
Volkswagon	(Germany)
Firebird	(Pontiac)
Cougar	(Ford)
Marquis	(Ford)

Name others not included.

VISITING A MOTEL DINING ROOM is all a fantasy in discussion.
What is it: Arabian coffee; escargots bourguignonne; flambée; filet de boeuf ǎ l'ambassadeur; boeuf stroganoff; riz pilaff; crěpes suzette; borsch; shashlik; chicken Kiev.

If they had unlimited funds, what recreation would be featured at the motel they owned?

Seventeenth Meeting

LISTINGS in team competition. How many motels can they name in the area? How many auto ferries? Can they list all cities of ten thousand in a hundred-mile area? The leader, with atlas in hand, makes corrections.

WHAT WOULD ONE PACK for the following trip to Ontario, Canada, given the following description of a motel in a tour guide book?

Exceptionally well-kept lodge rooms with shared baths, 7 tastefully furnished chalets and motel units and 9 comfortable cabins, cottages and cottage units; some with TV; many with radios; 17 with portable heaters; 17 with baths. Single rates $13.50 to $24. Playground. Lake swimming, fishing, rental boats and motors. No pets. Lower rates for groups of twelve or more before June 28 and after Sept. 2. Open May to Oct. 13. Reservation deposit required; refund notice 2 weeks. Phone. Dining room and snack bar; 7 to 8:30 A.M., noon to 1 and 6 to 7 P.M.; dinners about $3.00 to $5.00. In season rates, one room $24.00 to $36.00.

How much money would two people need for a week?

Eighteenth Meeting

LISTING PLACES OF INTEREST could be part of a souvenir folder. They remember a visit to Chicago (Milwaukee, a big city) at some time in their lives. What are tourist attractions in the state? In the surrounding states? Can they list ten in each state?

1. How many license plates (nationally) feature tourist attractions?

2. What is meant by jeep authorized service? Welding? Steering correction? Exclusive gas drying oven? What would be found in a body repairing and paint shop? Can they list thirty items? What would one find in an automobile air conditioning equipment shop? Can the group list twenty-five?

3. Do they think Americans have outgrown the idea of "keeping up with the Jones's" when it comes to cars?

Does the price of cars measure up to their true worth? How necessary is the second car? Why has the car become so "prestigious"? What used to be the status symbol before cars?

RACERS AND RACING could be a specialty of some club member. What are names of some famous racers? What physical skill is required? How many of them have seen a big race (or the movie of a big race)?

Nineteenth Meeting

THEY MAKE MINIATURE RACERS to give to children (see Appendix).

WHAT AN OWNER SHOULD KNOW ABOUT HIS CAR could be printed as a directive for new drivers. Would they like to take on this project?

"YOUR PREVENTIVE MAINTENANCE MEANS A CAREFREE TRIP" a slogan advises. To insure a safe, troublefree trip, what would they ask their serviceman to do in a checkup? They list items that should have attention: engine tune-up, spark plugs, battery, voltage regulator, muffler, wiring, gas, tailpipe, and so forth.

HOW TO GET HELP IN A HURRY prompts members to recall a number of traumatic situations. If a car breaks down or refuses to start, if there is a flat tire or no gas, what steps should be taken?

Twentieth Meeting

TWO LINES ARE FORMED for competition. How long will they stand as these questions are asked?

What is meant by custom body shop? By collision repair? Auto painting? Glass installation? Night towing? Painting and steam cleaning? Frame, body, fender work? Wheel balancing? Front end alignment? Wrecks rebuilt? Color matching? Fiberglass specialists? Metal flake painting? Insurance work? Credit cards honored? Complete overhaul? Electrical and carburetor work? Brake service? Authorized dealer? Sales and service dealers? Seat cover and top center? Axle service?

At the next meeting, each resident will be asked to submit a question about cars or transportation to stump an expert in the group.

Who can ADD UP THE MOTEL BILL first (listed on the blackboard at the front of the room)?

First Motel Bill		Second Motel Bill	
$18.17	two persons two beds	$22.40	four persons
3.43	telephone bill	1.45	towels for pool
2.00	for dog	2.02	telephone
3.14	breakfast, tip, and tax	4.98	breakfast in room
4.15	lunch, tip, and tax	13.44	lunch, tip, and tax
2.78	cocktails, tip, and tax	20.55	bus tour of city
11.16	dinner, tip, and tax	19.88	dinner, tip, and tax
23.69	casino	5.80	beauty shop and barbers

Twenty-first Meeting

DISCUSS the following:

In a Canadian tour book, what is meant by these items:

Central heating
Combination or shower baths
Infrared heat lamps
Full kitchen equipment
Lifeguard and instructor
Superb Chinese, French, and American cuisine
A la carte
Entrees
Winter plug-ins
Playground, pool
Portable heaters
Service charge in lieu of gratuity
Deposit required
Split-level motel
Suites
Wading pool
Featuring sole soufflé
Lobster in absinthe sauce
Fly-in trips arranged
Supervised swimming
Panoramic view
Social program and children's counselor
Sauna bath

The Queen's Highway
Refund notice one week
Rates quoted are in Canadian dollars
Port of entry open
The AAA emblem (CAA)
Duncan Hines
Informal dress
Ferry service
Touring bureau open
Lighted golf driving range
We honor Carte Blanche credit cards
24-hour all-risk trip insurance
Free continental breakfast
Coffeemakers in each room
Special winter holiday rates
Guides
Rope tows
Take-out service
Fisherman's cottage
Sunday smorgasbord
Children's menu
Checkout 11 A.M.
Change your money at a bank

STUMP THE EXPERTS. A member could volunteer to be the answer-man as questions are submitted:

Q. What can be done when car pep disappears?
A. Trouble possibilities include a sticking manifold heat valve; incorrect spark timing; improper distributor advance; bad coil,

points, or cable; restricted muffler or exhaust pipe; clutch or transmission slippage.

Q. My son just bought a used '72 which was a low-mileage demonstrator. It's a big car with a big engine and it takes regular gasoline, according to the dealer. I thought all new full-size cars needed premium.
A. The trend has been reversed. This engine has an 8.5 to 1 compression ratio and is designed to run perfectly on regular gas.

Q. Some slight chattering is more or less normal with nonslip differentials, but what else causes noise?
A. Noise also develops when the wrong type of rear axle lubricant is used.

Q. The motor vehicle inspector said more than half of motor assists reported by the state patrol involved tire failure. He said that about one third of all recreational vehicles are carrying loads in excess of tire manufacturer's recommendations. What can be done to correct this?

A. Luggage, food, water, recreational apparatus, and relatives are heavy. Often, drivers ask the service station to increase their tire pressure but have no idea how much it can stand. Proper tire size could be a corrective element, too.

Q. My grandchildren live in a hazardous traffic area and should be bussed. Money seems more important than the lives of the children. We've pointed out that other cities in the area are finding money in their budgets to bus children less than two miles who live in bad traffic areas. Why not this city?
A. They say "We are not aware of this." Maybe a letter to the board explaining this would help. The only solution they offered in the newspapers is to make the Highway 55 safer.

Twenty-second Meeting

HIGHWAY SAFETY. How do they rate as to importance, these separate sections in highway safety programs?

Laws	Police supervision
Accident records	Traffic courts
Medical care and transportation of the injured	

VACATION TRAVELING, a good subject for communication. With the use of free State Highway Commission information, questions for discussion can be brought up.

What proportion of vacationers do they think are out of state? What states would seem to make up most of the tourists?

What do they surmise is the average vacation length? Average cost per day? Two-week vacations are less expensive per day than short vacations of long weekend trips. Why? What are the pros and cons of toll-free roads? Are touring and sight-seeing more popular than fishing? Are there more women drivers than men? What age group would they say takes long weekend vacations?

How much is spent on advertising campaigns in state traveling? Should vacation advertising be slanted to men or women or children or young adults, if a choice had to be made?

They think of a joke about cars to tell at the next meeting.

Twenty-third Meeting

Sounding like back-seat drivers, can they make lists of DO'S AND DON'TS for drivers? (Checking tires; brake lights; car performance; claiming the right-of-way; yielding; choosing a lane and staying in it; bumper riding; stoplights, and so on.

They tell a JOKE OR ANECDOTE about a child and an automobile.

A little girl who was required to write an essay not exceeding two hundred words on the subject of automobiles, wrote: "My father bought a Ford. It stopped going up a hill about five miles from home. Father crawled under to fix it and it vomited oil down his neck and all over his new suit; then he cranked it and it backfired and broke his arm. This is about fifty words. The other one hundred fifty is what my father said while walking home and they are not fit to write down."

PRICE CEILING ON CARS, why or why not? Does anyone remember actually having the bill of sale in his pocket, the price $317, which included side curtains, a wrench, and a tire pump? (What, no sales tax?)

Should there be price ceiling on cars? The typical new car bought by the American family has more than doubled in price in the last twenty years. What are the factors involved? What are the largest expense items? The costs of depreciation, finance charges, insurance, and crash repairs? In general, what do they think about the quality of the latest cars?

WRONG-WAY talk may turn out to be the "best of anticalendar medicine." This resident, now blind, dictates into a tape recorder the following account:

> The N.Y.C. students employed here talking about returning to school soon, makes me think of my 1925 high school debut. Mother, sister and I were planning the bus trip home from Chippewa Falls so that we kids could be in time for school the following Tuesday. Grandmother was bidding us goodbye and like a bolt out of the blue, plans changed rapidly, at least for me. At the psychological moment, brother Bill roared into view on his then-new 1924 Harley-Davidson motorcycle. What he suggested to me might make me a fugitive from high school for a week but what did I care! I was riding back with him. Mother agreed but she did not know the route we were to take: for that part, we didn't either right then.
>
> To make a short story longer, we purred away in the wrong direction. Didn't Columbus do just that? Nightfall found us somewhere near Neilsville, our pup tent slung between the handlebars of the 'cycle and a post of a barbwire fence. A storm blew up to inundate our canvas hotel and a flock of sheep on the opposite side of the fence kept us from getting any sleep. I still see them and hear them as the lightning flashes.
>
> A foggy morning found us back on the road and still going in the wrong direction. By noon the sun was shining brightly, and with joy in our hearts, we reached our destination, a large farm near Pittsville, Wisconsin. The owner's son-in-law just happened to be a machine shop instructor at the school I was supposed to be registering for the next day. Old man Hutchins had a week's carpentry work laid out for my brother and his son-in-law. The machine shop teacher said that he would explain to my principal.
>
> I was off the hook: no school for another week. Brother Bill was busy hammering new shiplap siding on the house. The kids taught me how to ride their Indian pony and the pony taught me how to dismount over its ears. Only once did we leave the farm for a free outdoor movie in town. A dusty mile walk each way killed the last evening; then the rain came.
>
> Our departure next day took place between downpours and all the world was a sodden quagmire. Grandma Hutchins had insisted that we take back half of her orchard in the sidecar so I squeezed aboard somehow, legs protruding over the cowl.

Ten hours of puddle jumping, mostly growling along in low and second, finally got us to hard pavement somewhere near Black River Falls. There the rain caught up with the electrical system and repairs were accomplished while lightning silhouetted the jack pines and on we went.

At 2:30 on September 13, 1925, our faithful Harley-Davidson limped through the streets of La Crosse pounding on one cylinder. We were home though even if Father didn't recognize us right away.

I'll tell you, my *Chatterbox* friends, just writing about my delayed high school registration turned out to be the best of anticalendar medicine!

Have any of them had an experience going in the wrong direction? Can someone tell an experience of staying away longer than they intended, like the Man Who Came to Dinner? Are there stories to be told about deliberately playing truant from school? Getting caught? Other twists of fate?

Twenty-fourth Meeting

WHAT IS TO BE SAID about American automobile manufacturing ventures in other countries? Can they comment on the social involvement? Is there reason for concern over certain internal policies of foreign government? Should investigations be held in which pressure is brought to bear to modify alleged harmful policies?

Is it always a joint venture, give and take by both foreign government and American industry? Do the industries set up in these countries consider themselves always as guests of that country? What are the pros and cons?

The president of a truck corporation, for instance, which "receives a fair return on its investment of both capital and engineering skill, and expands markets for American products in overseas areas," says

The economy of the Republic of South Africa, and the standard of living for all its citizens of all races, receives assistance in the development of one of the most basic industries of any nation, transportation.

It is to the total nonwhite population that efforts should be addressed. The nonwhite South African can be trained to fill positions in a viable industrial society. Education, health services, housing and medical facilities are of little long-term value unless an industrial base exists to provide a means of livelihood for all citizens. Poverty, ignorance and poor living conditions are not the result of a modern industrial society: they result from the absence of such a society.

Nonwhite workers are being trained as welders, fabricators, plate workers, electrical wiremen, machine operators, operators of handling equipment, assemblers, storemen and planning assistants in manufacturing operations. In clerical and administrative positions, nonwhite are employed in job costing, machine accounting and timekeeping. . . .

Today the European work force in our plant at Paarl, South Africa, has increased by 82 percent while the nonwhite force has increased 120 percent in the last four years.

From a standpoint of wages, it is interesting to compare these wages paid at our Paarl facility. The average wage is $1,500.00 whereas the per capita income in Ghana is $224.00, Rhodesia $158.00, Nigeria $75.00, Congo $68.00, Uganda $63.00 and Tanzania $56.00.

Our lowest starting rate for nonexperienced married males is $720.00 per year which is higher than the combined total per capita income of all the above-mentioned countries.

The Industrial Conciliation Act legislates wages and working conditions, irrespective of color or race. Pertinent provisions of the act are as follows:

1. An agreed hourly rate for each job description.
2. Specific hours of work are not to be exceeded.
3. Overtime rates are to be paid.
4. Special rates of pay are established for holiday and weekend work.
5. Holidays are given and employees are paid while on holiday.
6. Holiday bonuses are provided.
7. Juveniles are not to be exploited.
8. Employees are provided for in case of injury.
9. Employees are provided for in case of sickness.

Have residents had experience in training a work force? What would be advantages both to the truck corporation and the African work force? What are the advantages in transforming an agricultural worker to a skilled industrial artisan? Is education of a worker of value unless an industrial base exists which gives him employment?

What other theories do residents have on corporate and social involvement? What are the pros and cons of joint ventures in manufacturing cars or trucks in foreign countries? Is industry brought into another country sometimes "the sole issue by which our friendship for another country is measured"?

ANAGRAM CALL. Anagram letters are used in place of playing

cards for this game. The letters are placed face down in the center of the table. As players turn up similar letters, they call out the name of a car beginning with that letter; the first to call out gets his opponent's letter.

The object of the game is to collect letters from opponents.

PARTNER ANAGRAMS. Partners sit opposite each other at tables of four. Anagram letters, face down, are in the center of each table. The leader calls out a name of a car to be formed—for instance, the word "Ford."

Players take turns at drawing out a letter from the pile in the center. Partners work together in forming a word. Until the first letter is drawn, all other letters must be returned to the pile face down; then the second letter must be drawn, and so on. Words are different in each round.

TO READ ALOUD

Automobile Quarterly

A very well illustrated magazine of motoring today, yesterday, and tomorrow. It has a hard cover similar to *American Heritage* and *Horizons*.

Beaumont, Charles and Nolan, W. F.: *Omnibus of Speed* 629.2

A collection of essays that describe the world of auto racing.

Bergere, Thea: *Automobiles of Yesteryear* 629.2

A pictorial record of motor cars that made history.

Burlingame, Roger: *Machines that Build America* 608-B956

Readable account of one aspect of America's greatness.

Clymer, Floyd: *Henry's Wonderful Model T* 629.2

A Ford album of photographs, cartoons, ads, songs, jokes, and informative text.

Clymer, Floyd: *Those Wonderful Old Automobiles* 629.2

Another collection of photos, jokes, cartoons, ads, and fond memories of American cars of yesterday.

Clymer, Floyd: *Treasury of Early American Automobiles, 1907-1925*

An album of photos, advertisements, songs, cartoons, test memories of the early days of the automobile.

Fox, Jack C.: *The Indianapolis 500* 629.2

A pictorial history of the greatest spectacle in auto racing.

Holmes, Fred L.: *Side Roads; Excursions into Wisconsin's Past*
977.5-H749
Hough, Richard (Ed.): *The Motor Car Lover's Companion*
629.20
A potpourri of nostalgic essays for those who still love motoring in spite of everything, and for those who once loved it.
Humphrey, J. R.: *The Lost Towns and Roads of America* 917
A leisurely journey on the forgotten roads which lead into quiet towns. Interesting photographs.
Jewell, Derek: *Man and Motor: the 20th Century Love Affair*
629.29
It is everyman's guide to, bedside book on, history and picture gallery of the greatest love affair of our times. A British publication.
Rinehart, Mary R.: *Best of Tish*   Fiction
Humorous stories about a woman driver in the early days of the automobile.
Schuster, George and Mahoney, Tom: *The Longest Auto Race*
629.2
A description of the 1908 race from New York to Paris via America, Japan, Russia, and Europe as told by the last living member of the winning crew.
Shippen, Katherine: *Miracle in Motion*   x338-S557
Survey of three centuries of American industry with accounts of the contributions of great inventors, capitalists, labor organizers.
Smith, Philip H.: *Wheels within Wheels*   629
A short history of American motor car manufacturing.
Stern, Philip: *Tin Lizzie*   629.29
This book, with its photographs, recollections, and anecdotes offers an opportunity for indulging in the past.

MEN'S CLUB
Introduction
Where Are the Men?

They're sitting in their rooms, sometimes with heads in hands, or wandering lonely up and down the halls. Why do they refuse to attend the Home parties, picnics, craft sessions? They are often afraid of being identified with an activity they think of as feminine, since women residents predominate in these groups. They are afraid of doing something which seems unmasculine, beneath their dignity and intelligence, and they refuse to stoop to such activities, afraid of being laughed at.

But what about the men joining forces in a "Stag Party" or "Smoker"? Would they enjoy being together, all males exclusive, to make their own rules, play their own games, conduct their own discussions?

Goals (of the Resident)

These include the following:

1. To make friendships, keep alert and active.

2. To learn new games and skills, submit new ideas, to take responsibility and stretch horizons.

Motivation Techniques

Motivation is an important factor.

1. The resident is encouraged to believe he is helping by being publically thanked, or being honored along with other committee members. His activities will grow as he becomes involved.

2. Beginning with visual aids (such as a sample craft or a picture of what is expected of him, or a chart showing his growth in activity, or a score or ladder tournament diagram), he is helped step by step into more and more important activity. The leader starts with what is understandable to him.

3. Completion of an unfinished job gives satisfaction. An unfinished item on the table waiting to be repaired or finished could lure him in.

4. The "reward" system could be used: the gold star after the resident's name on the wall chart, a cigarette, a piece of candy, a cookie, or a cup of coffee.

It is desirable to find a continuity of interest. The group can predetermine a thread of thought or theme to be carried through all the meetings: something to study or discuss, or something active to do.

First Meeting

See "The First Meeting" in Part III, "How to Lead a Club."

LEARNING NAMES, residents list their names on a sheet to be posted where the names can be learned. Or, the first person turns to the second and says his own name. The second repeats this and adds his own. The third must repeat the first and second names before adding his. The list lengthens as club members are able to repeat correct names.

In a circle, the resident to whom the bottle points after it's spun, tells his name and something about himself.

Resident committees can be set up to greet people, to furnish equipment and supplies for each program, to take roll, to read the minutes (optional), to prepare the room for the meeting, to arrange for refreshments (optional), to help escort wheelchair patients, to post notices, and so on.

Someone interviews a number of residents in the Home on a tape recorder, to be played back and identity of the interviewee guessed at the next meeting; residents interviewed might be asked to tell a joke or give an opinion without giving his name.

RELAY WARMUP. It's important to begin the club venture with some good games.

Equipment. Two beanbags.

Procedure.

1. Two circles of men are formed, one circle inside the other.

2. Each circle has a beanbag and starts tossing it to the person at his left as the signal is given, counting as each person catches it and passes it on. If someone misses, the count begins again.

3. The group tries to see which circle reaches the highest count.

Second Meeting

RESIDENTS DISCUSS some question of the day, each around the circle giving an opinion on the topic.

1. Without naming names, do they think today's politicians are as ethical as people in other professions? Why? What professions would be listed as more ethical? Why are these accusations made toward politicians? Has this always been true? They are asked to name politicians in history who were highly ethical. Has the code of ethics changed? How?

2. Should the Federal Government intervene in a strike? In what instances has it? Is it effectual? What would happen if it hadn't? In what instances are strikers justified in rebelling? In

what instances is the government justified? What are the losses to the public and to strikers? How does it usually end?

Can members volunteer to use names of songs to tell a story, to stump the club members at the next meeting? Could a committee work on this?

The tape is played giving interviews, residents identified and introduced, if present.

AMUSEMENTS. How many kinds of dance steps can they name? (Round dance, square dance, tap, clog, skirt, sand, shuffle, reel; rigadoon; saraband; hornpipe; bolero; fandango; tarantella; minuet; waltz; polka; schottische; two-step; rumba; tango; foxtrot; shimmy; ragtime; cakewalk; jazz; Charleston; jig; fling; mazurka; quadrille; polonaise ball; masquerade; fancy dress ball; cancan.)

Can they describe a festivity or special party that was unusual or memorable in some way? A carnival? Banquet? Wake? Picnic? Garden party? Track meet? Shivaree?

How many places of amusement can they name? (Rodeo; speedway; racing track; ring; gymnasium; swimming pool; shooting gallery; tennis court; bowling green; rink; roller coaster; carrousel; merry-go-round; swing; scenic railway; theatre; concert hall; ballroom; music hall; cinema; vaudeville; hippodrome; circus; park; golf links; cricket—football, polo, croquet, archery—field; hunting ground.)

Third Meeting

A SING-A-LONG ROMANCE starts them out, the purpose to guess the name of the song. One of the Homes presented the following:

> A pianist familiar with old-fashioned songs plays a few bars of the songs to be identified, or the leader hums the tune in the mike.
>
> Men call out the song as they recognize it, connecting words read aloud by the leader.
>
> *Oh How Lovely Is the Evening*, when *Juanita* and *Charlie, My Boy* were married *Down by the Old Mill Stream* while the *Wedding March* was played by *Sweet Adeline*. They were married at *Three O'Clock in the Morning*, and were attended by *Yankee Doodle* and *Margie*. On their honeymoon they sailed down the *Suwannee River* and saw *Amer-*

ica the Beautiful and after following *The Trail of the Lonesome Pine,* they crossed *Maryland, My Maryland* and finally reached *London Bridge.*

After a happy month they *Followed the Swallow Back Home.* They were met by *Old Black Joe* who drove them across the hills to their *Old Kentucky Home* where they had their first quarrel because he left her *All Alone, In the Evening by the Moonlight,* while he and *Sweet Sue* were down on the corner singing *Hail, Hail the Gang's All Here.* Then *Juanita* went back to the *Old Folks at Home* and Charlie said, "I suppose it's *All Over Now,*" but he wired *"I Love You Truly"* and she replied, *"Pack Up Your Troubles* and meet your *Kentucky Babe* in *Dixie."*

He met her *In the Gloaming* and they started back for their own *Home, Sweet Home* and from that time on life for them was one *Perfect Day* after another. Each Sunday they went to *The Little Brown Church in the Vale* and even after Father Time had sprinkled *Silver Threads Among the Gold,* their romance was just a continuation of *Love's Old Sweet Song.*

Residents are asked to compose another.

Fourth Meeting

RUNAROUND is a stunt with toothpicks. Arrange ten toothpicks so that they form the equation in Roman numerals: XI + I = X This equation is of course, incorrect. Players must make it read correctly without touching anything. (Answer: Walk around to the other side of the table and look at it.)

TAX REFUND.

Equipment. Paper and pencil for everyone.

Procedure. Tax due date could be the club meeting date. Forms are distributed to people interested in a tax refund (money donated to the fun fund).

> Since taxes have become the style,
> We've come up with a dilly;
> We'll have some fun and make some dough
> For this tax is really silly.
>> Just figure up the things you own
>> And gladly pay your fee.
>> For you can see that we are taxing
>> Your dearest property!

Now when the tax is finished,
You'll know just what you owe—
So bring the form straight back to us;
But don't forget the dough.

I live in a single room	15¢ each	$
I live in a double room	10¢ each	$
I have a TV set	10¢ each	$
radio	01¢ each	$
car	10¢ each	$
telephone	05¢ each	$
My wife owns a wristwatch	02¢ each	$
diamond rings	05¢ each	$
fur coats	02¢ each	$
fur stoles	02¢ each	$
fur neck pieces	01¢ each	$
My age is under 70	20¢	$
My family consists of a wife	10¢	$
unemployed son-in-law	15¢	$
children	10¢ each	$
grandchildren	05¢ each	$
(No charge beyond five grandchildren)		
brothers	05¢ each	$
sisters	03¢ each	$
My name has ___ letters	01¢ each	$
My room has ___ numbers	01¢ each	$
I have ___ pets	05¢ each	$ *

* You may claim exemption for any amount in excess of a total tax of $1.25

Tax status might be listed on the bulletin board; money refunded could be paper money good for a prize, credit toward a commissary fund, or some other reward.

—Submitted

Fifth Meeting

CAREER TALKATHON could begin by each resident telling something about the work he once did.

As a young man, he was raised on a farm; would he now plan on making farming his career? Why or why not? He describes changes in this work. As a young man, he was apprenticed in carpentry. Would he continue in this line if he could "do it over again"? Would he recommend it to others? Why? What experiences does he recall? Was he successful? In what way? In what ways did fate interfere?

DOUGHNUT FRY can be scheduled when the cook gives several men the use of the kitchen for a few hours. A Home newsletter describes their activity:

> We had our second doughnut fry with the assistance of three volunteers; five of the residents mixed the dough and twelve rolled and cut out the doughnuts and two fried; many ate them.
>
> Bob said the doughnuts were the best he's eaten. Along with the eggs being beaten, the dough being rolled and doughnuts being fried, the *Chronical* photographer was busy taking pictures. When the batter was ready, we worked in couples, one rolling the dough and the other cutting. Even the holes were fried. Some of us haven't made doughnuts in forty years and it sure was fun. A tape recording was made as we worked and was played back to us afterward.

Baking Powder Doughnuts. (If dough is chilled for several hours before rolling, reduce flour ½ cup.)

3 eggs
1 cup sour cream
1 cup sugar
1 teaspoon soda
4 cups flour
A little grated nutmeg.

Beat eggs, add sugar gradually. Add soda to cream. Combine the two mixtures and add the flour, nutmeg, and 1 teaspoon salt. Roll ¼ inch thick. Cut and fry in deep hot fat. Dust with confectioners' sugar.

Each is asked to discuss a great American at the next session.

Sixth Meeting

HALL OF FAME. Citizens can send in nominations to the national Hall of Fame. Working in couples or groups, men are asked to nominate ten great Americans for busts in the Hall of Fame. From club members present, seven names may be selected from the lists submitted as most frequently appearing.

Only famous people who have been dead at least twenty-five years can be nominated. The nominations may be made by any citizen of the United States. (Send nominations to the Hall of Fame for Great Americans. New York University, Dept. H, Washington Square, New York, N.Y. 10003.)

The final choice is made by a committee of electors, at least one from each state, who are appointed by the director of the Hall of Fame. This committee is made up of people from seven different groups: university or college; executives; historians or professors of history or literature; scientists; authors, educators and artists; men and women of affairs; high public officials; national or state justices.

To be in the Hall of Fame, the person must receive a majority of the electors' votes.

These Americans are now in the Hall of Fame: Thomas Jefferson, Abraham Lincoln, Robert E. Lee, Edgar Allan Poe, Daniel Boone, Mark Twain, Stephen Foster, Booker T. Washington, Thomas Edison, Woodrow Wilson. Members are asked to discuss who might already have been nominated.

Residents may want to discuss nominees, think about them until the next meeting, and then vote.

This is not a game but the real procedure; the results can be mailed in by the club.

Seventh Meeting

Discussion can take place on the Hall of Fame nominees, voting results mailed.

THE GOOD FELLOWSHIP CLUB resumé as contributed by a county home newsletter, is read aloud for discussion; are there ideas here which could supplement the club activities?

> The Good Fellowship Club had its monthly meeting, called to order by the president; the secretary's and the treasurer's reports were read and approved. . . . The new business was in regard to bingo and guessing games, in which all members will participate. It was also approved at the meeting to subscribe for the *National Enquirer* for another year at the cost of $5.00. The Good Fellowship Club subscribes to the *La Crosse Tribune,* which all patients enjoy reading. . . .

> * * *

> The superintendent takes a man resident to the local Rotary Club to a weekly luncheon meeting, as his guest. . . . The Home always considers wheelchair winners for separate competition in games. Four of our men are in community Sheltered Workshop projects. One of our members almost totally handicapped, writes the Home news which is then

taped for the local radio station WGLB and broadcast every Friday. He announces the Home news every noon over the PA system—weather, birthdays, maxim for the day, menu, etc.—which he compiles.

There might be several ideas here for some club.

SOME QUESTION OF THE DAY is investigated; each member gives an opinion around the circle.

1. What do they think the chances are of winning the title (some local team)? Who are outstanding players? They rank the others and discuss players on the opposing teams. Who is outstanding there? What special abilities does each have? How do the coaches compare? What is the scoring history of each team? Predictions?

2. What type of driver do they fear most on the highways? Could a law control this? Have they any dangerous experiences with this type of driver? Can they describe drinking tests? Are they valid, do they think? Do they know how other countries, other states, control this problem? Could mechanisms on the car alleviate or correct the problem of drunken driving?

Eighth Meeting

AUTHORITY AND LAW AND ORDER are deliberated. Is the general public losing respect for authority? Consider the middle-aged and aged: do they feel differently than a younger person regarding obedience? Define discipline. Are there advantages to oneself or to others? Does it make for a stronger government, a stronger person? If there were no authority, who would judge rightful power? How can one help in support of authority?

ANOTHER MEN'S COOKING CLASS could be a jovial adventure revealing hidden talent. After finding the interested residents, can the leader get permission from the superintendent or cook perhaps to prepare a complete meal? Can the men plan their own menu? How will ingredients be obtained? Where will the meal be served? To whom?

Ninth Meeting

GAMBLING GAMES can be revised so that no money changes hands. Chances are the men in the club know a dozen simple dice games they once played. Will they teach the others a dice game? Games of chance are always successful unless, of course, men have moral scruples against playing with dice; their feelings must be respected.

But most men seem to enjoy gambling games. If an aphasic (a patient who can't speak) is able to hold up two fingers to "place a bet," he can take part in the game. Residents too confused to learn the rules of a new game can play if placing a bet is all that's involved and the "banker" is there to pay him.

Twenty-five 1″ squares of colored construction paper, a different color for each player, are used as chips and placed in an envelope to begin the game.

The resident can play as long as he likes and as long as his "chips" hold out. A predetermined award may be given the winner, if this seems necessary; residents should not play for money in a Home or hospital club, of course!

CHUCK-A-LUCK is a standard Las Vegas game.

Equipment. Three dice and one layout or betting cloth numbered one to six; each player starts with the same number of chips (see above). The banker has an extra supply of each color of "chips" to make change.

Procedure. Any number of persons may play at one time, one being selected as banker.

1. All bets are laid down on the layout, or betting cloth, each player determining on what number he wants to bet and how many chips to place there. He places as many as he likes anywhere.

2. The banker rolls the dice.

3. The three numbers rolled are the winners. One number rewards the player with chips on that number: a sum equal to the amount of his bet, plus the same amount, given to him by the banker. Two of a kind pays twice the amount of the bet (2 to 1); three of a kind pays three times the amount (3 to 1).

4. The banker takes the remaining chips on the cloth.

5. They again place bets and continue; the leader determines at what point they stop, perhaps giving the player with the most chips at the end of the game a prize.

ARGUMENT. The leader baits them with an argument, for example: Is there a "right" way to fight in a marriage?

Tenth Meeting

CLUB SPONSORSHIP BY A LOCAL MEN'S CLUB can be highly successful. Can a committee look into the feasibility of a local club holding some of its meetings in the Home, so that residents may attend, too? Can a local men's club come in as hosts for the meetings? Can members invite a guest for beer and cards?

Eleventh Meeting

ROULETTE, one of the most popular sports, is an amusement needing equipment.

Equipment. A discarded bicycle wheel is mounted to spin. Numbers are 6, 27, 13, 36, 11, 30, 8, 23, 10, 5, 24, and so on, red or black, numbers on cards around the wheel.

Chips are needed, a designated color for each player since it is necessary to know whose bets they are; a rake; dice.

Procedure. Roulette is a banking game and all bets must be placed against the bank (proprietor of the game).

1. As many players may bet as can get near the table, a large oblong table, at either end of which there is a red and black layout.

2. "Place your bets, gentlemen," the banker says. Players place their bets on the layout to indicate the number or classification of number (color).

3. The banker spins the wheel in one direction. When he sees that the wheel will soon stop, he says "The betting is closed," and no bets may be placed thereafter.

4. He announces the winning number and whether it is red or black, odd or even.

5. The bank pays winning bets at the established rates and collects all losing bets gathered in with a rake.

For a winning bet on red, black; high, low; even or odd—the bank pays "even money"—the amount of the bet.

For a winning bet on the dozen (1 to 12, 13 to 24, or 25 to 36), the bank pays two to one.

On wheels with thirty-eight compartments including a zero (0) or a double zero (00)—if either of them occurs, all bets are taken.

A volunteer who has played at the gambling tables and who can take charge is a big help!

A LAS VEGAS PARTY could be the natural follow-through after learning these games. An activity aide describes theirs:

> Our horse racing game has been improved by using a long rubber-backed mat which we roll out on the auditorium floor for the marked racetrack. (Halls are terrazzo, not blocked off in squares, can't be used for designated distances and the craft shop is too busy a place for the space needed in a horse racing game.) (Horses are moved as the dice is rolled.)
>
> Scores for horse racing and bowling are kept on a six-month basis and awards given at a banquet dinner for the residents with high individual scores, the top team, the individual who increased his average the most, etc.

> We held a Las Vegas night with roulette, chuck-a-luck, casino, keeno, 26, and blackjack with residents wearing eye shades and striped vests as dealers. It was a dress-up affair for the women residents too, who wore formals among all the glitter of a night club with gambling equipment.
>
> High school students put on a show during refreshments, like a sophisticated supper club. Our volunteers' husbands ran the games. Residents made string bags with the residents' names attached to the bags. In each bag were fifty poker chips, donated by the volunteers, to start the gambling. . . .

Twelfth Meeting

TEST YOUR MANLY INTUITION is the barker's come-on!

Equipment. Three wrapped gifts; cards; paper and pencil.

Procedure.

1. Residents draw for highest card.
2. The player (A) with the highest card receives three wrapped gifts.
3. Someone volunteers (B) from the group.
4. A's intuition is tested by being asked the following:
   a. Does B have more than $1 on him? (A guesses, and if wrong, A must forfeit to B one of his gifts. In each case, B is asked to write the answer prior to A's guess.)

b. What is B's middle initial? (Again A guesses and if he is wrong, A gives up another gift.)

c. Is B's birthday in the first six months of the year? (If A is wrong, again he must give up another wrapped gift.) A may keep the three gifts if he gets two out of three correct answers.

Other questions: Does he wear a size 10 shoe? Own property? Have children? Sleep in pajamas (nightshirt)? Did he ever milk cows, walk behind a plow, need spectacles to read, win at bingo yesterday?

Thirteenth Meeting

GIVING AN OPINION on some topic of the day, each one around the circle is included. For instance:

1. Should the city charge an admission fee at the city park? Who benefits? Who is hurt? What would be the advantages of the change? How should the revenue be spent? What experiences have they had with this problem? Is any legality involved?

2. Should the city build a public swimming pool? What are the needs? Who would use it? How would it be financed? Where should it be built? What drawbacks should be considered? What other privileges or luxuries would have to be sacrificed?

BOARD BASEBALL is played on a cardboard field marked off in bases.

Equipment. A board 35" square, such as the top of a packing case; hooks are arranged and labeled as on a baseball diamond (below); three rubber rings.

Procedure.

1. The board is hung on a wall or set on a table against the wall, wheelchair height.

2. Players sit at a designated distance, scoring individually or in teams.

3. Each player tosses rubber rings at the hooks on the baseball board. 1B means one base; 2B means two bases; 3B, three bases; HR, home run; GO, grounded out; FO, fly out; W, walk; SO, struck out. Some of the hooks he is trying to ring, and some he's trying to avoid.

4. The number of innings may be determined by the players.

Fourteenth Meeting

TOURNAMENTS. A tournament is a way of deciding individual or team champions from a group. A tournament can be set up for many men's activities: dominoes, euchre, sheepshead, ring toss, horseshoes, pool, and so on.

Round Robin.

1. Every team or player must play every other competitor in the tournament.

2. Give each man a number.

3. Each man plays every other man. First, second, and third places are determined by the percentage of games won.

4. Divide the number of games won by the total games played to get the percentage. When twelve games are played and four of them won, four is divided by twelve and equals 33 percent.

5. Each contestant's name is listed with his percentage.

Challenge Tournaments (ladder tournament).

1. Draw lots and place players in order.

2. Write names on cards that can be placed in a slot or hung on a hook.

3. In a ladder tournament, a player may challenge anyone one or two rungs above him.

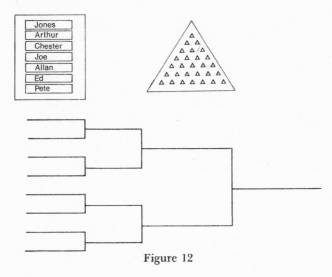

Figure 12

4. Then he exchanges places with the person he has defeated.

(Triangle tournament).

In a triangle tournament, the player challenges anyone in the row above him and then exchanges places with the person he has defeated.

Fifteenth Meeting

HORSESHOES is a favorite game of men. People with the use of only one hand or who sit in wheelchairs can play. An OT says

> Horseshoes is the big game event of the week in the Home section. The only requirement is that you are present at 2 P.M. sharp to draw a number, determining your partner and the game in which you will play.
>
> A man and a woman play as partners, each week changing partners for more equal competition. Rubber horseshoes are a good weight for handicapped people. The game can be played indoors or out.

Horseshoe rules are listed below.[5]

The Horseshoe Court.

1. Two pitchers' boxes with stake in the center of each, ten feet wide and fifty feet in length. (The pitching distance depends on the player's handicaps and can be adjusted anywhere.)

2. Foul lines surrounding the pitcher's box are defined, measuring to the nearest side of the box frame from the stake.

Horseshoe Equipment.

1. Stakes shall be of iron or steel (indoor sets have wooden stakes attached to a rubber base).

2. Rubber horseshoes (if indoors or if used by infirm players).

Playing Rules.

1. No contestant shall touch own or opponent's shoe or shoes until winner of point has been agreed upon. Referee shall declare foul and shall award points to the opponent according to position of his shoes.

2. No contestant shall walk to the opposite stake or be informed of the position of shoes prior to the completion of an inning.

---

[5] Permission given by Diamond Tool and Horseshoe Co., Duluth, Minnesota, from "How to Play Horseshoe" booklet.

3. A player, when not pitching, must remain on the opposite side of the stake to the rear of a line, even with the stake.

4. Any shoe delivered while the pitcher's foot extends on or over the raised foul line shall be declared foul and removed from counting distance.

5. In delivering the shoe, the pitcher shall stand within the pitcher's box, but outside the radius of the stake.

6. In delivering a shoe, the pitcher must remain behind the foul line until the shoe leaves his hand.

7. Choice of first pitch or follow shall be determined by the toss of a coin. In successive games between the same players, the loser shall have choice.

8. A foul shoe:
    a. A shoe pitched while contestant stands beyond the box foul line.
    b. A shoe striking outside the opposite pitching box.

Foul shoes are removed from the opposite pitcher's box at the request of the opponent. A foul shoe shall not be scored or credited except in the score sheet headed "shoes pitched."

9. Measurements to determine points won shall be made with standard rulers.

Scoring Rules.

1. A regulation game shall consist of 50 points (or any other number acceptable to the players).

2. A game is divided into innings and each inning constitutes the pitching of two shoes by each contestant.

    a. A shoe must be within six inches of the stake to score.

b. Closest shoe to stake scores	1 point
c. Two shoes closer than opponent's	2 points
d. One ringer scores	3 points
e. Two ringers score	6 points
f. One ringer and closest shoe of same player score	4 points
g. Party having two ringers against one for opponent scores	3 points
h. All equals count as ties and no points are scored.	

    i. In case each contestant has a ringer, the next
closest shoe, if within six inches, shall score   1 point

    j. In case of tie, such as four ringers or con-
testants' shoes are equal distance from the
stake, causing no score for either, party pitching last in the inning will start the next inning.

    k. A leaning shoe has no value over one touch-
ing the stake.

3. The points shall be scored according to the position of the
shoes at the inning's end—that is, after the contestants have each
thrown two shoes.

Ringer credits shall be given on the same basis.

Winner of points shall call the result. In case of tie, the party
pitching last shall call.

4. Definition of a ringer: A ringer is declared when a shoe en-
circles the stake far enough to allow the touching of both heel
calks simultaneously with a straightedge and permit the clearance
of the stake.

5. The recording of results shall be as follows:

W—games won; L—games lost; P—points; R—ringers; DR—
double ringers; SP—shoe pitched; OP—opponent's points; PR—
percentage of ringers.

Sixteenth Meeting

CHECKER TOURNAMENTS are set up as detailed here by a therapist.

    This year's checker tourney received great interest, and thirty-two
men signed up to play. They were divided into two flights of fifteen
men each and played four round match games to decide the best player. The eventual winner of the A flight group was the winner of last
year's tournament who breezed through all opponents without a loss.
The champ of the B flight group also won all his matches.

    The men, many of whom were stimulated by the match games, de-
cided to continue their checker games, and have set up a pyramid tournament. After players are eliminated according to finishes in regular
single elimination play, any player may challenge any other player in
the same horizontal row. If he wins, he may then challenge anyone in
the row above, and so on.

    This arrangement calls for constant attention to one's game to be prepared for a challenge from a player in the rank below and keeps the level high.

BOWLING TOURNAMENTS were a scheduled feature in the infirmary.

A successful bowling season was concluded; a group of thirty-six residents met once a week for twelve weeks, on a scheduled basis and with team handicaps. The group began right after New Year's and practiced bowling for the first five meetings to determine abilities and to select men and women for individual teams.

The careful placement of bowlers on the four teams (Blue Jays, Robins, Cardinals and Orioles), and weekly up-to-date handicaps were balanced and produced a close race for first place. Two teams, the Blue Jays and the Robins, finished in a tie for first place with identical records of seven wins and five losses. The second-place team, the Cardinals, was only one game behind with a six and a six record. After leading the league for the first three weeks, the Orioles faded and ended with a four win and eight loss tally.

The four teams and their bowlers knocked over 16,000 pins in the twelve-week season; the Blue Jays had the high mark for total team pins in one game, 370. . . .

Residents are asked to plan a letter to a legislator on a bill which the group or an individual supports or rejects, for the next meeting.

Seventeenth Meeting

It's said to be dangerous to discuss politics, though it is often a man's favorite topic. Rather than discuss it, maybe it's safer to write about it.

CONTACTING LEGISLATORS is discussed by club members interested; suggestions for letters to legislators are given below:

1. Describe the bill by number or the issue by its popular name.

2. Present a concise statement of the reasons for this position. Some of a legislator's most valuable help can come from a citizen with specialized knowledge of the problems.

3. Make your letter short, but sensible.

4. Time the letters to arrive while the issue is alive and hot.

5. If the legislator is on a committee, relay the information on the bill for study.

Some Don'ts.

1. Don't write to a legislator from any district except your own.

2. Don't threaten a legislator with defeat. Make a reasonable and sensible approach, not extremist.

3. Don't write a chain letter or form letter.

4. Don't write a dozen letters on the same subject. Give quality, not quantity. Have other persons write if they support your position.

5. Don't demand a vote your way. Give your legislator your feelings on an issue.

6. Write a letter of thanks when your legislator has done something of which you approve.

Eighteenth Meeting

MOTIVATED TO USE THEIR HANDS, men could come into a club meeting, the tables littered with a broken alarm clock, typewriter, radio, or some other mechanical problem for their solution.

A surprise activity in the carpentry room or craft shop could arouse their interest in joining other clubs as well.

Inexpensive Skill Sticks, available from most craft companies, are popsickle sticks grooved in fancy notches, which come with directions to make Christmas crèches, frontier towns, western corrals, and other items to be sold or given away to children. Newspapers on the tables, Elmer's glue, a Skill Stick kit, and the members of the club can be happily busy for weeks on their own.

Derby Kits, available from any department store where Boy Scout uniforms are sold, come with eight balsa wood racing cars cut out for further wood filing and sanding and staining, not a messy project but an intriguing one and the product makes an acceptable present for a child.

This can be the time and place to see who's interested in leather kits, tile, bird feeders ready to assemble, paint-by-number sets, or mosaic pictures, all available in craft catalogues.

Nineteenth Meeting

AROUND THE CIRCLE, they discuss a topic of their own choice, such as

1. In what respects can men and women never be equal? How did this emancipation start? How does the role of American women compare with that of the women in other countries? In what fields of work should there be more women?

2. What is their opinion of fashion's new skirt length? What is the best length in their opinion? What's this thing about stock prices going down when hemlines go down? How is this explained? What dates and hemline lengths can they recall?

BOWLING TOURNAMENTS can be adapted to equipment on hand.

Equipment. A volleyball; two rows of milk cartons weighted.

Procedure. The player rolls the volleyball between two lanes of milk cartons, avoiding knocking them down; low score wins.

Twentieth Meeting

Residents nominate and next meeting vote on a favorite writer, movie star, game, employee in the Home, and so forth.

THE ART LINKLETTER HOUSE (use one idea). Men guess what's inside the cardboard house with these clues:

It's pink, it's round, it's happy, it's mechanical (musical ball).

It's major, it's minor, it's held in the mouth (mouth organ).

Lucky in four, so find some more (four leaf clover).

Matrimony, love affair, give her one, if you dare (ring).

Twenty-first Meeting

WHAT'S MY LINE? This should be easy for people who remember the TV show. Residents answer ten questions on a real or imagined profession by replying Yes or No. The individual who provides the question wins if the group fails to guess it.

CHESS BY MAIL. For those who play, information is given (see Appendix).

READING THE HOME CENSUS, they list names of residents a few years back; some residents are still in the Home, of course; residents give impressions of those gone.

A short anecdote or quotation such as those appearing in monthly digest publications is to be submitted by each resident at the next meeting, and read aloud.

Twenty-second Meeting

PUNCHING A BAG in competition, men can vie with each other as to the length of time they can keep punching (see Appendix).

A punching bag set on a floorboard, extending up three feet (the proper height for a wheelchair patient) can be purchased for $10.50 plus shipping costs, from the local sport equipment store. The leader may set it in the rec hall, carpentry, or pool-room areas. In passing, men residents sit and give the punching ball a few swings with fists, wrists, or arms.

"GUESS THE FAMOUS MAN," they're told. Residents call out when they think they have the answer; they are eliminated from the game if they're wrong. Ten points go to the resident who gets the right answer on the first clue, nine on the second, and so on down.

Clues to identify the man:

1. He invented bifocal lenses.
2. He became postmaster general.
3. He founded America's first subscription library.
4. He was influential at Paris peace talks.
5. He wrote antislavery papers.
6. He was a signer of the Declaration of Independence.
7. He was editor of the *Pennsylvania Gazette*.
8. He suggested sending a cargo of rattlesnakes to London parks to retaliate for British injustice.
9. He is author of *Poor Richard's Almanac*.
10. On January 15, 1752, he conducted a kite experiment. (Answer: Ben Franklin.) The beginning clues should be most remote and difficult.

A resident is asked to be responsible for clues for another famous man for the next meeting.

Twenty-fourth Meeting

BASEBALL (outside, with ambulatory players).
Equipment. A ball; a baseball diamond of suitable size; teen-age volunteers as runners.

Procedure.

1. There are two teams, four members in each, a team of teen-agers and a team of residents.

2. A resident player stands at each of the four bases and catches the ball as it's thrown from first base to second and around the diamond.

3. The teen-ager does the running. The teen-ager runs from the home base to first, while the man at home base with the ball throws it to the man at first who catches or picks it up from the ground and throws it to second, second to third, and third back to home base as the teen-ager attempts to get there first.

4. The game is scored by teen-agers who touch each base without being tagged with the ball by the basemen. The game is won by the first three teen-agers reaching home base safely or by the residents if the teen-agers fail to reach home safely.

NO RUN BASEBALL.

Equipment. A Ping-Pong paddle; a small ball; a baseball diamond or lawn area.

Procedure.

1. A member of one team stands at each corner of the diamond and another in the center to pitch.

2. The opposing team member up to bat at home plate hits the ball with the Ping-Pong paddle; if the ball goes outside the baseball diamond, he scores; if it stays inside, he does not and is out.

3. The game is scored the same as in baseball; when three outs are made, the teams change positions.

FATHER'S DAY CELEBRATION. A Home reports on such an occasion.

Twenty-eight Lions Club members met here at their regular meeting for a meal in the Home, their initiation, and talks by the staff.

Father's Day was observed with all our gentlemen wearing corsages made of gilt-colored pine cones, a colorful pipe stem cleaner and a bit of cedar branch. Special recognition went to the oldest father, grandfather of the most children, fathers born in other countries, etc. There was a sing-a-long. We hear tell someone received a couple of kisses as she pinned all the corsages on the men Sunday morning.

Could some of these ideas be used in the club? Could a class of Sunday school children be invited in for a party with cookies and Kool-Aid? Or could a teen-age group come in to entertain, play cards, and shake hands with the oldsters?

TO READ ALOUD

Good Stories.

Adams, Samuel: *Grandfather Stories*   818-A217
   Stories about the author's grandfather and the building of the Erie Canal.

Andrews, Mary: *The Perfect Tribute*   Fiction
   An incident connected with Lincoln's Gettysburg speech.

Barrows, Marjorie: *The Family Reader*   813.8-B278
   "Friendly" stories in which the reader shares the gaiety and warmth of human experience.

Brown, Joe: *Stars in My Crown*   Fiction
   Courage, common sense, and humor characterize this story of the author's grandfather, a Southern minister.

Chase, Richard: *Grandfather Tales*   x398.2-C487
   Imagination and humor pervades these American-English folk tales.

Chase, Richard: *Jack Tales*   x398.2-C487j
   North Carolina folklore.

Connolly, Myles: *Mr. Blue*   Fiction
   Story of a man who wanted happiness more than wealth or success.

Doyle, Arthur: *Adventures and Memories of Sherlock Homes*
                    Fiction

Edmonds, Walter: *Cadmus Henry*   Fiction
   Story of the Civil War.

TRAVEL CLUB

Introduction

"Faraway places with strange sounding names, keep calling, calling. . . ."

Most people are interested in either telling about their travels or listening to someone else recount theirs. Unfortunately, many aged people feel they've never been anywhere and have nothing to talk about, but is there anyone who hasn't *wished* for a trip to see the Redwoods of California or the live alligators in Florida, longed to have fished at Cape Cod, to have returned to an old family landmark in Texas, or to have visited a daughter now living in Arizona or Oregon? Foreign travel may not be of as much interest, unless it leads to an ancestral home in Ireland, Bohemia, Greece, or some other land dear in memory.

This can be an easy club to organize, since "the world is so full of a number of things" and its study is limitless. Also, looking at slides and pictures is one of the most pleasurable of pastimes, especially if there's discussion with it and not "just a dark, warm, drowsy place to go to sleep, if we don't watch out!"

A small nucleus of people in the Home can be recruited on the basis of having "always been good at geography," having some travel experience, knowing a friend who will come in with slides even though they're only pictures taken within the boundaries of the state. Who doesn't want to join a merry group around a table with a game, or become part of a circle in alert discussion laughing together at a joke or puzzle, or perhaps take a little trip outside the Home to a travel lecture!

Goals (for the Residents)

Two main purposes exist.

1. To learn more about other countries and our own!

2. To appreciate the good company of other residents in armchair trips.

Motivation Techniques (May Be Applicable to All Clubs)

To motivate the members, try the following:

1. Appeal to the recognition of a resident's potential as a club member.

2. Watch for any leads which he exhibits.

3. Serve coffee.

4. Contact the new resident who has just been admitted to the Home.

5. Plan the theme of the club, something appealing to the resident.

First Meeting

See "The First Meeting" in Part III, "How to Lead a Club."

For a portion of each club meeting, residents can enjoy travel slides, free films, amateur travel movies, or reading travel stories aloud (see Appendix).

However, some other new ideas could be experimented with; if the ideas fail, it's no disgrace since there are many other activities to be tried. However, they should be ready immediately, so that the program moves along.

From memory, residents could try to draw freehand the map of a foreign country; who can make the longest list of its native products or landmarks?

It is helpful to be well supplied with maps, even if nothing better than state road maps posted where all can see, and a pointer. Maps can be used in dozens of ways—settling arguments and creating new games of distances, boundaries, extent of areas, locations of cities, and so forth.

Residents are asked at the next meeting to tell of a precarious trip.

Second Meeting

PUZZLES often animate people with this special knack.

How many words having to do with weather can be made of these letters used in any order, but only as often as they appear here?

A W I N D C B T L O M R E F H S (not a word)

(Hot, wet, wind, snow, warm, cold, mist, storm, fair, air, blow)

Residents invent another which has something to do with travel: how many words can be found in the following:

T I C K E T A G E N T, or
T O U R I N G I N A N O L D S M O B I L E

Here are the names of three forms of transportation. Residents find out what they are by rearranging the letters in each word.

S A K S E T	Skates
L E Y C B C I	Bicycle
A N W O G	Wagon

WALKEE-TALKEE. Would-be travelers talk about getting around on foot. Residents describe the longest walk they ever took. Why did people formerly do so much more walking than they do now? Were there special walking clothes or shoes? Anything unusual they have seen in walking? Dangers? If they have lived in other countries, what are the walking habits there (Germany, Ireland)? Has anyone had to retrace steps in walking, perhaps having lost something? Can they relate stories of long distance walkers? Have they later suffered ill-effects? Who was the best walker they ever knew? What descriptive words can be listed as characteristic of walking: sauntering, lumbering, mincing, and so forth.

TELLING OF PRECARIOUS TRIPS, the following is an illustration:

> Very spry for his eighty-six years, he sometimes walks with one of our blind residents, accompanied by his sturdy two white canes. One brisk morning they discussed vacations of former years, recalling a trip —— and his wife had taken in a 1941 Chevrolet. They drove from Iowa to Denver, taking in both the Iowa and Nebraska state fairs. The most exciting part was driving to the top of Pike's Peak. His wife was not at all frightened on the way up, but coming down was another story. He said she hung onto him and moaned in distress, for there were no posts or railings to guard the side of the steep road.

Third Meeting

COOKING FOREIGN FOOD could be a subject to talk about and perhaps to try. Club members make up a "One World Taste of Travel" recipe book in the following several meetings.

PASTIES, A CORNISH DISH, delights people from Cornwall, as it did these.

> With the help of volunteers, residents spent a morning making pasties served for dinner. Potatoes, onions, suet and meat were prepared the afternoon before. The ladies were brought to the kitchen around 9 A.M. to begin, some making at least five pasties.
>
> The dough was rolled and cut the size of a dinner plate. The ingredients and suet were put on a half of the dough, the other half closed over the fixed half, then baked and ready for dinner.
>
> Pasty is a famous Cornish dish popular in this country, made especially famous in Wisconsin through the Mineral Point area.

Ingredients.

1½ cup flour
1½ tsp. baking powder
¾ tsp. salt
½ cup shortening
6 tbs. hot water
2 tsp. lemon juice
1 egg yolk.

Method.

Sift flour, baking powder, and salt. Melt shortening in hot water, add lemon juice and unbeaten yolk. Stir together and then add dry ingredients. Mix together well, cover, and place in icebox to chill. Use this as under and top crusts for meat pies or cobbler. Glaze top before baking with slightly beaten egg. Bake in 425-degree oven for 25 minutes. It can be kept in the refrigerator a week.

Fourth Meeting

SWEDISH CAKE.

Ingredients.

½ cup butter
¼ cup sugar
1 egg yolk
1 cup flour
1 egg white, unbeaten
¾ cup nut meats
salt

Method.

Form into balls, dip into egg white, then into nuts. Place in greased cookie sheet and press fairly flat with bottom of a glass. Bake in slow oven for 5 minutes, remove from oven, press *centers* down, bake 15 minutes longer. When cool, put drop of jelly in center of cookie.

Fifth Meeting

HONEY MACAROONS (Greek).

Ingredients.
  1 cup butter (melted and free of salt)
  3 cups salad oil
  1 cup water
  2 heaping tsp. baking powder
  1 orange (the juice)
  ½ tsp. cinnamon
  flour

Method.
Mix with mixer—melted butter, salad oil, and water until light color. Add 2 tsp. baking powder to orange juice, then add to mixture with cinnamon. Add sifted flour until enough to roll. Knead very well and add more flour.

Filling.
  1 lb. walnuts
  2-3 egg yolks
  ½-¾ cup honey
  nutmeg

Method.
Grind nuts coarsely—mix egg yolks beaten with honey. Add cinnamon and nutmeg and put on slow fire. Let boil up once and cook until thick. Roll small balls of dough and flatten. Put little dab of filling, pinch dough together and roll. Bake in medium oven for about 20 minutes. Bake just like cookies. Let cool. Then pour on honey. Sprinkle with sugar mixed with cinnamon.

Sixth Meeting

JEWELED PINEAPPLE BAVARIAN CREAM

Ingredients.
  1 pkg. lemon Jell-O®
  1 cup hot water
  1 cup crushed pineapple undrained
  1 tsp. vanilla
  ½ pint cream whipped

Method.

Dissolve Jell-O in hot water. Add pineapple. Chill until well thickened. Add vanilla. Fold in whipped cream. Pour into individual molds or single quart mold. Serves six to eight.

Seventh Meeting

KOREAN YOOT.[6] Yoot is the most popular game of Korea and has been played for centuries.

1. *This diagram* can be marked on the floor or ground in less than a minute. In Korea, the game is usually played on a straw mat on the floor or ground.

2. *The players.* The game is played by two, three, four, or six persons. When four play, it is a partner game, and partners sit opposite.

3. *Counters or men.* Four "men" of contrasting size or shape are needed for each side. When three play, each one has three men. The men may consist of any convenient stones or pieces of papers. (Men were originally called "Horses.")

4. *The playing sticks.* The most important equipment is the four Yoot sticks. The shape is half-round, about 7″ long, the size of a man's finger; they are white on the flat side, and dark on the convex side.

Yoot sticks are made of hard wood, often highly polished, usually slightly tapered toward the ends. Round side may be darkened by charring, or indicated by burned or painted designs.

---

[6] Permission to use by World Wide Games, Box 450, Delaware, Ohio 43015.

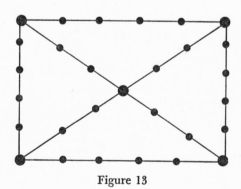

Figure 13

5. *The moves.* The object of the game is for the players to move one to four men (as may be agreed) around the field and off the board, the shortest way.

Scoring is as follows:

One white (flat) side up gives 1 point.

Two white sides up scores 2 points.

Three white sides up scores 3 points.

Four white sides up scores 4 points and permits a free throw.

Dark side (round) up scores 5 points and permits a free throw.

The one who starts the game is determined by throwing the sticks, the highest score leading.

A player may move his partner's counters.

Players all enter their men at the same starting point, and move around counterclockwise. To bring a man home and off the board, it is necessary to throw exactly the points needed to go one beyond the finish.

6. *Throwing the sticks.* The sticks are held in one hand and dropped, or thrown down. Some players toss them with much flourish, attempting to influence the result, but whether the light or dark side shows is largely a matter of chance.

7. *Doubling up.* If a player throws so that one of his men is moved upon another of his own counters, he can double them up, and they ride around together as one piece, but counting for both men. Of course, they can both be sent back at once. Three can ride together, but not four.

8. *Sending back.* When one player moves a counter to a spot occupied by an opponent, the opponent's piece is sent back to start over, and the player who captures an opponent is given a free throw. (Free throws are usually taken before moving the counter.)

9. *Short cuts.* If a counter lands on the corner spot, or the intersection of the diagonals, it can take the shortest way home on the next move. (For example, a throw of 5 would permit placing a counter on the corner, a free throw might give 3, to place the man on the middle spot, and throw of 4 would bring it off the board.)

If you have a man on the turning spots, you are obliged to take the shortest way. (That is, it is not permitted to take the longer way in order to bounce an opponent.)

10. *Winning.* The player or team wins which first brings all men around the playing area and off the board.

Residents next time think of some sculpture for others to guess as to location.

Eighth Meeting

STATES ARE IDENTIFIED as a brushup in geography. Using a fairly large map of the United States pasted on colored paper, they cut out each state along the border line. They mix all the pieces well and then paste them or pin them in jumbled order on a large piece of cardboard with the colored paper backs showing. They write a number under each state. Residents then try to identify states by number.

SCULPTURE LOCATIONS. Discussion is promoted. Where could one find this sign: "To the World's Largest Sculpture"? (Mount Rushmore, South Dakota; the sculpture busts of Washington, Lincoln, Jefferson and Theodore Roosevelt.)

They name famous sculpture for others to locate.

SURVIVAL can be associated with long-forgotten tales. How hard is it to survive on a raft in the middle of the ocean? In 1943, a steward in the British Merchant Navy was on a raft in the middle of the ocean, after his ship was torpedoed. He floated around alone in the Atlantic on the raft for 133 days until he was finally picked up by a fishing boat and saved.

Can residents describe other survival episodes in the woods or across the prairies in a storm?

What major improvements could they see in travel in the next ten years?

A TRAVEL COLUMN in a Sunday paper is read aloud.

AN IMAGINARY BUS TRIP through Europe indicating stops and days scheduled in each country is planned.

AN IMAGINARY TRIP TO A FARM. A sulky pony ride is just one of the many activities that city slickers could enjoy on a vacation on a farm. There are four hundred of these agricultural settings in fifty states and Canada that welcome visitors. Where would they like to go and what would they like to do on the farm?

Tenth Meeting

OPINIONS are given as to differences in people in other countries. The widow of one-time Senator Borah of Idaho, when she was one hundred years old, at a party in Washington, D.C., made a comment about men: "All men are different and all husbands are alike."

Are men in other countries different? Alike?

The word "teen" dates back to the 10th century. It has undergone some changes in meaning, but that depends a lot on one's point of view. The old meaning of the word when used as a verb was to vex, harass, cause grief, or to enrage. When used as a noun, "teen" meant harm, danger, irritation, and malice.

What are teen-agers like in other countries? They describe teen-agers they love.

QUIZ. Here are names of three cities in the United States. Letters in each word are rearranged to form the name of a city.

N O S B O T	Boston
T R I T O E D	Detroit
N A L C D E V E L	Cleveland

Next time, countries are identified by pictures. Each resident brings significant pictures, perhaps from *National Geographic,* for others to guess at the next meeting.

Eleventh Meeting

MOVIES (or slides) on travel are shown (see Appendix). Travel pictures from magazines, contributed by residents, are discussed.

Reservations are made for residents desiring to eat out at the next club meeting.

Twelfth Meeting

"EVENING OUT" can mean eating in a foreign restaurant. Arrangements are made to have dinner downtown with another nursing home or hospital group, Dutch treat, ordering from a foreign menu.

Thirteenth Meeting

AN EXCHANGE STUDENT is asked to come in and talk (local high school or college). The student could bring a display of articles from his country: beads, baskets, figurines, cloth woven and dyed by his people, jewelry. Or, pictures of his family and of the countryside.

Fourteenth Meeting

CERAMICS ARE DISPLAYED or other displays brought from the vocational school class. An instructor from the school could come with a craft and an informative talk on the history and countries represented in this craft.

Fifteenth Meeting

AN EXCHANGE OF GIFTS is a custom in travel. Each member brings a ten-cent gift, wrapped and to be exchanged. Gifts can be passed in a circle as music is played, members keeping the gift they hold when the music stops.

FOREIGN FOOD, a good topic for entertainment. Residents bring pictures cut from magazines of foreign food. Can the others identify the food from the pictures?

Sixteenth Meeting

SCRAMBLED FOREIGN STATESMEN can be a difficult stunt. A list (available from the newspapers) is made of prominent statesmen and the countries they represent. Each club member is given a scrambled list to discuss and to match up, country and man.

GUESS THE MILEAGE is a stunt prepared by a resident with a map giving distances. Residents guess the mileage between two given cities; closest guess wins.

Seventeenth Meeting

IN INFORMAL DISCUSSION, the leader asks a few leading questions, such as "What would you do if you were program chairman?"

FARAWAY PLACES could be a regular weekly activity in the club.

1. Residents ask the Carpentry Club to make a large frame for a big map of the world to hang low enough for wheelchair people to examine. Such a map is often inserted in the *National Geographic* or could be available from the library.

2. Members stick jeweled hat pins, dime store variety, in countries which the club has studied.

3. They clip pictures of faraway places and frame them, or shellac pictures and mount them with masking tape.

With a WORLD GLOBE, residents may discover misconceptions as to distances. For instance, it's shorter from New York to England than New York to Chile; from Wisconsin to Bolivia via Miami, than Wisconsin to Bolivia via New Orleans; from Oregon to Moscow via the Arctic, than from Oregon to Moscow via New York; it's the same distance from the Philippines to Hawaii as San Francisco to Hawaii.

Residents list other discoveries verified with the measuring tape and the globe.

COUNTRY AND RACE. Can residents name each country and the race predominant in that country? A dictionary or encyclopedia has a list of countries.

Eighteenth Meeting

TRAVELING ON A SHOESTRING can be adventurous, even in short distances. Each couple is given a road map and asked to route a trip to the nearest cave, forest, state or national monument, park on a river, skiing point, beach for bathing, lookout tower, new urban development, nearest kiddy camp, freeway, fish hatchery, and so on, depending on the state and what it offers by way of travel interest.

Winners could be the ones finding all the places listed in the shortest time, or the nearest places. But perhaps it's most fun just learning about the state, with no competition.

PUZZLER. Can club members change the word "Trip" in four steps to "Dray" by changing a letter at a time? (Trip, trap, tray, pray, dray.)

Nineteenth Meeting

POPULAR TRAVELER. Who gets the vote? What traveler do they say did the most for his country: Lewis and Clark, Johnny Appleseed, Bob Hope, John Glenn, a President? Each member defends his decision.

FLAGPOLE RELAY gets people up out of their seats.
Equipment. Two canes, two Coke® bottles; two small stakes with miniature flags.
Procedure.

1. Miniature flagpoles are placed as goals for two rows of players.

2. Players with canes push the Coke bottles to the flagpole, around it and back to the relay row to the next player.

3. The row completing the procedure wins.

They NAME FOREIGN FLAGS from pictures in the encyclopedia or describe a flag for others to guess.

Residents are selected to practice stunts for the next meeting (see below).

Twentieth Meeting

STUNT I. (The leader works with an accomplice, a resident with whom he has practiced the stunt.)
Procedure.

1. Objects which everyone can see are placed in a row on a table or stand. The leader and accomplice have mentally given each object a number previously.

2. The accomplice, briefed on the stunt, goes out of the room.

3. Residents in the room select an object for him to guess.

4. To secretly inform the accomplice as to which object has been selected, the leader calls him back by giving the same number of words as the number of objects on the table: "Come" for the object number one; "Come on" for object number two; "Come on, please" for object number 3. Other objects can be added and additional words added to the greeting.

5. The group tries to guess how this is done by going out of the room themselves and responding to the leader's greeting if they can.

STUNT II. The leader says: "Schenectady, Milwaukee, Minneap-
olis, St. Paul, spell 'that' and I'll give you a ball." Residents try
to spell these cities, and may even spell them correctly, but the
winner is the one who spells "that."

These FRIGHTENING EXPERIENCES, as told by residents, are read
aloud:

My sister and I were going to Lansing from La Crosse on the J.S.
Excursion Steamboat on a Saturday in 1909. The boat caught fire, it
was thought from a lighted cigarette. It came to shore on Bad Axe Island, near DeSoto, where all the people got off. There were a thousand
people on the boat. Of those, two lost their lives, and the boat was
completely burned.

* * *

One day, while living in Montana, my husband, son and I were
chased by range cattle while crossing grazing land going to a neigh-
bor's. The cattle ran toward us and we knew we would be trampled if
we didn't get out of their way. There was a fence a short distance
away, so we ran for that. I put my son over and couldn't climb over,
so rolled underneath. The cattle were close behind, but stopped when
they couldn't get to us, and started grazing. We were badly frightened
but continued on our way.

* * *

We were out for a ride in a car with some friends. We were on the
Midway hill when something went wrong with the coil in the car, causing us to tip over. None of us were injured but we were all pretty
much frightened.

How many personal experiences can be narrated in the group?
Can each resident add one?

Twenty-first Meeting

ALPHABET VISITS can be made by wheelchair tourists. Players sit
in a circle; the first player takes the letter "A" and says "I'm going to the *Arctic* by *airplane;* when I get there I am going to dig
angleworms." He can use any place that begins with "A," any
means of transportation that begins with "A," and when he gets
there, he can "do" anything that begins with "A."

When the first player has completed his turn, the second one
uses the letter "B." He could say, "I'm going to *Brazil* by *bus*
and when I get there I'm going to buy *bananas.*"

The third with "C": "I'm going to *Cairo* by *camel* and when I get there, I'm going to eat *cookies*." They continue.

HOW MANY WORDS IN A CITY? A resident suggests a city and the group together lists as many words as possible from the letters in that word.

Twenty-second Meeting

TALKATHON. If one could live a week's time in some other country and some other era of history, where and when would he choose?

Each resident REPORTS ON A COUNTRY, perhaps for the others to identify.

WORLD TRAVELERS, well known, are subjects for reports by residents: Livingstone, Lindbergh, Columbus, La Salle, de Soto, Kit Carson, Ponce de León, and others they can name. How was civilization changed because of their travels?

Residents NAME FAMOUS SCHOOLS or other objects in countries outside the United States.

For the next meeting, residents bring travel gift pictures cut from magazines. They also bring a foreign costume or item of clothing to wear or display.

Twenty-third Meeting

COSTUMES to wear or an item to display can be something residents exhibit with pride. Each describes his.

They present a guest of honor with TRAVEL ITEMS, pictures they have cut from magazines: photo album, camera supplies, guides to points of interest or customs, diary, address book, stationery and stamps, dictionary of foreign phrases, books to read while traveling, small sewing kit.

Twenty-fourth Meeting

JIGSAW PUZZLE is, for the visually handicapped, put to interesting use by a volunteer.

Most of us studied U. S. geography so many years ago we are very vague and uncertain of the shape and arrangement of the states on a map.

We spent an interesting and informative Sunday afternoon when we opened a new jigsaw puzzle for our sightless pal. As he held each separate state in his hand, his delicate Braille touch outlined the edges. Surprised at the large size of Idaho in relation to the small size of Vermont, he was full of questions.

We found we were indeed "rusty" when it came to fitting together some of the smaller eastern states. We did fine on the west coast, but does Nebraska fit under South Dakota and how in the world did Arkansas get right under Missouri?

As we talked about each state and the surrounding ones which border it, we decided it would be fun to make up our own quiz for the *Chatterbox* readers. Try it and see if you are smarter than we:

1. What state touches only one other state?
2. How many states border Wisconsin?
3. Which is farther west: Reno, Nevada, or Los Angeles, California?
4. One state touches eight other states. Which is it?
5. Which is farther north: Maine or Minnesota?
6. At least two states are touched by seven others. Name them.

(These questions are all based upon the original 48 and do not include Alaska and Hawaii.)

TRAVEL AGENCIES are usually willing to contribute travel brochures. A different brochure can be obtained for each resident and passed around the group. Each resident finds something he would like about the trip, something he would not like. When discussion is finished, the brochure is passed to the person at the left, who gives his reactions.

TO READ ALOUD

Gilman, Coburn: *Week-end Book of Travel* 910
Exploration, adventure, and romance over far horizons.

Gollomb, Joseph: *Albert Schweitzer: Genius in the Jungle* 92-S41
Biography of a medical man in Africa.

Humphreys, J. R.: *The Lost Towns and Roads of America* 917
A leisurely journey on the forgotten roads which lead into quiet towns. Interesting photographs.

Jimenez, Juan Ramon: *Platero and I* Fiction
Simple tales of a donkey in a little Spanish town.

Lindbergh, Anne Morrow: *North to the Orient*   915
    This book is the beautifully written description of the flight
    the Lindberghs made to the Orient. Her account of the trip
    and the places visited is warm and personal.
Mallery, Richard: *Masterworks of Travel and Exploration: Di-*
    gests of 13 Great Classics   910-M
McNeer, May: *The Mexican Story*   x972
    The country and its history from the Mayan civilization to the
    present.
Pillsbury, Dorothy: *No High Adobe*   814
    Sketches about the author's Spanish-speaking neighbors near
    her New Mexico home.
Rittenhouse, Mignon: *Amazing Nellie Bly*   92-C66
    About the adventurous woman who proved she could travel
    around the world faster than anyone else of her time.
Street, Julian: *The Need of Change*   Fiction
    Humorous skit with an English setting.

HOBBY CLUB

Introduction

Often, when interviewed about his special interests, the resident doesn't know what is meant by the question, "What are your
hobbies?"

What does that mean? What is that word? He spent his life
earning a living, he will hasten to say, raising a family, paying
his taxes as a citizen in routine struggle. He had no time for such
nonsense. He worked, ate and slept, minded his own business, and
did what was expected of him.

The creative leader tries to know him better: going for a walk
with him, playing his choice of card game, listening as he talks,
discussing him with the aides on the wards who see him constantly. What can be learned about each resident? That he was a railroad man, a draftsman, that he played dominoes as a youngster,
used to write (or recite) poetry, bet on the horses, that he loves
candy, raised purebred cattle, is preoccupied with religion, likes
pretty girls, has always been interested in the history of the county, was devoted to a pet dog, is critical (or idealizes) the labor

unions, belonged to a city pinochle club, is vocal about politics, was once a professional skater, lives only to eat, and so on. There should be at least *one* item of interest on each resident that can be converted into a hobby.

Given a stack of discarded newspapers or magazines and a scissors, could he be set to making a scrapbook of pretty girls, pure-bred cattle, the history of the county, poetry selections, or race-horses? (One such subject.)

Is correspondence with some hobbyist possible?

Are there local citizens or other residents in the Home with the same hobby whom he could meet? Are there library books or free brochures on the subject? Could he write expressing his opinions or findings? Could he talk on a tape recorder in an interview featuring his hobby? Would he attend club meetings to hear about other hobbies which could surprise and interest him, watch residents tieing flies or polishing stones; or, as an ex-Navyman, could he teach others how to make a foursquare knot macramé belt?

OTHER MOTIVATION TECHNIQUES

Additional techniques will serve to stimulate interest.

1. Appeal to the recognition of his accomplishment.
2. Ask him to please some person whom he likes.
3. Encourage him to help others in the group.
4. Give him competition with other residents.
5. Label the item with the resident's name, if it will please him.
6. Persist in continually coming back to talk with him.

Goals

The following goals are to be kept in mind:

1. Special interest groups give residents a unique chance to be creative; they give the leader a similarly important chance to bring the community to the hospital or Home through groups with common interests.

2. Hobbies give residents an experience which can carry over to daily life on the wards, weekends and evenings, and help one to make new friends.

3. There are probably as many hobbies as there are individuals; any interest could be recognized by the club.

A possible reason for forming this club could be to continue an established hobby among club members or to introduce them to something new. Limitations in selecting the primary hobby could be costs, area, equipment and materials needed. For instance, photography might not be practical.

Members could decide to form a single hobby of interest to all, instead of branching out in the many ways presented here.

Helps

Some ideas here may be helpful.

1. If the Home is in a town large enough to draw on, visits and an exchange of information and ideas can be made.

2. The YWCA and YMCA often sponsor clubs, as do churches or recreation centers.

3. There are hobby magazines available from which articles and information can be reported by residents. The encyclopedia is of great help!

4. Hobby Club activity publicized in local newspapers suggest subjects for residents' meetings in the Home. Other sources can be exhibits, night classes, local club meetings to which residents may be invited once residents let the community know they're there!

5. As certain hobbies become especially popular, they can be further developed and extended.

Special Interests

With the use of a library or a set of encyclopedias in the Home, a variety of special interests can be developed by a group or individually, such as the study of pyramids; mob psychology; breeding horses; the study of our penal system; training dogs; magic; etiquette; genealogy; French; dreams; the study of narcotics; the study of Eskimos; the study of space; unusual business ventures; environment; first aid; paper weights; biographies; weather forecasting; crime; railroads; politics; our Presidents.

First Meeting

See "The First Meeting," Part III, "How to Lead a Club."

Residents make a list of collections and special interests among their friends in the Home: stamp collecting, postcard collecting, match collecting, coin collecting, and so on.

Can they list values in such hobbies? Have they collections of their own? What new interests can they suggest? Are there local collectors in the community or the county who could talk to the group? Could exhibits in the Home help promote membership and interest in the club? They decide on a speaker for next time. Each member could bring in an unusual button as a start in finding a club hobby.

Second Meeting

BUTTONS are small, light in weight, easy to mount and handle, easy to store. They make a good collection for people in Homes and hospitals.

The beginning collector could mount his buttons on 12″ × 18″ pieces of cardboard, classifying them before they are mounted. Divisions can be made from the standpoint of color, size, shape, age, use, type of fastening or material.

Visitors to the Home could be notified that contributions of buttons are requested, and they are encouraged to drop in for more frequent visits. Also, correspondence can be started with members of other button clubs.

Someone is appointed to lead the discussion on a new collection next meeting.

Third Meeting

STAMP COLLECTIONS are a popular resident hobby. Members from a local club demonstrate a stamp auction, if possible. Or, residents could attend a local meeting of stamp collections.

Collectors desiring first-day cancellations can send addressed envelopes, together with remittance to cover the cost of the stamps to be affixed, to the Postmaster, Washington, D.C. 20013. The envelop to the postmaster is endorsed: "First Day Covers six cents

(Polish Millenium Stamp)." Announcements of new stamps are often listed in stamp columns in local papers.

Residents are urged to bring unusual postcards to discuss at the next meeting.

Fourth Meeting

POSTCARD COLLECTIONS are of no monetary value and are easy to acquire. Some residents can have a small start in saving postcards by notifying personnel in the Home to save cards.

What observations can residents make about the cards: postmarks, the picture itself, the variety of cards from foreign countries or parts of the United States. What is the best way to mount the cards, exhibit or preserve them? What uses could such a collection have?

They are asked to bring an unusual coin to the next meeting.

Fifth Meeting

COIN COLLECTIONS can be begun by a resident finding a single curious coin among his belongings. Stamp and coin collections have probably been the two most popular collector items in America. Information about forming stamp groups can be applied to coin collecting. Valuable stamps and valuable coins should not be left in hospital or Home rooms, however, but always put in safe keeping, under lock and key.

Good information about United States coins can be obtained by writing the Bureau of the Mint, Treasury Department, Washington, D.C. 20220, and to Superintendent of Documents, Government Printing Office, Washington, D.C. 20402.

A practice that could be of interest to hospital and Home collectors could be getting unused specimens of all the new United States coins issued during the year from the Bureau of the Mint. They will usually be one penny, one nickel, one dime, one quarter, one fifty cent piece, and occasionally special commemorative coins. The total cost is generally less than $2 and they usually increase in value in a few years.

Pieces of unusual money or bills could be observed at the bank, in a collection at the local museum, or at a cigar stand where coins and stamps can be bought. A local citizen could come to the club with some interesting items in his collection. The club can talk about the coins residents collect and display some of their treasures.

For the next meeting, residents are asked to bring in a "show and tell" item, an item of sentiment or of history from the old country, perhaps of little worth to anyone else but displayed by them with pride.

Sixth Meeting

"OLD COUNTRY" COLLECTIONS. A piece of lace, a handkerchief, a china figurine, a watch from the land of his ancestors can be informative and motivating.

Each resident is requested to bring a match cover not likely to be duplicated by the group, for the next meeting.

Seventh Meeting

MATCH COVER COLLECTIONS could start with friends, relatives, and employees bringing in souvenirs from trips. How many cities are represented by the match covers? States? Any from out of the country? How many colors are represented, kinds of business, resorts? What are the slogans on each? Any unusual designs or gimmicks? Were the match covers acquired in any unusual way? Are there residents who would like to trade with others, passing them around? What were some of the first matches like? What are the uses of matches in this day and age? Could they have had more uses fifty years ago? Are there any match covers unique in safety?

Residents are asked to bring in an American antique, a small item, for the next meeting.

Eighth Meeting

ANTIQUES are not hard to come by. Antique combs, button hooks, Bibles, photographs, marriage certificates, jewelry, laprobes, account books, chests, or diaries are sometimes seen in private rooms in nursing homes, and can be displayed at the meeting.

Have residents seen one like it? How does it differ? How was it used? Why is the item no longer produced like this? Does it have any monetary value? Sentimental value? How many people have owned it? Each resident in turn describes his antique.

Residents with a seashell are asked to bring it to the next meeting. Someone volunteers to bring a short item on shells to read.

Ninth Meeting

SHELL COLLECTIONS were sometimes begun following a winter vacation. How did each individual obtain the shell he has? Where could it have been found? Any ideas as to how old it is? What colors does he see in it? What was the animal like that lived inside? Eventually, what happens to shells on the beach? Has a resident seen the ocean?

Are there residents who have made decorations with shells: earrings, pins, bookends, shell kits in craft work?

For the next meeting, members are asked to share an antique letter or a letter of some significance.

Tenth Meeting

PEN PALS. Correspondence with foreign language students could be a new and happy adventure. The local high school foreign language department has the address of an exchange of pen pals in other countries. A fee for the name of the student is usually required. Often, residents read and write in another language and would enjoy the experience of making a friend in that language.

Other exchanges can be made through other Homes and hospitals.

Ancient letters could be read and discussed if the owner is willing and feels they would be of interest. When were they written? How did they happen to be saved? Will they be valued by others in another generation? What part of history have they seen? Was the mail service different at that time?

For the next meeting, residents are asked to bring in a joke, story, anecdote, picture, or model of a plane.

Eleventh Meeting

The "show and tell" items are displayed and discussed.

MODELS (see Appendix) can be of interest to a few or only a

single person. Model airplanes make good projects, if they can be supplied by a volunteer, some club in the community, or if the resident can buy his own materials.

Club time is taken up in discussing construction of the models. If members are new at model-making, they could begin with balsa models. Autos—antique and hot rods, boats of all kinds, railroad cars and engines are also available through hobby shops.

Model railroading boasts a large group of enthusiasts, but this is an expensive and probably unsuitable choice. Local gauge groups could host residents in their homes for an evening's demonstration of model trains, however.

At each of the following meetings, announcement is made of the theme for the next meeting and the responsibility and assignment given residents in preparing for it. Suggestions for the item for display and discussion will be made by the leader from here on.

Twelfth Meeting

COLLECTING AUTOGRAPHS. This hobby could be introduced by getting one another's signatures. A collection built up by the club writing letters to sport stars, radio and movie personalities, actors and other "well knowns" whom residents admire is an easy start.

Thirteenth Meeting

KEEPING SCRAPBOOKS needs no special direction or supervision. This activity can help residents work together and make friends; scrapbooks can be useful given to local hospitals, clinics, doctors' offices, pediatric wards, and so on.

Residents collect and file or paste newspaper clippings on a subject of interest to themselves: articles on the Home, historical features on a city or county, farming, news of neighbors and friends, and other such items.

Mounting snapshots in photo albums for friends and relatives or recording interests using community sources can take a great deal of time and involve many contacts.

Fourteenth Meeting

GENEALOGIES can be absorbing. Paper and pencil are distributed. Who can give the birthdate, name, and place of his parents, children, grandchildren? Grandparents? Sisters, brothers? Are there residents who can distinguish themselves further back in a genealogy? Could county records be helpful, clerk of court files? Family, neighbors, friends, a family Bible? Residents keep the list and add to it as they can.

Are there achievements and accomplishments which could be recorded regarding any of these people?

Fifteenth Meeting

HISTORY OF THE TOWNSHIP, COUNTY, OR STATE could be equally absorbing. Again, with paper and pencil, can each record the date and place of some significant piece of history in one of these areas? Taking a one year or a five year or some other period, can they each contribute important facts which could be noted? Can newspaper files, an interested librarian, a local history buff, the Historical Society members, a visit to the museum or to wayside plaques be useful?

Finally, in résumé, can someone write a summary; or, taking the most interesting historical events, can they feature them for the local newspaper?

Sixteenth Meeting

COLLECTIONS OF FOLDERS, MENUS, OR THEATRE PROGRAMS. What collectors are present who have saved items such as these? Are there other related collections? What ones do they especially treasure? Why? What part does sentiment play? What is the story behind each?

Seventeenth Meeting

PRESSED FLOWER COLLECTIONS. In each instance, how was the flower picked, preserved, and mounted? Are there different ways of pressing flowers most successfully? How will the collection be used (framed, for paper weights, scrapbooks, etc.)? (See also "Nature Club" and "Garden Club.")

Eighteenth Meeting

STONE COLLECTIONS, though few and small, contain specimens available for display and discussion. How many colors are seen in each? Why was it selected and saved? Have any of them been polished or retouched? How long has the resident had it? Have they picked up stones as youngsters? Are there local lapidaries who can visit with their collection to help in the discussion?

Nineteenth Meeting

CHESS AND CHECKER SETS can be collectors' items. Are there sets to be found locally which can be studied if there are none in the Home? What makes the sets unusual? Valuable? Do they show wear? Can someone give their histories? Can someone report on unusual sets, the history of the games? Play an exhibition game?

Twentieth Meeting

MINIATURE CHINA COLLECTIONS can be found in almost any room in the Home. What special associations does each piece have? Which piece is the oldest? Most valuable? Came from another country? Is unusual in some way? Is a family heirloom? Most colorful, most delicate? Are there any items with a special use in their day which are no longer needed?

Twenty-first Meeting

RECIPE COLLECTIONS. Do residents still own favorite recipe books? What was the family's favorite dish? The typical dinner when the minister came? A handout for a tramp? A winter meal? Summer? Most quickly prepared? Longest in preparation?

Residents could read them, discuss ingredients and their origins, primitive cooking facilities and utensils. Could some of them be tried by the cooks in the Home kitchen? (See "Homemakers Club.")

Twenty-second Meeting

A DOLL COLLECTION with an antique doll on display for discussion. Residents describe a favorite doll. How old was it? How do dolls differ: what are the varieties of materials used in manufactured or homemade dolls? Have they played with dolls of clay or wood or other improvisations? What was the most unusual doll they've ever seen? The most elaborate? What names did they have for dolls? Did they have boy dolls, dolls with special clothes?

How do dolls from other countries differ? Modern dolls could be brought in for display and discussion.

The men present could be more interested in a discussion such as the following, which concludes the meeting:

MY MOST UNFORGETTABLE CHARACTER. Who would each name? What description fits him (her) best? How was he different from others? How did one get to know him? Where did he live, when? What were his beliefs, habits, feeling toward others? Work? What things did he value most? What were his living habits? Who were his friends? In what qualities would the resident like to resemble him? What episodes in his life should be remembered?

Twenty-third and Twenty-fourth Meetings

COMMUNITY CONTACTS. City classes sometimes make further study of a hobby possible whether in caning chairs, carpentry, beauty culture, or literature. "Now You Have Time for It," the vocational school sign reads. Whether residents matriculate as students or for diversional activity, the classes can be worthwhile.

Volunteer groups like League of Women Voters, Daughters of American Revolution, Federated Women's clubs, study groups, church circles, or men's lodges often provide and direct study projects for special interests.

The Historical Society, Conservation Department, schools and library, foreign exchange students or local travelers, bird watchers, doctors, inventors, businessmen or club leaders can all contribute to discussions on a regular or occasional basis.

Other Activities

The range of collecting cannot be covered, but periodicals relating to special topics can be found in the Appendix for addresses.

Other hobbies of interest in working with residents could include birth announcement collections, diaries and journals, bead, earring, or buckle collections.

Any hobby can start a resident on a pursuit that will add to his purpose and interest in life.

TO READ ALOUD

Duncan, Kunigunde: *Earning the Right to Do Fancy-Work*
92-E335
   An informal biography of President Eisenhower's mother.
Graham, Elinor: *Maine Charm String* 917.41
   Picture of Maine and its people and of the author's hobby of button collecting.
Moses, Anna: *Grandma Moses; My Life's History* 927
   Biography of the woman who learned to paint after she was eighty.
Sumner, Cid: *A View from the Hill* 92-S 95
   A woman of sixty-odd years tells how to enrich later life.

GARDEN CLUB

Introduction

Gardeners, as onetime farmers or farmers' wives, amateur horticulturists, or people who find gardening a happy hobby are found in every county home.

Because it must be assumed that most members will be wheelchair patients or ambulatory residents unable to get out to a garden area, it is necessary to plan special activities. Appropriate work areas must be found large enough for wheelchairs, with a long rough table where plants can be potted, flower arrangements made, and flats prepared for seeding.

Protective newspapers can be placed on tables which have other uses, and clean peat moss can be easily swept up from the floors as a peace measure with the housekeeper.

Basement areas, patios, or roof gardens seem preferable, if accessible to semiambulants or wheelchair patients. If nothing better is available, the sun room, recreation room, or other multipurpose rooms are acceptable, and some of the "planting" projects omitted or simply discussed.

Ambulatory residents can be invited into community garden shows, parties, or tours. Several county homes have won numbers of blue ribbons for garden produce of flowers and vegetables at county fairs.

In one Home, the only incentive for one woman resident ever to leave the building in the summer is to walk out daily to the garden area, pull an onion, and eat it.

Hopefully, too, bed and room-bound patients become interested in the seedlings the community Garden Club members bring to them to care for, in the bulb to nurture, in the plants to grow in water, in the winter bouquet assembled of straw flowers or weeds or pulled from the floral bouquets contributed by greenhouses.

Local garden club members coming in to the Home are a great help in conducting meetings, planning and organizing special projects such as making bird feeders, visiting flower shows or wayside gardens, setting up flagpoles, and so on.

Goals

Certain goals should be kept in mind.

1. To share in community garden projects, in good community-Home relationships, and to find ways in which residents can be useful.

2. To add to knowledge of horticulture in beautifying the Home, improving Home living, contacting more room-bound people.

Residents can approve or disapprove these goals and after discussing them, draw up their own goals and bylaws.

First Meeting

See "The First Meeting," Part III, "How to Lead a Club."

A landscaping plan designed to beautify the Home grounds can be a good way to start. The group could cooperate with local organizations interested in roadside beautification, realizing that highway projects must be approved by local and state highway officials.

Other activities appear at the end of the chapter, as supplementary material.

CLUB MEMBERS KEEP AN IMAGINATIVE GARDENER'S LOG, getting plants started month by month in an imaginary seed bed.

At several meetings, residents pool their experience and information by making up a gardener's log for the various months of the year. What should the gardener be busy doing (indoors and outdoors)?

January, for instance, could include the following:

Start fuchsia, geranium, rose, heliotrope, ivy. Train one central leader upward and eliminate side growth as it occurs.

Keep temperatures even.

Sow seeds of calendula, candytuft, carnation, felicia, labellum, pansy, hybrids, sweet pea, viola.

Plant bulbs of pink and yellow callas.

Divide and repot orchids; repot early geraniums.

In a warm house, plant amaryllis and gloxinia bulbs.

Divide and repot African violets, begonia.

Sow seeds of African violets, begonias, gloxinia, gypsophila, marigold.

February (indoors and outdoors):

Don't start too many seeds too soon. Wait to sow fast-growing annuals and vegetables later. Repotting time for permanent plants—ferns, crotons, palms. Fall-sown annuals will be going into their final pots. All plants need regular feeding now and increased watering.

For later transfer to cold frame, start seeds of leaf lettuce, cabbage, cauliflower, broccoli.

Sow lobelia.

Start cuttings of dusty miller.

Bring in dormant miniature roses now to force; start them cool.

Start calla bulbs.

Start cuttings of acalifa, ageratum, lantana.

Sow seeds of ageratum, felicia and gypsophila, lobelia, petunia, snapdragon, verbena.

In a warm house, plant bulbs of amaryllis, tuberous begonia, caladium, gloxinia.

Start cuttings of allamanda, clerodendrum, coleus, croton, gardenia, lantana.

Divide and/or repot abutilon, African violet, begonia, orchids.

Sow seeds of African violets, azalea, begonia, cactus, eggplant, gloxinia, pepper, stevia, tomato.

Are there residents physically able to garden outside? If not, they could find pleasure in drawing up plans for one, as illustrated below, reported in the summer issue of a county home newsletter.

> Did you see the four formal garden beds on the south side of the building? . . . This project began in June and involved planning, real spadework, clearing of grass, bringing in black dirt and plants from the infirmary greenhouse and planting.
>
> Later there was watering, weeding and harvesting. A resident who used to work for the city parks used his knowledge and skills to lay out the bed. Others dug, carried, pushed the wheelbarrows and replanted for days. They usually had spectators. Numerous residents have already enjoyed the beauty of the flowers when on walks as well as from the ward and other windows. In their prime they rivaled those in parks. . . .

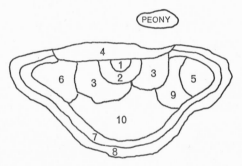

Figure 14. 1, President Canna; 2, King Humbert Canna; 3, Cleome (Spider Flower) ; 4, Vegetables; 5, Zinnia; 6, Marigold; 7, Coleus; 8, Lobelia; 9, Carnation; 10, Commanche Petunia.

Each resident at the meeting can WRITE AN ITEM for the Home newsletter regarding garden club projects or a gardener's observations.

Second Meeting

SMOOCH PRINTS resemble a Japanese painting but can be made by novices. Residents who have good use of their fingers can make a gift for a friend. A leaf is pressed (a new leaf for each print), pinned to the paper, and edges rubbed over with chalk, crayon, paint, or ink. The prints are used to decorate stationery, wastepaper baskets, lamp shades, wall panels, and so on.

Third Meeting

A volunteer is invited to show HOME MOVIE OR SLIDES of a local or foreign garden, to be discussed.

Or, a resident is asked to report on a Japanese, German, or American Indian garden.

Fourth Meeting

A GARDENER'S FISHPOND. Fortunes are placed in a box or on the other side of a curtain, each fortune typed and with a paper clip attached. The fish pole with a string, a small magnet attached to the end, picks up the fortune as it makes contact with the paper clip. Each member reads his fortune aloud:

You are ambitious and given to investigation and botanic experimenting.

Your nature is so sympathetic and sensitive that you hate to use pesticides.

Your back is subject to giving you excuses for not weeding.

Friday is your lucky gardening day, April and August your best months.

You never seem to "get in a rut," and have new gardening ideas each year.

You are energetic, active to the point of restlessness when it comes to seeding and hoeing.

You are kind, courteous, and seldom lack companionship in your garden.

You like to make money from your garden and are happiest when your gain is substantial.

You are idealistic and fond of all gardening projects.

You are at times restless, anxious, high-strung, and diffusive about your gardening.

You have the ability to make use of your green thumb.

You are fond of home and family as well as gardening.

Your fear of ridicule or criticism of your garden makes you cautious.

Fifth Meeting

During the week, club members volunteer to work with bed patients unable to attend meetings.

A GARDEN PROJECT IS GIVEN BED PATIENTS.

Variety Gardening.

1. Seeds of various kinds could be selected, purchased, or obtained from friends who have collected them on hikes.

2. Small labeled bottles are used as containers for seeds.

3. A box of the right size and shape for a windowsill is needed. If possible, there could be another box for cuttings or for plant resetting.

4. The bottom is filled with small pebbles and sand for drainage. It is covered with earth from a garden which has been fertilized or which has woods dirt.

5. Seed catalogues tell how much warmth, shade, and sunshine the plants will need.

6. Plants for quick growth are pumpkins and gourds, which sprout quickly.

HERBS are grown as a hobby. Ten kinds of herbs can be grown together in a separated box. Flavoring herbs are used in food flavoring. Sweet herbs are put in bags for bureau drawers, clothes bags, and glove boxes. When the leaves are broken off, they are replaced by new ones growing.

Common flavoring herbs are sage, basil, sorrel, savory, thyme, parsley, mint.

Common aromatic herbs are rosemary, lavender, sweet marjoram, thyme.

Sixth Meeting

GARDEN KERCHIEF is a relay.

1. Residents stand in single file with the same number of persons in each line.

2. The first resident is given a large cotton handkerchief.

3. When the whistle is blown, he turns and ties it around the neck of the player behind him.

4. When the bow is tied, the second resident unties it, turns and ties it on the third.

5. The line that first passes it down to the last player this way, wins.

A coat may be put on, buttoned, unbuttoned, and passed on in the same way.

FLOWERS ARE ARRANGED AND BOUQUETS AND CORSAGES MADE. A volunteer instructor can use magazines for pictured arrangements. A local florist or accomplished flower arranger, a county fair flower judge, a blue ribbon winner, or better yet, a proficient resident whose skill is generally accepted, can do the teaching.

If no other flowers are available, the donated funeral bouquets which usually come in abundance can be taken apart and rearranged. Special supplies like florist tape, wire, putty, miniature cattails, and so on, could be donated by the local florist.

Seventh Meeting

BULB PLANTING. Plan a bulb planting day in the fall; if getting outside is impossible, plant the bulbs in pots indoors.

1. Plant tulips or daffodils in individual 5″ pots, three or four bulbs per pot. Soil mixture should be as follows:

2 tbs. bone meal
1 tbs. charcoal
1 part leaf mold or peat moss
1 part sand
2 parts good garden soil

Cover the bulbs with the soil and keep the pots in a dark place with 2″ of soil above the pot. Don't let the soil dry out. In about six weeks, if leaves are showing, place the pots in a sunny spot in the Home and permit the blossoms to develop.

Keep the soil well watered.

2. Narcissus bulbs will bloom indoors in shallow bowls with water, gravel, and charcoal. Keep the bowls in a dark place for two or three weeks, checking daily. When the leaves start to come up, place the bowls next to the window.

3. Hyacinths can also be grown in a specially designed vase, narrow at the top to hold the bulb and wide at the bottom for water, roots, and a lump of charcoal. The narrow waist of the vase holds the bulb. The water should come to the bulb base.

Residents are asked next time to bring pineapple tops, onions, carrots, avocado seeds, or sweet potatoes for planting. Volunteers and employees can be useful in saving these for club use.

Eighth Meeting

PLANTS ARE GROWN IN WATER. The meeting could be devoted to green plants that grow readily in water: coleus, a foliage plant; sansevieria of the lily family, philodendron, and ivy. A lump of charcoal is put in each vase or bowl to keep the water sweet. The water will remain clear if the base does not admit light.

Pineapple tops and the others should have root ends exposed to water with the rest in the air. Charcoal again is used.

For the next meeting, residents save the roses brought into the Home and spread the petals on a table in a cool place.

Ninth Meeting

A ROSE JAR MAKES A CHRISTMAS GIFT.

1. A layer of rose petals is put into a one gallon lidded stone or china jar, about ½″ in depth, then a very thin layer of salt placed over it.

2. Rose petals and salt are alternated until the jar is half full.

3. The jar is stored in a dark place for ten days, the mixture stirred in it each morning.

4. After ten days, the rose petal mixture is transferred from the jar to another container.

5. An ounce each of cloves, allspice, and stick of cinnamon is ground and mixed together.

6. Some of the spices are scattered in the bottom of the jar from which the petals were removed and then put in a layer of the rose petal mixture.

7. Layers are alternated until the spices and petal mixture are used up. The jar is set in a dark place for three weeks. This is the stock or base for the rose potpourri.

8. In three weeks, the stock is properly aged and ready for the final steps. The following ingredients are assembled and mixed together:

¼ ounce each of mace, allspice, and clove, all coarsely ground

½ ounce nutmeg, grated

½ ounce cinnamon

1 ounce powdered orrisroot
4 ounces dried lavender flowers.

9. The jar or jars are filled with alternate layers of stock, and this last mixture packed firmly. If a rose geranium plant is available, add a few of its leaves. If not, a small vial of rose oil from the drugstore is purchased and a few drops put on each layer.

10. Finally, an ounce of cologne is added to the entire mixture, or in proportions appropriate to the size of the jars used.

A gallon crock half filled with salted petals will produce enough mixture to fill two one-quart jars, allowing a space of about one inch at the top of each jar. This space is essential, no matter what size the jar.

To perfume the room, the lid is removed for half an hour or so at regular intervals.

SUNFLOWERS ARE GROWN. A journalist resident writes the following in the Home newsletter:

> One of our residents planted some sunflower seeds back of the Annex last spring. In the fall I went over and cut the heads off and brought them back, a big box full and some of the heads a good foot in diameter. We have quite a bit of seed for the birds this winter.
>
> We understood that (the lady who planted the seed) topped hers and had them under cover outside and thinks the sparrows got them. Others, including this writer, are willing to wager that it was gophers or field mice. Well, ———, since it was your seed to start with, you can help yourself to some of ours.

Tenth Meeting

ROSE SACHETS can be another gift project. Sachets are made of little bags filled with rose petals, which have been allowed to dry thoroughly. They are very acceptable gifts when tied with pretty bows.

BULLETIN BOARDS are kept decorated in season by volunteer members. A bulletin board holds two large wallpaper vases filled with flowers, each flower with the name of a resident with a birthday that month. For residents who like the art-craft type of thing, another flower project involves decorating flower pots, cut flower containers, and discarded detergent bottles by wrapping yarn around them and decorating them with felt flowers.

TRIPS. The club could meet following a trip to the nursing home garden or the garden of a volunteer. Residents can become interested in a flower and weed show of their own, quart jars serving as display containers. Residents can decide to work on this project during the week and display it at the next meeting.

Poems about flowers are brought next time to read aloud.

A hat decorated with a flower, once worn by a woman member, is described next meeting.

Eleventh Meeting

Poems are recited or read aloud, flowered hats described, flower and weed bouquets exhibited.

Residents volunteer to take on committee assignments to FEED THE BIRDS AND SQUIRRELS.

A resident submits news to the Home paper:

> When I used to feed a hundred blackbirds after supper each day, we noticed that the birds are very smart. If the bread we gave them is too dry, the birds take the piece over to a tree where there is water and dip it once or twice and then fly away with it. Some of the same birds come back every year, one of them with a broken leg.
> We have a patient here, a great guy, who feeds the squirrels. He has them so tame, they come right up to him. He calls and holds out peanuts in the shell and the squirrel stands up and very carefully, so as not to bite him and takes the peanut.
> Now if a friend is with him the squirrel will ignore him. They really know him and fasten their bright eyes on him as he calls them and the fun begins. He also puts out water for them, which they appreciate. By the way, ———— has folks who keep him supplied with peanuts.

BIRTHDAY FLOWERS. Committee are appointed responsible for flowers for celebrants of birthdays (or at the monthly birthday party).

Twelfth Meeting

A HANGING CARROT GARDEN. Growing carrots to hang in the window is a novelty.
Material. Five carrots; a knife; a needle and some black thread.
Procedure.

1. A carrot is sliced 2″ from the stem end.

2. In the center of the cross section is a small ring marking the core. With the point of a knife, the core is dug out to make a hollow center as wide as the ring.

3. At least ¼″ of carrot flesh is left between the bottom of the hole and the stem end of the carrot.

4. Turned upside down, the carrot now looks like a little basket.

5. A darning needle threaded with black thread is pushed through the carrot about ¼″ from the top.

6. The thread is pulled through the carrot and hung on a tack at the top of the window.

7. Similar baskets of the four remaining carrots are made and hung by black threads.

8. The holes of the carrots are filled with fresh water and kept filled each day. If, in addition, the carrots get plenty of sunshine and warmth, they will soon begin to sprout.

9. Because nature sees to it that leaves grow up toward the sun, the feathery growths on the carrots will soon curve upward as they grow, finally covering the whole carrot. The resident will then have five green balls hanging in his window.

Or, a carrot top will grow in water.

The top and three quarters of the lower part of a carrot is cut off and placed in a dish surrounded by pebbles to hold it in place; covered with water, fern-like branches will soon grow from the top.

By the same process, horseradish and sweet potatoes can be grown, but a sweet potato should be put in a jar of water and horseradish, in wet earth.

People impatient to see something green in a very short time can wet a sponge and set it in a dish with a small amount of water. The sponge, covered with flax seed, will be green in three days. By the same process, radishes will show green in five days.

A living shamrock can be made by unrolling a large sheet of absorbent cotton and cutting out a giant shamrock, the width of the sheet. The cotton is kept wet and lettuce seeds sprinkled on it. Growing, it comes up green, a large living shamrock. Remember, it must be kept wet. If it's started the first of March, it should be ready for St. Patrick's Day.

A large pine cone put in the warm oven opens wide. Stood on end and filled with black dirt, it is sprinkled with grass seed and soaked with water. Standing in a glass for support so it's upright, the grass will grow a foot high if the dirt is moist. Gardeners in one Home trimmed it at Christmas time to look like a Christmas tree, shaping the grass to a point.

Thirteenth Meeting

HELPFUL GARDEN CLUB MEMBERS can do the following:
1. Prepare garden vegetables for the kitchen.
2. Make seasonal flower posters for the bulletin board.
3. Take wheelchair residents outside to see the garden.
4. Make markers for the garden.
5. Dig dandelions.
6. Water flower beds, window boxes.

Will members volunteer to serve in assignments requested by the Home and suggest other ways of being useful and needed?

DISCUSSING FAVORITES, what would each say?
1. If he were reincarnated, what flower would he like to be?
2. What's the biggest job in gardening he ever had to tackle?
3. If he had $100 to invest in gardening, how would he spend it?
4. What's his favorite plant (tree, shrub, flower)?
5. He makes a prediction on the local rainfall this month. (The lowest temperature, the high for tomorrow, and so on.)

Fourteenth Meeting

SING-A-LONGS can be impromptu; the leader calls out a line at a time.
(Tune: *Clementine*)

> I'm a palm tree, I'm a palm tree,
> I'm a palm tree through and through,
> I would rather be a palm tree
> Than a coconut like you.

I'm a tomato	I'm sweet marjoram	I'm a sweet corn
Pepperpot	Horehound	Rhubarb
I'm a daisy	I'm sweet William	I'm viola
Wallflower	Pansy	Scabiosa

How many wild flowers can residents name: ten? fifty?

"ON A WILD FLOWER GARDEN," a resident entitles her essay.

I never cared much for domestic flowers but I once had 125 varieties of wild flowers in my yard. Some of these, I was told by an authority, could not be grown in a yard. I had seven kinds of wild violets, seven kinds of ferns and three kinds of gentians, as well as many more. In my two fish pools, I grew some fine California lilies as well as pond lilies, also wild iris. I never grew spatterdock which I would rather call a pond tulip.

I think the most important flower I had in my collection was not a flower at all but a toadstool, commonly called the ghost flower. It grew on a stalk about 6" to 8" high and produced a flower-shaped crest which looked like an albino pasque flower. I found it in a dark cavern on the bluffs where it was feeding on rotting wood. I found a dark place for it at home and it grew all summer, but it did not come back in the spring. I talked to many people who never saw a ghost flower or never heard of one, but I had one growing in my yard.

Once I grew a pasque flower which is a hybrid with a fringed flower like an aster. The state gave me permission to grow lotus, but my flowers got the worst of it when I was assigned to a mail run so far from home I could not care for them.

There are three kinds of blooming wild cacti in this state. I had one that produced yellow blossoms. I was told by the natives it wouldn't bloom but would only grow new leaves. I took one home and planted it in a pile of sand to be used in concrete and it thrived. The natives had watered theirs and the bud shoots had turned into foliage. By starving the plant for water, nature had provided seed from blossoms to insure the life of the plant.

Discussion follows.

FLASH CARDS. From discarded seed catalogues, large pictures of vegetables and flowers are mounted separately on cardboard, to be used as flash cards. The group names the pictures as they are held up.

Fifteenth Meeting

A GARDEN IN A BOTTLE is an easy indoor project. For a garden novelty in a jar or bottle, enough pebbles and sand are put in the bottom of the jar to take care of drainage; rich earth covers it. A long stick and tweezers can be used to place seeds in different parts. The top of the bottle or jar is perforated to give air and regular moisture.

STUMP THE EXPERTS. Each resident contributes to the list to identify the following:

1. Seed tapes (consist of seeds properly and accurately spread for growth).

2. Gazebo (an outdoor structure for summer entertaining).

3. Heat cables (bottom heat cables to help germinate seeds).

4. Pelleted seeds (coated with material to make them easier to handle, space).

Sixteenth Meeting

GARDEN PLOT is a game for more than five or six players.
Equipment. Blackboard and chalk; paper, pencil (with eraser) for each resident.
Procedure.

1. For each letter in a proverb, the leader makes a cross on the blackboard. "All that glitters is not gold," would read XXX XXXX XXXXXXXX XX XXX XXXX.

2. Each resident draws in front of him a little outline of a garden marked off in ten plots.

3. The first player names any letter of the alphabet.

4. If he has chosen "G," the leader writes this letter under the first letter under the third and last word. That resident is safe for this round.

5. The second resident announces a letter. If he happened to choose one which is not in the proverb, the leader tells him to erase one square of the garden.

6. If he is unsuccessful in selecting another letter when his turn comes around again, he must erase another square of the garden. Each time he misses, he loses a garden square.

7. The game continues and the outline diminishes until it is completely erased.

8. The resident who first guesses what the proverb is has the privilege of selecting the next proverb.

9. Each player draws a new garden for the next proverb.

SCENIC GARDENS. Small figures or animals are made of hairpins or wire and placed in a large glass globe with plants.

Or, builder's cement mixed in a glass is built in high and low spots: mountains, valleys, and streams. The high spots of cement are painted to blend with the scenery, mountains, bridges, little figures, huts, etc.

Seventeenth Meeting

ZODIAC FOR GARDENERS is read aloud around the circle as residents give their birthdays.

March 21-April 19: Money may come to hand unexpectedly, when you harvest your karats.

April 20-May 20: Your own judgment's more reliable than others' in petunia planting.

May 21-June 20: Influential person will be watching your work.

June 21-July 22: Good results if you try out modern growing methods.

July 23-August 22: Take advantage of a friend's successful insect spray.

August 23-September 22: Give more heed to judgment of your partner.

September 23-October 22: Find what is badly needed for your onions.

October 23-November 21: It's your time to shine at the county fair exhibits; display your talents.

November 22-December 21: People will pay well for your services in horticulture.

December 22-January 19: A tendency to impulsive haste should be curbed when it comes to expansion of your garden plot.

January 20-February 18: Dare to be different; do the unusual with hedges.

February 19-March 20: What you do today lands you on top.

BIRD FEEDING STATIONS.

1. Set up a board with holes in it large enough to accommodate a number of earthenware cups.

2. Put this outside the window and place tidbits of bird food in the cups, and soon the visitors will come.

3. If there is a garden window box in the windows already,

dip pine cones in melted suet in which seed has been mixed and hang outside of window.

Foods. Pork rind, cooked meats, cut up apple, birdseed, buckwheat, cocoanut meat, cracked corn, dog biscuit, and suet.

Eighteenth Meeting

IN MY OWN BACK YARD. They discuss what they did there, describing it, drawing a picture of it, talking about plants and care of each.

FENCES. They discuss corrugated, fiberglass, brick, redwood boards, panels of glass, concrete blocks, rail, board fence, hurricane fence, peeled picket or stockade fence, smoothed lumber. Others?

"FIT THE MEANING," the leader says and mimeographs or writes on a blackboard for residents to do orally.

Each sentence has a word which is obviously wrong. The game consists of rearranging the letters of a word to form another that will fit the meaning of the sentence.

One point is scored for each correct word written opposite the sentence, and ten extra points are awarded if all the words are correct.

1. The ores needs mulching (rose).
2. Each fowler is a gift of God (flower).
3. The gardener drake the compost (raked).
4. "Cares crows suggest a human figure, set up to frighten crows, terrifying without danger" (scare).
5. The typical gardener is attired in sun bent-on (bonnet).
6. The blue ribbon at the garden show beast the red (beats).
7. The tiller and also the worse were responsible for horticultural success (sower).
8. A framer conducts or manages a farm (farmer).
9. Field, meadow, forest, arbor, grande—all are part of the good earth (garden).
10. Wine of that tagvine is regarded superior (vintage).
11. Tiller of the oils, is our gardener (soil).
12. Lady Bird Johnson encouraged planting the roadside with brush (shrub).

13. The seed-plot or grass-plot is often found in a slags-house (glass).

14. A botanic filed is used for experiments (field).

15. Of all the seasons, twiner is the season for dormancy (winter).

Nineteenth Meeting

A GARDEN ONE CAN MOVE. Plants in pots, hanging baskets, or vines can be brought inside or put outside. What preferred combinations could be practical?

A MEMORY WALK they might like to build, they talk about instead, recalling bits of family history.

Footprints, pawprints, leafprints are easily pressed into concrete, along with designs showing important dates, names, outlines, maps, or symbols. They cut silhouettes from heavy roofing felt or make line designs of wire or rope and imbed them in the surface of wet cement, then remove as soon as concrete sets.

MAKING PICKLES can be a delight! In a Home craft shop, residents made pickles from the cucumbers they grew in the garden. They put them in a crock and ate them when they wanted one.
Easy Cucumber Pickles.

small cucumbers	1 cup salt
2 quarts vinegar	2 cups sugar
1 quart water	1 cup ground mustard

Soak cucumbers in cold water to freshen. Mix dry ingredients and cold vinegar gradually to dissolve mustard. Pour over as many cucumbers as it will cover. If a large crock is used, fresh cucumbers and pickling brine may be added from day to day until crock is full. Then cover with plate and weight down. Ready for use in several weeks.

Twentieth Meeting

WHIZ QUIZ can add variety in starting a meeting. Residents given paper and pencils are asked to write all the words they can think of: flowers, foods, vegetables, insects, and so on (one classification) with the letters "S" and "T." One point is scored for every two words listed.

GARDEN CLEANUP is a relay. If residents are physically unable, volunteers could compete instead.

1. Residents stand in relay formation along the starting line.

2. Each team has in front of it a crooked stick about 12″ long.

3. When the whistle blows, the first player kicks the stick to the goal and back, leaving it in front of the next player who repeats it. The sticks are to be pushed along the ground, not kicked up in the air.

4. The line finishing first is winner.

ASTRONOMY. From 50 to 160 degrees of sky can be seen from an average hospital window. Charting what is visible and learning to identify heavenly bodies can become a nightly phase of recreation. A small telescope can be used, but most of all a reliable volunteer who can work individually with the few interested residents is needed.

FRUIT SALAD. Seeds from breakfast fruits (grapefruit, apples, oranges) are planted in a small pot or bowl of good dirt. Little plants will soon pop up which can be used as table decorations.

Twenty-first Meeting

FLOWER PETAL SCRAPBOOKS promise residents almost endless activity.

Materials. Glue, scrapbook, or the makings of a scrapbook—cardboard, strings, cloth or leather for the cover.

Procedure.

1. Petals are pressed until they are dry and flat, preferably between waxed paper, then under a book or other heavy object, like a telephone directory. They are pressed until dry.

2. They are tipped very lightly with glue and arranged in flowerlike designs on the pages of the scrapbook. A tiny daub at the end of the petal is usually enough to hold it in place.

3. The name of the flower is printed or written in next to it.

4. The designs are made as much as possible like the growing flower if one were to look straight down on it. Saran Wrap® and a spray over the page will protect it.

Flowers that make especially interesting groupings were poppies, iris, marigolds, pansies, roses, Jack-in-the-pulpits, violets, pinks, nasturtiums, tiger lilies, gladioli, tulips.

How many kinds of ROSES can the group list? Each member describes his favorite flower and tells what he knows about growing it.

"REPORT ON AN ARTICLE," the leader assigns his club members. Members volunteer to report on a short article or read a paragraph or two on something of interest found in *Flower and Garden, Home Garden,* or *Horticulture* such as "How to Start Conifers from Seeds," "Box Elder Bugs," "The New Flowers," "Tree Care," "Flowers That Bloom at Night," and so forth.

Twenty-second Meeting

VISIT A FLORIST SHOP OR GREENHOUSE. Residents did and wrote about it.

> With a blue sky and the sun shining brightly, interested residents toured the greenhouse back of the infirmary. Under genial guidance, our green thumbers had opportunity to view hundreds of potted plants and flowers, many in bloom and others soon to burst forth in an array of colors.
>
> Numerous questions were asked. In turn, the visitors were informed of the various procedures and year-round duties of the greenhouse employees.
>
> Most of these plants will be set out in the Home grounds around Memorial Day. Those making the tour were. . . .

Twenty-third Meeting

MAKING COAL FLOWER GARDENS is a winter diversion.
Materials. Three or four odd-sized pieces of clean, washed coal; a bowl; a cup of water; six tablespoons of table salt; four teaspoons of household bluing; water-soluble dyes.
Procedure.

1. Place the pieces of coal in a bowl. Pour one cup water over it.

2. Add six tablespoons of table salt, four teaspoons of bluing.

3. Set it in the sunlight or on a well-ventilated shelf.

During winter months when it is often difficult to have colorful flowers in the rooms, this artificial garden is effective. Oldsters can see before their eyes the chemical action transforming coal into a colorful bouquet in a few minutes' time.

Little buds of salt crystals appear and in a few days crystals will completely cover the coal.

Water must be added from day to day to keep the water level. Color, such as Easter egg dyes or standard clothing dyes, can be added; for strong color, use concentrated dyes. Add the dye to crystals with an eyedropper, a drop at a time. If more is used at one time at a given spot, the crystals will melt. Within a few hours, the hues of the dye will spread and mix into a colorful bouquet.

Twenty-fourth Meeting

MAKING IMPRINTS OF LEAVES is done with a stamp pad or inked glass.

Equipment. Pressed leaves; a pane of glass; rubber roller; paint or thick ink.

Procedure.

1. Paint or ink is smeared on the glass and the pressed leaf placed on the glass.

2. The leaf is rolled with the roller, until both sides are well inked.

3. The leaf is carefully placed between the clean sheets of paper and pressed lightly.

4. Papers are pulled apart and both top and bottom side of the leaf are clearly preserved.

For very small leaves, one can get dainty results by rolling them on an inked stamp pad. Or, instead of rubber roller, residents use small glass jars to roll and ink the leaves.

A KNOWLEDGE TEST.

1. They name all the things that could be found in a greenhouse.

2. They name holiday plants (gift plants): poinsettia, cyclamen, Christmas pepper, calotropis: gift plant studded with little oranges, African violets, crocus, azalea, chrysanthemums, Christmas begonia, primroses, bulbs: amaryllis, kalanchoe plants. Can they name others?

Other Activities

THEY EXAMINE something new. Residents displayed a live peanut plant to aid in conversation about this legume. The plant was viewed by other interest groups in the Home as well.

CHAT SESSION can bring out the following:

1. What each would have in his dream garden.

2. What a typical old-fashioned garden would have: hollyhock, bleeding heart, coreopsis, love-lies-bleeding, red salvia, coleus, white phlox, roses, coralbells, sweet alyssum, begonia, dwarf iris, bachelor's buttons. What else?

3. Exchange experiences in cold country gardening.

4. What would be raised in a garden in a hot climate; temperate climate?

5. How to raise grapes or some other berry fruit.

6. A favorite tree when it was first seen—why one feels it's something special; its annual changes.

7. A favorite vegetable. What is easiest to raise; hardest?

8. Old-fashioned garden equipment. How did it differ from today's?

9. Plants that can be started from leaves; from tubers; from seeds.

10. A wine-tasting party; what wines would the group request?

11. All the shrubs that have berries.

12. A tropical garden, such as found in California or Florida —palms, cycads, ferns, orchids, bougainvillea, bird of paradise, firecracker plant, shaving brush tree, silk cotton tree, Malay jewel vine, buchnera, bromeliads, umbrella palm.

A CONTEST.

1. Residents make up quizzes to stump the club members.

2. They name all the flowers they can think of that are red (or some other color).

3. A Home garden contest is held for the largest vegetable, fruit, or flower grown.

GUESS THE FLOWERS.

1. Name a preacher flower (Jack-in-the-pulpit).

2. What flower belongs in the sewing basket (bachelor's button).

3. What flower leaves its first syllable in the kitchen (pansy).

4. What flower, by dropping its first letter, becomes a suitor (clover).

5. What flower is combined with bread and milk to complete the lunch (buttercup).

6. What flower combines a dude and a beast (dandelion).

7. What flower suggests traveling over a great distance (carnation).

8. What flower reminds one of winter (snowball).

9. What flower joins an untruth with a girl's hair (lilac).

10. What flower shows grief (bleeding heart).

GUESSING GAME from a seed catalogue. Each resident describes a flower or tree for the others to guess. He gets five points for each clue he gives in which there's no response or an incorrect response.

The following clues describe creeping phlox:

1. It has dwarf masses, bright colors.

2. It's an early spring flower with perfectly rounded balls.

3. It's 4″ high.

4. It stays green year-round.

5. There are masses of color in early spring when few other things are in bloom.

6. It's wonderful for ground covers and borders.

7. It grows in part shade or full sun.

8. Its colors are red, blue, pure white, and pink.

The following clues describe a red maple:

1. One of the fall's brilliant trees.

2. In the spring, it's loaded with small red flowers.

3. In the summer, its green leaves gives loads of wonderful shade.

4. It's very majestic, a lawn or street tree, fairly fast growing.

The following clues describe a periwinkle:

1. For shady areas between shrubs; it grows in other dim places.

2. It grows even where grass won't grow.

3. One can have a twelve-month, thick, abundant carpet.

4. There will be lavender blue flowers in May, a beautiful flower that makes the dullest part of the yard look like a showcase.

5. It grows vigorously; it will grow in poor, stony soil on steep banks, in rock gardens, anywhere.

6. It does better in the shade than grass, but likes sun, too.

7. It spreads and spreads—one plant will grow to fill two square feet.

8. It gets 4'6" tall.

The following clues describe peonies:

1. There are giant flowers, sometimes double blossoms.

2. It's planted by root divisions.

3. It has rich color assortments in satin rose, red, crimson, snow-white, salmon, pearl-pink.

4. Roots sell for about $2 each.

The following clues describe cushion mums:

1. Hundreds of blooms on a single plant the very first year they're planted.

2. It continues as a perennial.

3. It has so many flowers one can't see the leaves.

4. It's a rounded plant that seldom grows more than 12" high and 2' wide.

5. Each flower is perfectly formed and shaped; blooms from late August until frost.

6. It's very hardy.

7. It has red, shell-pink, sunshine yellow, snow-white colors.

8. It grows even in poor soil and with little care.

The following clues describe the blue spruce:

1. This is a strong northern-grown tree that starts at 10-18".

2. It has seedlings for transplanting.

3. It's excellent for use as cover groups.

4. It's also used as individual specimens.

5. It can be shaped as you like.

The following clues describe the creeping red sedum:

1. This is a ground cover for masses of summer flowers, rock gardens, border edging, under shady trees and steep banks.

2. It's hardy, grown in northern nurseries.

3. They're planted a foot apart.

4. They will fill troublesome areas with a neat 3-4″ cover that spreads fast but doesn't need pruning.

5. It has bright red, starlike flowers from June through September.

6. It has attractive, thick, semi-evergreen foliage the rest of the year, even in subzero weather.

Men's Crafts Relative to Gardening

A STRAWBERRY BARREL may be an old skill for some men in the club.

Equipment. A large wooden barrel with a hole at the bottom for drainage; a saw; soil; strawberry plants; broken clay pots.

Procedure

1. Four-inch circles are cut at various places in the barrel; a large-size barrel could have thirty circle openings.

2. Broken clay pots are put in the bottom for drainage.

3. Soil is put into the barrel at levels, a strawberry plant placed at each open circle, and finally filled to the top with soil.

Experience has shown that the plants blossom but often do not produce with any great success. The barrel could have a number of plants. It covers only a small area of a garden and is high enough for an oldster to water and weed without having to bend.

BOTANICAL BOOKENDS are a useful novelty.

Material. Discarded half-pint floor wax containers; sand; enamel and brush; can opener; decal transfer.

Procedure.

1. The top of the can is removed with a can opener that leaves a smooth, noncutting edge.

2. The side surfaces of the container are given a smooth coat of quick-drying enamel.

3. A colorful decal transfer is applied; or, if the resident is artistic, he may paint on his own design. The cans are decorated in pairs.

4. They are solidly packed with sand.

5. Cacti or other house plants are planted in each.

The bookends can be sold, given to friends, or used in the Home.

In the carpentry shop, men may make garden markers, as well as bird feeders, planters, and birdhouses.

FIN AND FEATHER CLUB

Introduction

This is another attempt at getting men together in a group, since fishing and hunting are often two of their most favored sports. Fin and Feather interests in several county homes have merged into clubs. Members of the group can suggest topics for study, discussion and activity such as

1. Hazardous experiences out-of-doors (bad weather conditions, misunderstanding in following directions, being confused or lost).

2. Building a fire (read aloud Jack London's short story, "To Build a Fire," one of the great short stories of all time).

3. Rescuing something or someone.

4. A most memorable outdoor trip or other experience worth retelling (as to beauty, terrain, breaking the law, companionship of other hunting and fishing characters).

Variety in amount and content of program between meetings can be the key to the club's success, perhaps reducing the number of meetings and replacing them by outside study.

Goals

Residents could set their own goals. The following could be discussed:

1. To relive and learn hunting and fishing techniques and adventures.

2. To make friends in the Home.

3. To use as carry-overs in conversation following club meetings.

4. To join other social groups in the Home and to become interested in other activities.

Resource material can be read at each meeting; it is available from the recreation section of any Sunday paper. Men visiting from the local Conservation Department can take residents on trips to marshes, fields and streams, parks and conservation farms.

Inquiries can be made to large industries in the state, public library, and ecology departments for films, displays, and pamphlets (see Appendix).

Motivation Techniques

Several approaches to obtaining motivation can be used.

1. Use the resident as a leader, if capable.
2. Show him the value of the activity.
3. Give him competition with others.
4. Encourage him to help others.
5. Watch for any leads about special interests, talents, and strengths which will contribute to the club.

Each meeting begins with a guessing contest. From local conservation material, the leader gets answers to questions on county hunting and fishing, such as the following: What's the deepest lake in the county? How many hunters were registered last year? Where was the biggest fish ever caught in this area? Name five lakes (parks, streams) in the county. What's the lightest-weight gun used legally? What's the largest animal ever trapped here? Some resident can be responsible for this part of each program.

Variety is an attention-getting device.

First Meeting

See "The First Meeting" in Part III, "How to Lead a Club."

INTRODUCTION GAME. Around the circle, each resident takes a turn at giving his name. "My name is ———— and I like (some food beginning with the first letter of his first name." (My name is Bob and I like beets.)

Afterward, they try taking turns around the circle, giving one another's name without help.

"WHAT IS IT?" The player thinks of an object, then gives clues such as I have four legs, one body, two arms; you can sit on me (a camp chair).

"WHAT'S IN THE BAG?" In a bag, an object is placed which everyone has seen or used before; it's passed around the table with everyone guessing what it is.

FISH AND BIRD QUIZ.

Equipment. Assuming there are ten players, the leader writes a different word on thirty slips of paper: hatchery, water, fisherman, fishery, fishpond, feather, or the names of birds and fish.

Procedure. A player draws a slip and gives one word as a clue, until ten clues have been given for others to guess.

The person who guesses it draws another slip and continues.

Even people in wheelchairs can prepare a meal. Appointed committees check on equipment and on the food for the cookout at next meeting.

Second Meeting

COOKOUT. The old days of beans, bacon, and flour are gone and sourdough recipes are a thing of the past. Now campers enjoy beef stroganoff on a mountain and chicken a la king in a canyon. Dried food packages to which only a kettle of hot water is added may interest residents, assuming proper cooking areas are available.

Or, a hobo dinner: enclose in individual packets of foil, chopped beef, onion soup mix, diced raw potatoes and carrots and seasoning. Grill the packet over the open fire until vegetables are tender.

Third Meeting

CAMPERS' RELAY is for people in a seated position.

Equipment. Two baskets, each containing a number of identical items which a camper would use and which can be passed down the relay lines, such as a can opener, matches, bottle opener, compass, stick, glove.

Procedure.

1. Club members sit facing one another, preferably at a long table, and preferably fifteen or more players.

2. A player starts by passing an item from the basket down the

line, one at a time; no player may hold two items at the same time.

3. The last player in line drops them into a paper bag.

4. When he has received all the items, he passes them back one at a time.

5. The side completing the returned items first, wins.

EXCERPTS FOR DISCUSSION can be obtained from conservationists' columns. Information such as the following can be continued by questions:

Nature Notes.[7]

> The drake wood duck is generally considered the handsomest of all waterfowl. Sought by gourmets and by manufacturers of colorful flies for anglers, it became so scarce that seasons were closed in both the United States and Canada from 1918 to 1941. Fortunately, they are reestablished in safe numbers.
>
> The ruffled grouse may be the wildest of game birds. His explosive takeoff has unnerved experienced hunters. He likes second-growth timber country and plenty of underbrush, briers and berries. On a wintry night he may bury himself in a snowbank.
>
> The pine siskin is a happy-go-lucky gypsy. He may migrate, but to no certain place. He has a taste quirk that is not understood. He picks up salt deposited by highway crews.
>
> The painted quail of southeastern Asia and Australia is about the size of a sparrow.

Have they seen or hunted these birds? What other characteristics do they have? Can they describe unusual habits of their favorite game bird?

THE LOCAL BIRDHOUSE CONTEST WINNERS are invited to bring their winning birdhouses to display and discuss.

Residents volunteer to debate next time on camping, roughing it or doing it the easy way.

Fourth Meeting

DEBATE: When he dug his own toilet, carried and purified the water from a stream or lake, ate off a flat rock, cooked pancakes outside and ate in the rain, *or* when he nestles his tent down be-

---

[7] Reprinted, courtesy of the *Chicago Tribune*.

tween many others next to a laundromat, shower, hot water, as people do now. What are the pros and cons of these camping conditions?

Patients are benefitted by some type of exercise, but permission from the PT or doctor should be obtained for them to participate in the following exercise:

FISHERMEN AND HUNTERS.

Equipment. A ball; a large number pinned on each player: half the players with red numbers, half in blue, no duplicates (one color for Fishermen, the other for Hunters).

Procedure.

1. The player with the ball stands in the center of the circle of players.

2. He calls two numbers in the circle and the two step toward the center.

3. Center man tosses the ball to the first player who steps forward.

4. If he misses, the man with ball tosses it to the second man and repeats.

5. First man to catch the ball, keeps it, and in turn calls two numbers in the circle. Residents may develop some way of keeping team or individual score to make the game competitive.

Assignment: Next time, everyone comes wearing a fishing hat or a fishing fly in his lapel. Each brings an anecdote about a fishhook.

Residents are asked to prepare a list of one-, two-, and three-day trips.

Information is available from state newspapers which feature conservation; they should enclose a stamped self-addressed business-sized envelop.

Fifth Meeting

FAVORITE FISHING SPOT. Where would he go in the state? Out of the state?

STORIES around the circle.

1. Favorite fishing spot.
2. Hunting lodge.

3. Sport store.
4. Gun.
5. Bait.

A DIRECTORY of the nearest boat launchings is made, as well as a list of one-, two-, and three-day trips.

ANECDOTES are told about accidents with fishhooks. A Home newsletter has one:

> I've heard a lot of fish stories in my day, but none to match this one. It seems a certain lady and her husband had been fishing and were driving home. One of them had carelessly left a plug lying loose on the dashboard.
>
> The plug, if you know your fishing gear, was a "lucky 13," good, they say, for catching fish, and as it turned out, other things.
>
> Just about the time the couple reached home, the plug bounced off the dash and the lady felt a sudden sharp pain.
>
> A gang hook at one end of the "lucky 13" had imbedded itself into the inside of her leg, just above the knee.
>
> Now, no lady likes to sit on the front seat of a car and try to remove a fishhook from her leg, for goodness sake! So, after a couple of short unsuccessful tries, our heroine decided to go into the house to do the job.
>
> This was a mistake. Because just as she was cautiously easing herself out of the car, she felt another sudden sharp pain. This time the hook at the other end of the plug had imbedded itself into the inside of her other leg, also just above the knee.
>
> By now the lady was not only in pain, she was embarrassed and utterly frustrated. Clearly she couldn't just stand there with her knees together.
>
> Equally clear, she couldn't move, not without making things worse than they were already.
>
> Came her gallant husband to the rescue, picked her up, carried her into the house and laid her gently on the couch. Together they worked to remove the hooks. They couldn't manage it.
>
> At the hospital, the hooks were eventually and expertly removed and now the wounds have healed, all except our lady's dignity. After all, how would you like being carried into the emergency room of a hospital with everybody looking at the strange way your legs are hooked together by a "lucky 13"?

Committees are appointed to work on Jackrabbit Shot and Wild Animal Pistol Range props for next time.

Sixth Meeting

JACKRABBIT SHOT can be tried with teen-agers.

Equipment. Four jackrabbits cut out of stiff cardboard on individual stands, each about 14″ high, painted a different color and placed on a high shelf (a board balanced on two chairs) where they can be knocked off easily; gum; four tennis balls or beanbags; popguns with cork bullets. The rack may be decorated with green-brown paper.

Procedure.

1. It takes two teen-agers to run this concession, one to set up the rabbits and one to be a barker giving out the balls and keeping scores.

2. Residents stand at a 10′ distance and are given four turns to knock down all four rabbits. Scores could be awarded by a stick of gum for each rabbit toppled.

WILD ANIMAL PISTOL RANGE.

Equipment. Pictures of wild animals pasted on a board. On each picture is a red spot, a "bull's-eye" to hit; popgun; mints, or something else to pass for everyone.

Procedure. Players can decide to line up in teams and compete in hitting the bull's-eye. Great caution must be taken to supervise this game if darts are thrown. Popguns or suction darts can be used instead.

TALK-AROUND. Each member is asked individually to name the coldest year he remembers; the hottest summer. What work is especially difficult in cold weather? In hot weather? What effects does heat have on people, characterizing them in different parts of the country? What part of the country would he think was ideal as far as weather goes? What is meant by altitude? Air pressure? What is meant by squalls, weather-wise? In what ways is one dependent on weather (e.g. picnics, crops)? What rhyming weather prophesies does he know? ("If it rains before 7, it will stop before 11." "Rainbow at night, sailor's delight; rainbow at dawning, sailors take warning.")

Each next time brings something to tell about hibernating animals.

Seventh Meeting

After the discussion on hibernating animals, the following is read aloud:
Nature Notes.[8]

> The deer's summer coat is thin and sleek, and closely appears to be skin. Winter hairs are stout, crinkled and hollow, containing air cells, so that the body heat of a sleeping deer barely melts the snow.
>
> Being a browser, the deer's winter survival problem is food.
>
> Contrary to popular belief, the bear is not a true hibernator. Its temperature drops only 6 degrees from a normal of 99 degrees, and its respiration and heartbeat are about the same as during summer activity. You might call the bear's sleep a deep stupor.
>
> By contrast, a true hibernator, such as the ground squirrel, may have a temperature drop to 39 degrees or so, which approximates the temperature of its underground abode. In its deathlike sleep, it breathes about three times per minute, and its heartbeat cannot be detected even by a stethoscope.

HUNTER WITH A SENSE OF DIRECTION is an activity limited to ambulants (two teams). The first player is asked to walk to the goal with this right hand on his head; second, with his left hand on his head; third, with both hands on his head; fourth, with arms folded; fifth, with right hand on the left shoulder; sixth, with some idea he suggests.

Winning line finishes first, to the goal and back.

A GUIDE TO STATE ATTRACTIONS is compiled, a city by city listing; this could be produced in pamphlet form if there are typists and facilities for reproducing it.

Residents next time are asked to bring a small matchbox and a discarded greeting card.

Eighth Meeting

Members with good eyes and good hands like the detail of the following craft:

---

[8] Reprinted, courtesy of the *Chicago Tribune*.

DECORATED MATCHBOXES for open-house souvenirs or gifts to new members or friends.

Materials. Safety "penny" matchboxes; glue; rectangular pictures cut from greeting cards (or fish or birds); scissors; heavy, clear plastic.

Procedure.

1. A piece of plastic is cut to matchbox size; this is a pattern to draw around pictures before cutting them.

2. Picture is glued on matchbox after cutting.

3. The resident's name can be typed and pasted on the bottom of the box if he likes this idea.

OR, VISIT THE MUSEUM to see the wild game, fish and fowl, and other exhibits.

Arrangements are made for an exhibition by a local citizen for the next meeting.

Ninth Meeting

DOG OBEDIENCE TRAINING EXHIBITIONS sometimes bring trainers and their dogs to the Home for a demonstration. Or,

FREE CASTING INSTRUCTION BY EXPERTS involves inviting a volunteer to bring his equipment to teach casting. Or,

Residents with POPGUNS OR SLINGSHOTS compete in hitting a target.

Does someone have a recipe for turtle stew? An experience to tell about catching turtles?

A resident writes the following:

> Fishing wasn't so good for ——— but he came out OK after he cleaned up a large turtle that dressed out eight pounds of meat. Let's get another one and put on a "Smoker" for the men and serve turtle stew. Isn't it wonderful to know that the largest species of turtle in the world is the Marine Leatherneck? Its length is 9′ and its weight is often fifteen hundred pounds. Boy, wouldn't that fellow make a lot of stew?

For next time, they bring something to tell or read regarding survival and sustaining foods.

Tenth Meeting

This activity could take several meetings to develop, but a start could be made now with THE HUNTER'S GUIDE.

Major opening and closing dates for all types of Wisconsin hunting are listed below. Can a similar chart be drawn up by residents for another state?

October 3. Noon opening of statewide duck season. Good hunting opens everywhere except the Horicon zone. Ruffed grouse and squirrel hunting start statewide. Sharptail grouse become legal in northern zone.

October 4. End of early bear season in northern Wisconsin.

October 17. Start of Canada goose hunting in Horicon zone. Start of gun deer season on all Apostle Islands, except Madeline.

October 24. Noon opening on pheasants statewide and Hungarian partridge in southeastern zone. Rabbit shooting begins statewide.

October 25. End of sharptail grouse hunting in northern zone.

November 17. End of early bow and arrow deer and bear season. End of woodcock hunting.

November 21. Start of general gun deer season.

November 26. End of duck shooting.

November 29. End of gun deer season.

December 5. Start of late bow and arrow season.

December 6. End of pheasant hunting statewide. End of Hungarian partridge shooting in southeastern zone.

December 31. End of late bow and arrow deer season. End of ruffed grouse hunting south of Highway 64.

January 31. End of squirrel and rabbit season statewide.

Residents tell of emergency goods for SURVIVAL; someone reads aloud "Winter," found in a county home newsletter:

> February is the "hunger month." During winters such as we are having this season, Indians suffered because at this time of the year their winter supply of dried and smoked meat usually was exhausted. Fresh meat such as venison and fish was hard to get, so the Indians had to depend on emergency foods to survive.
>
> They gathered rock-tips of lichens, moss and even used buckskins to

make soup. The inner bark, twigs and buds of spruce, basswood, tamarack, birch and slippery elm were brewed for tea. Actually, these were famine foods. Many Indians perished during lean winters with much snow.

During such winters animals and birds also perished from lack of a steady diet. With the long duration of snow cover and subzero temperatures, game birds and animals must travel in the open and expose themselves to all predators, including man.

Deep snow is a gauge to survival for all wildlife. Deer congregate in deep swamps where the available browse is soon gleaned off trees. And even though ample browse may be just over the rim of the "deer yard," it may as well be a hundred miles away. Snow is a barricade of fear to most animals.

A winter such as we have this season culls the population of many species especially in areas where insufficient food and cover exist. As more marshes are drained and wooded areas removed from the landscape, the environment provides less protection needed for survival.

Each resident brings a riddle next time to stump the group.

Arrangements are made for suitable films and/or scouts and their leader.

Eleventh Meeting

RIDDLES are told.

FILMS FROM THE LOCAL LIBRARY are shown. Or,

SCOUTS and their leader lecture on camping or give a demonstration of some of their skills.

Twelfth Meeting

TALK-IT-OUT, something memorable on hunting and fishing seen on TV, in the paper, or heard on the radio, Or,

What's a satisfactory substitute for soap when camping and cleaning pots and pans? Or,

A buck deer leaves a different track from a doe. The buck drags its hooves, but a doe leaves a sharp, clean track. Can members describe other tracks in hunting? Or,

What is meant by marine courtesy? How many accepted rules of using waterways can be listed?

GUESS THE ANIMAL. A slip of paper with the name of an animal is drawn by each resident. Each in turn tells three or four facts about the animals for the others to guess.

Subjects for discussion at the next meeting are assigned.

Thirteenth Meeting

TOPICS TO EXAMINE.
1. Experiences in erecting an A-frame structure.
2. A log cabin.
3. Building a fireplace, or pointers to make in building.
4. How to set up sleeping bags in camping.

USE OF A GUIDE. Sometimes a Sunday paper recreation section contains large-size maps of the counties. Special maps show state parks, places to fish, hunt, or camp, as well as information on planning trips.

What's the hardest wood they can name? What indications have they seen of mother love among wild animals? Have they ever wondered how a parent bird allocates food? Can they name the bird that sits lengthwise on the limb and calls its name a hundred times without pausing? Can they locate white, wild sheep?

Nature Notes.[9] Each paragraph is typed on a slip of paper, drawn, and read aloud.

1. The Dall sheep of Alaska and the Yukon are the only wild white sheep in the world, and Chicago's Brookfield herd is the only one in any United States zoo.
2. In the Old West, to call a man a "coyote" was a fighting epithet, but the resentful bloke should have been so smart: of all North American predatory animals, the coyote is the only one that has increased, prospered and extended its range with the coming of civilization. Some hundred years ago, the coyote was confined to the plains and desert country west of the Mississippi River. Today, he is at home from Mexico to the Arctic Circle.
3. Interstate Highway 75 in Florida was routed away from a nest of bald eagles. Since eagles return to their old nest year after year, road construction too close would have caused them to abandon their home. Three fourths of all eagles die before they reach breeding age. Immature bald eagles do not get their distinctive white head and tail until about four years old, thus many are mistaken for hawks and are shot.

---

[9] Reprinted, courtesy of the *Chicago Tribune.*

There are only about 125 known active nests throughout the state of Florida.

4. Walking upright, the mother beaver often emerges from a swimming lesson with her tired youngster cradled in her arms.

5. When a parent bird joggles the nest, the infants react by gaping. The parent checks the gullets for unswallowed food. A nervous mechanism prevents any youngster from monopolizing: when he gets full, his throat muscles refuse to work.

6. The whippoorwill can repeat its call a hundred times and more without pausing for breath. The bird which incessantly repeats its own name sits lengthwise on a limb.

7. The coolabah tree of Australia yields a wood that weighs about ninety pounds per cubic foot.

Discussing these and similar bits of information is sometimes stimulating and provocative.

Fourteenth Meeting

Residents with good vision and nimble hands can learn a new craft if they have an instructor, materials, and the place to work.

FLY TIEING needs an expert volunteer or one of the residents who has mastered this art to instruct.
Material. Vise; new hooks; feathers; yarn or floss; deer hair or other animal fur; thread (fine silk); scissors; glue.
Procedure.
1. Place the hook in the clamp of the vise.
2. Fasten the thread to the hook.
3. Wind a bit of feather for the fly's tail.
4. Wind the yarn on for the body, hair or fur for flotation.
5. Wind the feathers on to protrude upward.
6. The hackle (one of the long narrow feathers on the neck of the bird) is wound on.

Residents retrace MEMORIES ON HUNTING AND FISHING.
1. The most peaceful site.
2. Best fishing.
3. Most beautiful scenery.
4. Easiest place to fall asleep.
5. Longest, loneliest hikes.
6. Best sunburn (or worst).

7. Coldest swimming.

8. Best food. They bring a recipe for the next meeting.

Fifteenth Meeting

COOKING CLASS is often one of the more successful meetings. A popular camper's classic is happily named "S'Mores." For each serving, four squares of milk chocolate are placed on a graham cracker. A marshmallow is toasted over a fire, slipped onto the chocolate, and the sandwich topped with a second graham cracker.

They discuss other favorites and how they're made.

The following stories illustrate a topic on FRIGHTENING EXPERIENCES for discussion.

My husband and I went fishing one evening and as the fishing was good, we stayed out late and it turned dark. When we started for home, we found we were lost, and called and shouted until someone heard us and came to the rescue.

* * *

My husband and I and one other couple were camping on an island out in the Mississippi when the mother of the other lady came to spend a day with us. That evening, the friend and I took the mother home to Onalaska by rowboat. It got dark before we got back to our camp; consequently, we got lost. We rowed around in circles for some time until we realized we weren't going to make it to camp that night. We did find our way back to Onalaska, where we stayed overnight. Meantime, our husbands became alarmed when we didn't return and came to search for us.

They were afraid we had drowned, until they found our boat tied up in Onalaska. We all had a frightening experience.

* * *

I went out swimming with a group of friends. There were some good swimmers in the group; I could not swim, but was anxious to learn. One of the group told me I should lie on my back and paddle my feet. I was practicing this, but didn't succeed very well, and I went under water. I came up for the third time before I was rescued. That was the end of my learning to swim.

Sixteenth Meeting

BIRD OR FISH.

1. Players are seated in a circle. One player (or the leader) is "It" and enters the circle with an object, such as a book which can be passed.

2. "It" hands the object to any player in the circle and names a letter of the alphabet.

3. The player to whom the object is handed passes it to the left and names three fish or birds beginning with the letter named before the object gets back to him.

4. If he fails, he becomes "It."

FIN AND FEATHER TIC-TAC-TOE is played with chairs.

1. Two teams are selected, the Fins and the Feathers, each of the latter with a large sheet of paper pinned on him for identity.

2. Nine chairs are placed in three rows, like the tic-tac-toe arrangement.

3. A player from one team comes up and sits in a chair.

4. A member of the second team comes up and sits in another chair.

5. A team attempts to get three players in a row, like the tic-tac-toe game.

6. There is no coaching from teammates when a player makes his selection of a chair.

BACKPACKING provides a topic of interest. Hiking to a secluded campsite while carrying all needed equipment takes an experienced camper. Why would it be necessary to use the following skills: read a map, use a compass, know weather forecasting, build a primitive shelter, identify animal tracks, and recognize danger?

Seventeenth Meeting

FISHERMAN'S KNOT is a trick which can be unfamiliar.
Equipment. A piece of string 36″ long is required for each player.
Procedure. Players are paired off.

1. One player ties his string to both wrists like a handcuff, leaving as much slack as possible between wrists.

2. The second player ties one end of his string to one wrist.

3. The second end is passed inside the string of his partner and tied to his second wrist, so that the two strings cross.
Stunt. Which player can first release himself? They try putting the string over one another's head, even stepping through it, but

this won't work. If they become too annoyed, one is told to try putting his string under the string at the opponent's wrist.

EXPERIENCED HIKERS have carried packs weighing as much as fifty pounds, but a beginner should limit his load to twenty pounds.

What do members say is the single most important piece of equipment in their load? Perhaps a pair of quality boots.

What bare minimum items would they include? Perhaps a good quality sleeping bag, a first aid kit, a mess kit, extra matches in a waterproof container, a lightweight rain poncho, an ax or hatchet.

A knife should be kept in one's pocket or belt, readily available.

What kind of areas should be selected for hiking?

Eighteenth Meeting

FISHING TRIPS are lined up with doctor's permission and dependable volunteers. They could fish from a dock, which is safer than a slippery bank.

An activity aide wrote regarding their club that the Hook, Line, and Sinker Club for men and women who fish, was disbanded until spring. One man got seventy-six fish in a stocked pond that spring. Residents cleaned the fish and the club had the meal in the craft room.

In another Home, the city newspaper helps with transportation and furnishes the bait (worms) and hooks.

MEMBERS DESCRIBE A FAVORITE MARSH. What is life in the marsh like? What birds or wildlife are found there? What are the sounds there? Smells? Changes? Dangers?

A trip is recounted by a resident below.

> Many of our residents who participate regularly in discussion groups were treated to an outing one October afternoon and went on a forty-mile trip around Horicon Marsh. Starting at the southern boundary, they drove along the eastern side and then stopped briefly along Highway 49 near the northern edge to observe some of the 110,000 Canadian geese reported to be feeding there.
>
> Following this trip, Canadian geese and the history of the marsh provided the subject matter for two remotivation sessions. Residents

enjoy watching the geese feed on the cornfield just east of Clearview. There is quite a difference of opinion as to the number but some believe there are several thousand.

Nineteenth Meeting

COOKING CLASSES are possible if the "rec room" has a hot plate. *Cheese Torte,* prepared on the spot.

Crust: 1 package zwieback or 22 graham crackers (crushed)

¼ cup melted butter

¼ cup sugar

1 tsp. cinnamon

Mix together and press into skillet, reserving one cup for topping.

Filling: 1 cup sugar

2½ pounds dry cottage cheese, unground

4 eggs, beaten

1 tbs. flour

1 tbs. cornstarch

1 tsp. vanilla

1 large can evaporated milk

1 tsp. lemon juice

Grated lemon rind

Pinch of salt.

Blend all together, spoon on top of crust, and cover with remaining crust mixture. Bake one hour or more.

The recipe says "until a silver knife comes clean," but who has one of those on a camping trip? Use a heavy cast iron frying pan on the Home "camp range" and cook the torte over a very low flame.

THE USE OF LOCAL CLUBS. A resident "took in" a fox hunt sponsored by the Sportsmen's Club. Are there other suitable local clubs to be used by the Fin and Feather members?

Twentieth Meeting

CLIPPING FILE. Special items on hunting and fishing can be found in the Sunday paper, recreation section, or in *Field and Stream*—good subjects for discussion and for a scrapbook or file.

GUESS how many fishhooks in the jar.

LAWS. Can the group list the laws effective in the county for hunting? What are the local fees?

RELAY. Sides compete in passing a fish pole down the line and back.

CAMPING for the aged and infirm can seem completely out of line, but it goes on all the time in isolated cases. An activity aide reports below that camping for the handicapped has much to offer.

> ———— returned and in real good condition, too, from another annual junket with the "River Rats," a group of fellows from the area who've gone on a camping trip every year since 1934.
>
> Anyway, he paddled his share of the ten-mile stint down the Namekagon in a canoe, and slept in a sleeping bag (cheated though, used an air mattress under it) and ate nice bland food like steak and onions and fried potatoes for breakfast!
>
> But then ———— is only ninety; you have to expect stunts like that from young fellows!

TRIPS. A jaunt looking for wild flowers is set up; in the fall, a nutting party or an outing to see the leaves from a bus window.

WHAT WOULD ONE FIND? In a zoo, in a virgin wood, in a sport shop, in a hiker's pack? There are hundreds of items to be named.

Twenty-first Meeting

FIND THE NORTH is a stunt for people with canes. "Scouts" are posted at various distances and each lays the point of his cane on the ground (floor), pointing to what he considers the exact north (or south) without using instruments. A compass will prove the degree of accuracy. A prize could be given for the closest.

QUESTION AND ANSWER MAN could be self-appointed; he reads the following and calls on others for the answers:

1. What is the big date for the fishing season for trout, muskie, northern pike and walleyes? bass? What other important dates are there for anglers: trout-fishing season, salmon, on the Great Lakes, and so on?

2. What is the danger of pounding nails into trees?

3. What water containers are recommended in camping? Precautions in using drinking water?

4. What is the use of flat fish bait, landing nets, preserved worms, fly reel, spin reel, firebird reel, cast rod, screen house, pontoon boats?

5. Have they ever made a walking stick? Of what wood? How was it whittled, sanded, polished, stained, hand rubbed? Where did they travel with it? How does one look for such a stick? How select it? Have they place-name sticks or people-name sticks; how do they identify them?

6. They describe cleaning squirrels.

Twenty-second Meeting

BIRD AND ANIMAL SOUNDS. They imitate the sound or action of a bird or beast: frog (croak), crow (caw), brook (babble), bee, squirrel, robin, blue jay, snake, bat, coyote, hyena, elephant, donkey, others.

How many birds can they name that call their names (whippoorwill, bobwhite, killdeer, and so on).

Residents volunteer to EXAMINE FOR DISCUSSION the following subjects:

1. Lake property as an investment.
2. How to cook bratwurst outside.
3. What he would look for in a cabin site.
4. The best trout stream he knows.
5. The pros and cons of snowmobiling.
6. Skiing, sites and skills.
7. Merits of canoe, fishing boat, pram, and outboard motor.
8. A favorite outdoor dog.
9. Houseboats.
10. Rod and reel techniques.
11. Waterfowl hunting.
12. Squirrel and rabbit hunting.

Residents bring a joke to tell at the next meeting.

Twenty-third Meeting

JOKES have always been attention-getters for fun-lovers!

Dice games are usually successful. Here is one:

GROUSE (played like Hearts, with dice).

Equipment. Six dice for each table—each die has a letter from G-R-O-U-S-E on one of the six sides (someone in the carpentry class can make the dice); score pad and pencil for each table.

Procedure.

1. Three to six players at a table. The six dice are rolled by a player. G counts 5, GR counts 10, GRO counts 15, and so forth. The whole word, GROUSE, counts 35, and is the end of the game.

2. The player gets one turn; his score is marked and the dice given to the player at his left, who repeats the procedure.

3. Whoever gets 35 first wins and the game is ended.

FISH AND GAME TYPES. Going around the group, each member names a different fish found in the state. Second time around, each names some wild game.

ITEMS OF INTEREST are written or typed and drawn from a hat. Each member draws one to read and comment on next time.

1. The great wandering albatross glides on the windiest ocean wastes, coming to land only to breed and rear one youngster each year. The 11′ wingspan is inefficient for flapping flight, and the windless doldrums at the equator are barriers that few of the birds succeed in crossing. (Has he heard of other strange and unexplained migration habits of birds?)

2. From 1869, when the railroad spanned the continent, and the breech-loading rifle was introduced, the buffalo carnage was so great, that by 1887, the once-mighty herds of millions were reduced to just a few stragglers. (What other animals and birds are disappearing because of the rifle?)

3. Fossil evidence indicates that the bison migrated across the Bering landbridge from Asia two thousand centuries ago. (What other fossil remains are in this hemisphere?)

4. Young opossums are less than an inch long at birth, and they normally spend the first two months in the mother's marsupial pouch, when they emerge. The whole brood travels on the mother's back. They remain with her for another month or so. (A koala bear has a tiny infant like this; do they know of others? What other animal has a pouch?) [10]

---

[10] Reprinted, courtesy of the *Chicago Tribune.*

Twenty-fourth Meeting

ITEMS ARE READ and comments made from the preceding assignment.

PHOTOGRAPH. A picture is taken of the group, a photo that can be used for a number of purposes.

BOARD GAME is easily made and will amuse the club members. A Home newspaper reports the following:

> Following a short business meeting of the Conservation Club, its nine members played a fishing game. Each player was given a "boat" for a marker with the object to "catch" fish as he progressed around the board by shaking dice.
>
> Along the way there were many pitfalls, such as "Broke your line, go back two spaces." ———— was the first to fall in the lake, and both he and ———— lost turns for catching turtles. ———— was the first to "catch a fish" and also the first to reach home.
>
> Each player catching a fish was given a cigar when reaching home.
>
> There was much laughter and joking and some of the comments heard were: "Look where he is . . . he's in a mess now." "Where am I now . . . still hung up on that stump?" "First he meets a skunk and now he falls in the lake . . . oh, that's bad." "I'm looking to catch a bottle-bass." "That cup of coffee spoiled my luck."

In the summer, the club, with a picnic lunch, visited local fish hatcheries.

Other Things to Talk about and Listen to

How does one back up a camping trailer? What about dead-end roads? Hitches? Bow and arrow hunting?

Has anyone attended an outboard meet? Was it a national championship? Where held? Sponsored by whom? Divisions? Finalists? Point system? Spectators? Two heats or more? Who qualifies?

How decoys are made.

The location preferred for camping.

How does one tell a coho or Chinook salmon from a trout? ("Just look in the mouth. Salmon have gray or black skin inside the mouth, the trout white or reddish skin," an Isaac Walton follower testifies.)

TROUT STREAM RULES. Is a license required? How long are the fishing periods? Could there be admission to onlookers? Who can give the starting signal? Could there be a signal marking the closing of the fishing period? Can fishermen stay on after the fishing period? Any rules about interferring with other competing fishermen? How can equipment be furnished? How about protection of this equipment?

Could there be several fishing periods? If so, can fishermen step aside and wait for the next period? After he selects a fishing position, could he step to another position? Who lands and nets the trout for weighing? What care will be taken to keep the identification of the fish caught? What procedure takes place before the fish is removed from the area? What part of the fish must be hooked? Are snagged fish accepted?

What could the admission fee be? On what merits would a prize be given—greatest number of fish? Will more than one award be given? What if there is a tie? Will previous winners be eligible?

Discussions. Each member is assigned an item.

1. How can one make a folding cot warmer while camping?

2. Definition of terms in an outboard: bow rail, running lights, walk-through windshield, lounge seats, vinyl carpeting, ski racks, ski eyes, battery box.

3. A camper which converts into a runabout; a one-man submarine; a hovercraft which cruises over the water and land.

4. Details of an inboard-outboard: convertible top and zippered boot, side and aft curtain, walnut wheel, fuel-amp-oil temperature gauge, insulated motor box, bow rail, teakwood trim, two jump seats, bilge pump and blower, fire extinguisher.

5. Characteristics of a good chain saw for weekend woodcutters.

6. Craft that can be ridden on the water like a motorcycle and can pull two water-skiers and float boats with seating up to twenty.

7. An ideal recreation cabin: size, stream or lake, woods, county facilities available, shade trees, road or isolated, frontage, sugar camp, size of house, rooms.

VERBAL INQUIRIES can be the most worthwhile of any activity that could be planned.

Discussion.

1. Boarding kennels for pets.
2. Hulls of wood, fiber glass and metal, aluminum or alloys.
3. Log rolling.
4. Hunting and dog training.
5. Eskimo dog teams.
6. Guns: revolver, automatic pistols, carbines. How is each used?

Discussion.

1. Camping cook stoves, air mattresses, other camping gadgets (folding chairs, bicycles).
2. Experiences with raccoons, porcupines, chipmunks.
3. A downpour or storm while camping.
4. With a 12′ sailboard, what would be the size of the beam, the size of the mast, the size of the boom, the size of the sail? What would be the total weight?

Discussion.

1. What attire would he consider important as a Fin and Feather man? Hats, gloves, jackets, boots, and so forth.
2. Worm fishing and plug casting.
3. Has his good luck fishing ever attracted a crowd? He tells of a most successful fishing trip. What kind of bait did he use? Rod? Reel?

TRAPPING experiences are exchanged. What tricks in handling animals can they distinguish in trapping?

A Home details below some of the novel discoveries of an Indian resident in their club.

> He decided to move to Wood County where he could trap game for a living: otter, mink, muskrat and coon. He would get quotations from different fur companies and sell his pelts where he could get the most money for them.
>
> There are many tricks to learning trapping and it takes years to learn the trade. Many times soneone would want to trap with him but he did not want to give away his secrets. After buying a trap he would boil water with green oak leaves in it and dunk the traps in this for ten or fifteen minutes. This process would darken the traps to make

them look natural with the surroundings and also removed any human scent from them.

When setting a trap he would kneel on a piece of canvas (always using the same side) so he wouldn't leave any human scent on the ground. He explained animals are very sensitive to odors, especially the fox which can sniff scent up to half a mile.

When he trapped beaver he would have a deputy warden working for the state, skin them for him for $1 a skin. Beaver are very difficult to skin as one can't leave any fat on the pelt. After the beaver is skinned, the pelt is measured lengthwise and across and double this figure. A beaver would then bring $1 per inch. A live otter will bring $150 or more. The otter, he says, is a very vicious animal and hard to capture alive.

His grandfather told him long ago if an Indian caught an otter and he didn't belong to a clan which could catch otter, he would have to release it again. He asked, "How?" as the animals are so vicious, and his grandfather explained that one kneels by the trap far enough away so it can't reach him. Then he talks to the animal in his own language for ten or fifteen minutes and it will quiet down. When it gets quiet he can walk in and pick it up. He tried this and found it to be true: he once wrapped one in an overall jacket and took it home.

Also, he explained, the wolf is a cowardly animal. If caught in a trap, one can walk right up to it: it will snarl and spit but if one keeps walking when he gets right up to it, it will keel over from fright.

He has the privilege of trapping on the cranberry marsh at any time; however, he has not trapped for about two years now.

PRESERVATION OF GAME was a subject for exchange of ideas in a Home.

The Indians in South Dakota had a way of taking care of freshly killed game, such as deer. They pulled it high into a tree to keep dogs away, and left it there to age, before they skinned it. The meat improved in flavor and tenderness by this waiting period, according to ——.

We discussed how cheese is aged until it is moldy, too, and the soft interior is a delicacy once the mold is removed. One of us had a friend in the meat-packing business who told of the choice steaks hanging in coolers for an aging period, crusted with mold. It is sliced off before the buyer gets it, and the steaks are butter-tender and juicy (and high priced!).

One of our residents told about an explorer in the early days of Alaskan territory who saw Eskimos eating fish that appeared to be rotten. When asked about it, one man replied, "We like our fish better when it is aged. You say this is rotten fish? You Americans eat rotten milk and call it cheese!"

Can each member recount an experience or custom about preserving game?

TO READ ALOUD
(Read short excerpts to discuss.)

Burnford, Sheila: *The Incredible Journey*   Fiction
The pleasure and the amazement which accompany the reading of this tale persist in the reader's mind long after he has learned that the two dogs and the one cat arrived safely at their destination.

Day, Beth: *Grizzlies in Their Backyard*   917
Adventures in Canada.

Disney Productions 1956: *Vanishing Prairie*   124 p., Golden
Based on a documentary film of the Great Plains which depicts the struggles for survival between buffalo, goat, bird, and dog.

Foote, J. T.: *Anglers All*   Fiction
Good fishing stories.

Gipson, Fred: *Old Yeller*   Fiction
Texas farm in the 1860's and a dog's part in life there.

Henderson, Dion: *Algonquin*   Fiction
Story of a great dog.

Hunter, John: *Hunter*   799
Wild game hunting in Africa.

Kantor, MacKinley: *Voice of Bugle Ann*   Fiction
A sentimental and dramatic story of Bugle Ann, a foxhound, and of her master's devotion.

MacDougall, Arthur, Jr.: *Under a Willow Tree*   Fiction
Dud Dean's stories about angling, hunting, and camping in the wildlands of Maine.

Meredith, Scott: *Bar 5 Roundup of Best Western Stories* Fiction
Eleven top stories.

Schaefer, Jack: *Shane*   Fiction
Wyoming in 1889.

Waldeck, Theodore: *On Safari*   Fiction
Romance and adventure in Africa.

NATURE CLUB

Introduction

Many of the suggestions from the Fin and Feather Club and Garden Club are equally applicable here and vice versa. However, the Nature Club may attract as many women as men, so both sexes could be considered in planning Nature Club activities.

Will this club have different objectives from other clubs?

A vocal myna bird or a parrakeet taught to speak by listening to tapes could be the hobby which launches an indoor nature study.

Training a pet chipmunk gives pleasure to people in wheelchairs on a patio in the summer. Residents who spend their savings buying him peanuts as eagerly await his appearance each spring as they do the return of a friend. An imaginative resident wrote charmingly of "Chip" and what his private life was like in an amusing, happy series in the Home newsletter.

Residents have assisted in the raising of deer and young pheasants, the latter brought in large numbers to the Home grounds by the Conservation Department. Residents raise corn and sugarcane for the winter birds and teach them to come to be fed at regular times. One man taught goldfish in an outdoor pool to surface at a fixed meal time; another attracted blackbirds in the yard with crumbs.

What type of resident is interested in joining the Nature Club?

Residents who have worked in circuses have much to contribute in recounting experiences with handling wild animals and in describing habits, instincts, and characteristics of many animals.

Retired farmers and their wives, knowledgeable in making things grow, are sometimes authorities on wild birds, weeds, bees, flowers, storms, and seasonal changes.

Lumberjacks can furnish information on identifying trees, their growth and diseases. Individuals can be discovered in the Home who have their own theories on weather predictions and offer superstitions or facts for discussion and comparison. Others quote Indian beliefs or data from the *Farmers' Almanac*.

Many residents have lived alone in isolated country areas

where great adventure took place in treacherous clashes with the elements and can recount surprising tales of nature's phenomena.

Forest rangers, fishermen, and miners have experiences to contribute. Even modest backyard gardeners may have kept simple records of edible weeds and mushrooms, the cycle of bird family life and migrations, mating schedules, and other events, all worth telling and perhaps worth entering in a Nature Club memoranda.

A good leader among the residents suggests a theme for the club's study through his own special interest, and stimulates others as well.

Goals (of Residents)

The following ideas start discussion:

1. Inform and stimulate imagination by reading aloud stories of animals, insects, birds, flowers, and so on.

2. Exchange experiences and information on nature, including woodcraft.

3. Promote friendships and better understanding of one another.

4. Help increase love of the land and out-of-doors.

5. Compare city and country living.

6. Enjoy and appreciate the natural beauty of the world in which he lives.

Motivation Techniques

Below are several methods for motivating residents.

1. The leader, as for all clubs, needs to know the resident, his interests, and his basic needs and drives.

2. Be persistent, but not too personally involved for the good of the resident.

3. Invite members of both sexes to attract one another.

4. Arouse curiosity.

5. Assign the handicapped to help the handicapped.

6. Watch for leads which residents can exhibit.

First Meeting

See "The First Meeting," Part III, "How to Lead a Club."

For the next meeting, residents are assigned to report on the life history of an insect, obtaining the materials from an encyclopedia or nature book. Or, they might read from prepared simple statements typed on slips of paper. These materials provide good subject matter for discussion.

Members are also asked to bring a little-known fact of nature.

Second Meeting

Can each define an insect? How many can the group name? Are there beneficial ones? Detrimental? What are the largest seen? Smallest? Are there any dangerous ones? Can each name bugs that help destroy more harmful bugs? What insecticides are known by the group?

PLAY A RECORD OF NIGHT SOUNDS, including those of insects, which add much to a meeting (see Appendix).

```
E  N  I  R  E  V  L  O  W  N  A  L  L  I  H  C  N  I  H  C
L  L  N  L  N  O  Z  O  A  R  M  A  D  I  L  L  O  L  P  H
E  J  O  E  O  A  L  T  L  A  M  R  B  H  R  O  E  L  K  I
P  A  O  M  I  F  U  E  A  U  E  E  T  E  S  O  M  R  A  M
H  G  C  A  L  G  R  R  S  V  X  O  T  U  P  D  C  P  N  P
A  U  C  C  N  R  D  K  A  D  N  A  P  A  K  D  E  P  G  A
N  A  A  A  I  V  R  E  N  A  C  Y  R  O  H  N  E  E  A  N
T  R  R  U  A  A  B  A  T  O  T  D  C  T  A  K  I  N  R  Z
E  O  Q  R  T  E  S  S  E  A  L  I  O  N  S  R  A  M  O  E
A  S  K  E  N  S  M  S  L  H  E  L  P  G  H  E  L  T  O  E
T  A  O  G  U  U  O  P  O  S  S  U  M  W  E  G  A  R  R  J
E  B  A  B  O  O  N  E  P  R  A  I  R  I  E  D  O  G  E  E
R  A  E  B  M  M  K  S  E  Y  E  G  P  I  P  A  K  O  G  L
R  I  X  S  W  W  E  R  H  S  W  Y  P  U  H  B  N  O  I  L
E  O  P  H  C  O  Y  O  T  E  O  M  A  T  M  U  U  K  T  E
F  P  A  A  G  T  C  H  I  P  P  O  P  O  T  A  M  U  S  Z
R  L  A  N  T  W  A  R  B  E  Z  S  K  U  N  K  P  M  C  A
E  S  I  O  P  R  O  P  B  U  F  F  A  L  O  I  I  A  S  G
P  D  M  U  L  E  F  F  A  R  I  G  D  G  O  P  H  E  R  I
P  O  L  A  R  B  E  A  R  S  L  E  N  I  P  U  C  R  O  P
```

FIND THE ANIMALS. (See page 252.) Copies can be made and distributed, or shown on the wall by lantern projector. The names of seventy-four animals can be found among these letters. They can be read forward, backward, up, down, and diagonally up and down. A complete list of the animals that can be found follows:

Aardvark	Monkey	Tiger	Dingo	Raccoon
Badger	Mule	Zebra	Gopher	Sloth
Chinchilla	Porpoise	Ape	Lion	Whale
Gazelle	Sheep	Bat	Deer	Kangaroo
Jaguar	Tapir	Cat	Opossum	Hippopotamus
Mole	Squirrel	Cow	Rabbit	Chimpanzee
Muskrat	Antelope	Dog	Skunk	Ferret
Platypus	Beaver	Elk	Weasel	Ibex
Rhino	Coyote	Fox	Baboon	Marmoset
Porcupine	Goat	Ox	Camel	Mountain Lion
Anteater	Leopard	Pig	Elephant	Orangutan
Bear	Moose	Wolf	Horse	Polar Bear
Chipmunk	Okapi	Wolverine	Mink	Prairie Dog
Giraffe	Puma	Armadillo	Mouse	Sea Lion
Koala	Shrew	Buffalo	Panda	

FACTS can be full of surprises. Residents add to this little-known fact of nature list, as it's read.

1. The red-breasted nuthatch makes a trap of balsam in front of its nest to trap intruders.

2. A deer waves a flag when it runs.

3. A white birch sheds its seeds in January.

4. The goldfinch stays in the north in the winter, only changing the color of its coat.

5. Witch hazel blossoms in late October.

6. The cowbird makes no nest; it lays its eggs in the nests of other birds.

7. The Destroying Angel is a very poisonous mushroom.

8. English sparrow and starling are two European birds which have become great pests in this country.

9. Flowers protected by law in Wisconsin: trillium, lady slipper, arbutus, bittersweet, lily, water lily.

10. Hummingbirds prefer flowers to worms.

11. A partridge beats a drum.

12. Insects domesticated by man: honeybee, silkworm, spiders (for their silk).

Next meeting, residents bring something related to the Nature Club for the group to guess: nuts, leaves, burrs, bark, pictures of nature.

Third Meeting

IDENTIFY TREES (BY PICTURES). This could start some serious study on trees. They discuss the growth of a tree: Where are some of the oldest trees in the world? What are they? How is age of a tree determined? What are some fast-growing trees? How old are trees on this property? Where are some of the oldest trees nearby?

KNOW THE TREES can be oral, or if mimeographed, a project for the week.

> There was a youth so ———— and neat (spruce)
> Who loved a maiden wondrous sweet.
> A ———— girl, with her he'd stray (poplar)
> Along the ———— beside the ———— (beech, bay)
> When breezes frought with ocean air
> Would softly touch her ———— hair (chestnut).
> Her rosy ———— in his he pressed (palms)
> To ask ———— was her request (pawpaw).
> Should he succeed with hope elate,
> She promised him she'd set the ———— (date).
> He sought her home that very night,
> Although he feared the ———— bite (dogwood);
> But yet for her sake he could dare
> So not a ———— then did he care (fig).
> Then spoke he to the ———— man (elder)
> "To win your daughter's hand I plan."
> "And for her constantly I ————" (pine).

—Submitted

Fourth Meeting

BIRD MIGRATION is a mystery to reflect upon. Local birds that migrate are discussed, as well as those that do not. What birds seen here failed to migrate in the winter? How do they survive? Where do local birds go?

Someone reports on an article on this subject.

Members identify bird songs on records from the local library, or welcome a visit by a local bird watcher, who encourages observation and listening (see Appendix).

Fifth Meeting

ANIMALS are featured.

MY WILD ANIMAL PRESERVE is a miscellaneous "come-on," a game to be played indoors or out. One resident begins by saying, "I have a ———— in my wild animal preserve," choosing an animal whose name begins with "A." The second names an animal with a name beginning with "B," and so on down the alphabet. Each repeats what the others have said.

LOCAL WILD ANIMALS are listed.

FILL IN THE BLANKS. With the following copied on the blackboard where all can see, residents discuss it together and take time to identify the animal which fits into these blanks.

. . a . . . (weasel)   . . . . . a . (muskrat)
. a . . . . . (wart hog)   . a . . . . (rabbit)
. a . . . . (walrus)   . a . (rat)
. . a . . (koala)   . a . . . . . (raccoon)

Residents prepare others.

TROPIC: TERRAIN. The leader shows slides or magazine pictures of terrain illustrating the time of year, indications of weather and climate, age of trees, types of vines, flowers, birds, and so on. Residents study and discuss them.

THE DOCUMENTARY MOVIES (15-20 minutes in length) promote discussion, available free from U.S. Dept. of the Interior, Office of the Secretary, Washington, D.C. 20240 (see Appendix).

Sixth Meeting

"I KNOW AN ANIMAL," someone says, which gets the group's attention and makes members think. This simple game calls for knowledge and imagination. The leader begins by describing some nature object in this way: "I know an animal. It lives near ponds and has sharp teeth. One can tell where it lives by the presence of something he builds there. Hats are made of its fur. It is a rodent." The first resident who guesses correctly must then describe some other bird or animal for the others to guess.

WHAT EXPRESSIONS GO WITH . . . ? Lion (come in like a, in the lion's den, lies down with the lamb, put one's head in the lion's mouth, lionhearted, others).

Fox (foxy grandpa, fox-trot, cunning, fox chase).

Lamb, bee, rabbit, snail, mouse, bird, kitten, and others are named.

THE MANY WAYS TO ATTRACT BIRDS TO A LAWN are enumerated.

1. Provide two level feeding stations with cornbread, crumbs, and peanut butter.

2. Provide an open feeder where wild birds can eat and watch for possible danger.

3. Provide feeding stations attached to a window.

4. Use wild birdseeds and sunflower seeds. Use a small container (top of a spray can) with small holes punched near the bottom for drainage for crumbs or peanut butter mix.

5. Use an inexpensive chromium soap dish nailed to a tree or post as a suet holder.

6. Make a birdbath: pea gravel with perforated black plastic.

7. Provide hollies and pyracantha berries (for insect eaters which can't eat seeds), dogwood, and mulberry trees.

8. Provide trees and shrubs for resting sites and cover.

What are others? Which seem most suitable? Are there committees who will start working? Where could the feeders be placed? What months will they be needed?

Seventh Meeting

Nature Notes[11] are each typed on a slip of paper for members to DRAW, READ, AND COMMENT ON.

1. A squirrel's front teeth never stop growing, but their length and keenness are normally maintained as the opposing teeth wear against each other.

If one of the incisors is damaged or malformed, the opposite tooth could grow unchecked with fatal results.

---

[11] Reprinted, courtesy of the *Chicago Tribune.*

2. The yearly cost of a lion at Chicago's Brookfield Zoo is about $2000. Each adult lion eats seventy-two pounds of meat per week at a cost of 33¢ a pound. Other expenses include minerals, vitamins, building maintenance, and keepers' wages.

3. The wandering Laysan albatross cruises over the entire North Pacific from California to China, following the wind pattern which old sailing ships used.

4. The caribou, of the far northern tundra, migrate more than four hundred miles southward in the winter. In the spring, while on the long trek northward, the young are born. The animals press on despite all obstacles, and mass drownings sometimes occur when they attempt to cross swollen streams.

5. The forward-facing eyes of an owl are virtually immobile in their sockets, but the owl can twist his head a full 180 degrees to see things.

6. The Western World first learned of the giant panda from missionary-scientist Peré David when he toured Western China in 1869. No live giant panda was seen by the Western World until the first zoo-owned specimen in the world went on a display in Chicago's Brookfield Zoo in 1937. Today there are three of the breed in zoos outside Red China: Moscow has one, and so has London and Washington, D.C.

7. Most birds remain quiet near their nests, but not wrens. Is their harsh chattering supposed to be a scolding, or a lullaby?

Residents tell their idea of THE GOOD LIFE. What instances of improving or destroying life can be attributed to ecology?

Do they think private possession of handguns should be outlawed? They list pros and cons and summarize them finally.

LEAF IDENTIFICATION. Each resident is given a leaf and asked to identify the tree. He is asked to bring back another leaf like it, if possible.

The club may be divided into teams to compete in matching the leaves correctly. Residents are asked to bring some pressed leaves next time.

Eighth Meeting

SPATTERPRINTS make greeting cards, pictures to be framed, souvenirs, program covers, and other items. Flowers and leaves lend themselves to attractive designs by means of spatterprints. Residents who have little artistic talent can still achieve beauty in this activity. It also makes possible permanent collections of flowers, ferns, or leaves.

Equipment. Pins; screen wire; paper; leaves; poster paint; a discarded tooth brush.

Procedure.

1. Pin the leaf or flower on a paper.

2. Hold the screen about an inch above the paper and brush the screen lightly with ink or thick paint.

3. When the paint is dry, pins are taken out.

4. The leaf is taken off, its shape shown by the paint spattered.

The brush should not be too wet, in order to have delicacy in the color.

SOME QUERIES are made around the group.

1. What type of tanager is found here? Where does it winter?

2. How long does a beaver live? How much does it weigh?

3. Why would a mountain goat require two hunters to get him?

4. What is the source of eiderdown for soft pillows?

5. What desirable use can be made of the ladybug?

INFORMATION TO START DISCUSSION.[12] Someone reads the following.

1. There are 222 members of the tanager family in the Americas. The best known of the four North American species is our scarlet tanager, which winters in the ancestral tropics.

2. The beaver never stops growing until it dies. Living about twelve years, it never reaches its full growth potential and averages between forty and sixty pounds, but a hundred and ten pound giant was taken in 1921 near Iron River, Wisconsin.

3. The mountain goat frequents the highest peaks and is usually secure in the knowledge that there is nothing above him, so he concentrates on possible dangers below. This can be his undoing; a decoy hunter shows himself below while another hunter keeps himself out of sight and tries to get in a position above the goat for a shot.

4. Common eider ducks of the North Atlantic coasts: The female eider plucks "down," a gray fuzz, from her breast to line her nest. Eiders nest in colonies, and when the young leave the nests, the down is harvested for market. It is the lightest and softest material that we know, and is used in famous eiderdown quilts.

5. Ladybugs are used commercially for insect control: one California firm engaged in ladybug business ships thousands of gallons

---

[12] Reprinted, courtesy of the *Chicago Tribune.*

(about seventy-five thousand per gallon) of these beetles annually. Cotton and alfalfa growers are the biggest customers, but orders come from gardeners and florists, too. Since the little predators can be kept dormant in cold storage for long periods, they can be shipped any time of the year.

Ninth Meeting

The leader promotes discussion, when relevant, on HALLOWEEN. He gives a question at a time and expects one or more answers. What does the word "hallowed" mean? What Holy Day is November 1? What are decorations for Halloween? What are weights of pumpkins? What color are the blossoms?

The rind is described; do pumpkins have seeds? How are they used? Where do farmers usually plant them? Why? Did residents go out Halloweening? Were they victims of pranks of children?

What color is an owl? What is the saying, ———— as an owl? Is an owl wise? What kinds of owls are there? What color are they? What are the horns made of? Why don't they see in the daytime? What are their enemies? Where do they hunt?

What do bats live on? How do they catch their prey? How does a bat drink water? When do they sleep? What position does a bat sleep in? Is its eyesight good? What about a bat flying in a woman's hair? When does it hunt?

KNOBBY GOURD PROJECTS. Members in a club added this idea:

Our knobby gourds cut out at the top like a jack-o'-lantern, are used for vases and will hold water and fresh flowers. Residents sometimes have painted faces on the gourds and exchanged them for comment, amusement, and admiration.

Tenth Meeting

CRAFTS. The leader, depending on the season when material is available, could bring a new craft for each meeting, or perhaps one for men and one for women.

Men's Crafts. In the spring, men make willow whistles to give small children. In the fall, they make milkweed-pod birds and animals, acorn toys and jewelry. They make totem poles, make bows of white ash, spruce, ironwood, hickory, or Osage orange, make wooden buttons, wood burl bookends.

Women's Crafts. Women make snail shell jewelry and mats of cattail rushes. They do cornhusk weaving or make cornhusk dolls. They make sachets of dried sweet clover, wild rose petals, or mint, and make pillows of pine needles or balsam needles.

SNOW SCULPTURE is part of winter nature study. Residents wearing heavy mittens and sitting in the sun at the picnic tables or in deck chairs on the patio are given snow with which they model animals or birds.

Eleventh Meeting

LEGAL PROTECTION OF FLOWERS. Could residents name wild flowers in the state which can be picked and those which are protected?

"WHO SAID THAT?" they will wonder. (This could be relevant to any club.) A resident jots down sayings characteristic of another resident, typical although casual. At the end of the meeting, or at some future meeting, he reads the list, the speaker to be identified by the group. (A tape recorder could be used instead of longhand.)

Twelfth Meeting

After a VISIT TO A LOCAL MUSEUM, residents make reports at the following meeting.

Thirteenth Meeting

SENSE OF DIRECTION is a blindfold stunt, which could be used in any club meeting. On a long table, a number of circles, each with a different number within it, are drawn at irregular distances. The blindfolded resident is turned around in his wheelchair (or is walked around his chair), turned to the table and told to put his finger on the circle.

If he places his finger inside the circle, that number is added to his score. Otherwise he gets nothing.

BREAKFAST ON THE PATIO in good weather will be enjoyable. Early morning breakfast provides a chance to observe bird life.

Club members are questioned: Do they know the story about the stone, the "Thrush's Anvil"? Do they know anything about the "nesting" habits of fish? Of what countries is the eagle a significant symbol? What birds use mud for building nests? Answers to such questions will be read at the next meeting.

Fourteenth Meeting

FIND THE BIRDS. Copies can be made and distributed, or shown on the wall by lantern projector. The names of the birds in this puzzle can be found in the list at bottom of page. The names may be frontwards, backwards, vertical, horizontal, or diagonal.

```
K   R   A   L   B   L   U   E   J   A   Y   R   A   N   A   C   B   L   R
K   C   U   D   U   U   R   U   F   F   E   D   G   R   O   U   S   E   E
E   A   O   E   Z   B   S   T   A   R   L   I   N   G   U   L   L   R   K
E   R   I   C   Z   G   R   A   C   K   L   E   I   B   I   S   U   I   C
D   D   S   W   A   L   L   O   W   L   O   R   H   D   S   T   N   R   U
A   I   N   O   R   E   H   N   E   R   W   T   N   W   L   G   O   F   S
K   N   L   I   D   G   P   C   K   D   H   N   A   U   F   W   L   H   P
C   A   K   T   E   R   N   R   R   R   A   N   V   I   L   I   E   U   A
I   L   O   O   N   E   O   I   A   G   M   R   S   L   A   P   E   M   S
H   S   U   R   H   T   B   S   I   H   M   H   I   U   M   E   L   M   A
C   D   S   E   S   W   H   M   A   N   E   W   Q   T   I   T   A   I   R
N   R   T   K   O   E   R   W   O   R   R   A   P   S   N   T   G   N   E
I   I   E   C   R   A   O   R   I   O   L   E   R   O   G   O   N   G   G
F   B   E   E   T   C   A   D   O   S   P   R   E   Y   O   R   I   B   A
D   K   K   P   R   U   O   P   U   R   P   L   E   M   A   R   T   I   N
L   C   A   D   N   N   P   N   E   L   G   A   E   K   W   A   H   R   A
O   A   R   O   B   I   N   E   D   N   A   C   I   L   E   P   G   D   T
G   L   A   O   H   A   N   Y   M   O   C   K   I   N   G   B   I   R   D
R   B   P   W   A   R   B   L   E   R   R   E   P   I   P   D   N   A   S
```

Blackbird	Cowbird	Grackle	Ibis	Oriole
Blue Jay	Crow	Gull	Kingfisher	Osprey
Buzzard	Duck	Hawk	Lark	Owl
Canary	Eagle	Yellowhammer	Loon	Parrakeet
Cardinal	Egret	Hen	Mockingbird	Parrot
Chickadee	Flamingo	Heron	Myna	Peacock
Condor	Goldfinch	Hummingbird	Nightingale	Pelican

Ptarmigan	Sandpiper	Stork	Tern	Warbler
Purple Martin	Sapsucker	Swallow	Thrasher	Whippoorwill
Quail	Sparrow	Swan	Thrush	Woodpecker
Robin	Starling	Tanager	Vulture	Wren
Ruffed Grouse				

DISCUSSION. Nature Notes[13] are to be read aloud and discussed.

The thrush relishes the wood snail, and to get to the succulent animal it seizes the snail and knocks it against a favorite stone until it breaks. The stone is called the "Thrush's Anvil."

Small-mouth bass build nests from April to June when the temperature becomes suitable at 60 to 65 degrees. The male bass constructs the nest on a bed of gravel or a coarse sand, removing all debris with fins and mouth.

The black-footed ferret is one of America's rarest animals, once thought possibly extinct until biologists found a colony in South Dakota.

In 1782 Congress chose the American, or bald, eagle for the Great Seal of the United States, rejecting the golden eagle originally proposed by the designer. The golden eagle has been for centuries a heraldic symbol of monarchies and dictatorships from ancient Assyria to the Roman Empire, Czarist Russia, Napoleonic France, the Austrian and Prussian Empires and Nazi Germany.

The cliff swallow of Capistrano fame builds a bottle-shaped nest of mud pellets under an overhanging cliff or beneath the eaves of a building.

The barn swallow plasters an open cup of mud to the top of a roughhewn rafter.

The tree swallow builds in cavities or nest boxes.

The bank swallow is a burrower.

STUDY CLASS. Each resident brings some specimen to study: insect, stones, four-leaf clover, a white pine needle, a heart-shaped leaf, or something else. These, with a magnifying glass, can be passed and scrutinized one at a time.

Fifteenth Meeting

RESIDENTS VISIT A LOCAL "WAYSIDE" or city park; on the way home, they try to name as many growing things as they can.

Can they MAKE UP QUIZZES for identifying flowers?

Baby talk for "and then me" (anemone).
Character in Little Abner (daisy).

---

[13] Reprinted, courtesy of the *Chicago Tribune.*

Fifth month fruit (May apple).
Bird swearing (crocus).
Azure gong (bluebell).
Red Man's brush (Indian paintbrush).
Bovine awkwardness (cowslip).
Fairytale shoe (lady's slipper).
A historical ship (mayflower).

Sixteenth Meeting

A sample NATURE STUDY TRIP is presented for discussion; can residents plan a similar jaunt?

Six cars were used to take residents for a drive along the river road to Nekoosa. On the return trip they drove to the zoo in Wisconsin Rapids to see the deer, bear, birds and monkeys. Volunteers from the nearby area drove their cars.

We were taken along Highway 54 to visit the cranberry marshes. We walked through the warehouse and a second building where the cranberries were processed, all very interesting. At the end of the tour we were treated to a glass of cranberry juice.

We were on the marsh road where we stopped to watch the men wearing hip boots, rake cranberries with the use of a mechanical rake and put the berries into big tubs. Some of us saw a duck on the marsh ditch dive headfirst into the water and come up with a live minnow in its bill.

Residents select a pressed leaf or flower to bring to the next club meeting.

EACH CONSIDERS: What could one do if lost in the woods? How could he find or make a shelter? How could he find pure water and food safe to eat? What berries, nuts, leaves, and roots are edible? Which are inedible or poisonous?

Seventeenth Meeting

SAKURAGAMI CRAFT. This simple technique of paper lamination can be used in a variety of arts and craft projects. Two most popular are for decorating note paper and pressed leaf and flower collections. Members can laminate fabric, pressed flower petals, leaves, hat veiling, and so on.

Equipment. An electric iron; brown wrapping paper; ruler; waxed paper; leaves, petals, etc.; Scott's tissue; stiff bristle pastry brush; Elmer's glue; paper; glitter.
Procedure. (See Figs. 15-21.)

1. Plan the desired finished size of the project and draw or rule outline on a piece of plain paper.

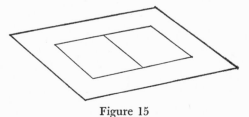

Figure 15

2. Place a sheet of ordinary waxed paper flat on table over the ruled outline.

3. Place leaves, petals, etc., on the waxed paper in pleasing arrangements.

Figure 16

4. Cover with a single sheet of Scott's tissue.

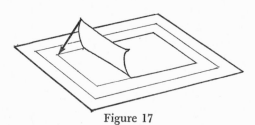

Figure 17

5. Using a stiff bristle pastry brush, apply a diluted mixture of Elmer's glue (50% Elmer's glue and 50% water) with a tapping motion to evenly saturate the paper.

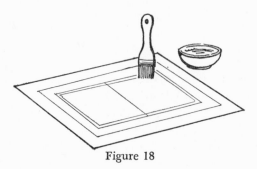

Figure 18

6. At this point, decorate with glitter by merely sprinkling it on where desired.

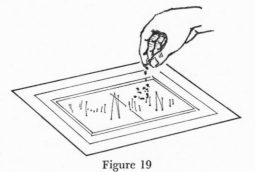

Figure 19

7. It must dry thoroughly overnight.

8. It is pressed to flatten by ironing between layers of brown wrapping paper.

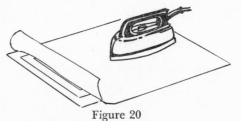

Figure 20

9. Using a straightedge, tear excess off edges for final size. This will produce a "deckle edge" effect.

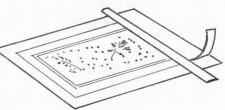

Figure 21

10. Decorative window hangings can be made, each creating actual scenes using various fern, petals, and dried leaves.

Eighteenth Meeting

They FILL IN NAMES beginning with letters of some month, a paper and pencil game.

```
         S     E    P    T    E    M    B    E    R
```
Tree sycamore elm peach tamarack elder maple beach evergreen redwood
Flower
Bird
Insect
Animal

A resident makes up another puzzle for the next meeting.

PETS. Everyone gives the name of a pet he once had, discusses breeding, feeding, training, responsibility for, care of, and so on.

BIRD CROSSWORD PUZZLE.

```
  . . g . . .  (magpie)
    g . . . . . .  (grackle)
. . . . g . .  (tanager)
    g . . . . . . .  (grosbeak)
    g . . .  (gull)
    g . . . .  (goose)
. . . . . . g  (starling)
```

Residents volunteer to make up another.

Nineteenth Meeting

PEACE AND QUIET is enjoyed by residents who just like sitting under a shady tree or in the sunshine beside the water, relaxing and absorbing surrounding peace and beauty. At any time of year, a ride down an old familiar road, looking at the world around them, is a heartening experience. Sometimes the greatest pleasure comes from quiet hours spent out-of-doors.

FORAGING residents can experiment cooking wild greens or making Indian or wintergreen tea. Can they develop other ideas?

Twentieth Meeting

THEY VISIT a maple sugar camp, or something typical of the locale. An outdoor project in the spring, if in the appropriate geographic location, could be driving to see the smelt run, early farm planting, blooming orchards; in the fall, wild rice harvests, sorgum mills, canning corn in factories, or county flower shows.

Residents enjoy a fishing trip, frying and eating the fish with friends afterward.

Each member brings a statement, a rare fact or event, or something of unique significance regarding nature, to the next meeting.

Twenty-first Meeting

Members submit statements of PHENOMENA OF NATURE to discuss. Here are other samples:

1. Witch hazel can shoot its seeds 40′ in any direction.
2. Native wild animals in order of intelligence are raccoon, bear, red fox.
3. A butterfly can produce a picture of itself when placed directly with photographic plate, and can be photographed without the use of a camera.
4. The crayfish can walk backward faster than it can go forward.
5. The tamarack loses its needles every fall.
6. The pitcher plant is a wild flower that likes to eat a piece of meat for breakfast.
7. The monarch butterfly migrates to South America.

PHYSICAL CHARACTERISTICS OF ANIMALS are given each of the following animals: lynx, raccoon, sloth, fox, skunk, armadillo, mouse, lion, dromedary, kangaroo, beaver, mongoose.

Of the following birds: skylark, oriole, stormy petrel, eagle, flicker, cardinal, bluebird, whippoorwill, mourning dove, jenny wren. They name others.

Twenty-second Meeting

SYMBOLS of the following flowers are given: lily, iris, bluebonnet, bluebell, tiger lily (purity, French coat of arms, Texas state flower, national flower of Scotland, spotted like a jungle cat).

What flowers are suggested by the following? A minister (jack-in-the-pulpit), wedding ring (bridal wreath), Christmas Eve (Star of Bethlehem), crimson wise man (scarlet sage), sweets (candytuft), broken romance (bleeding heart), frog steps (hops).

Can residents be responsible for maintenance of a BIRD FEEDING STATION? A study of bird migration charts is a natural follow-up. In the spring, birdhouses can be built and set up on the grounds, bird feeders in the fall.

Twenty-third Meeting

PROMOTING A NATURE COLUMN in the Home newsletter, a club member is responsible. "Have you seen the hummingbird's nest in the elm tree?" Each member at meetings can jot down an observation to be included in the weekly column, as one club did. Can members adapt ideas and offer suggestions?

Someone in a Home writes:

> Report to ——— anything of interest you observe about the outdoors.
>
> From 3 West we observe that several truckloads of young chickens, alive and kicking, were brought to the chickenhouses back of the farmhouse.
>
> I heard there is to be a pond on the adjacent farm to the east. Some dredging machinery we saw working there seems to bear this out. Perhaps the pond will be stocked with fish; it will cover one acre.
>
> Last month I spoke of a wren house in the back garden; at close range it was found to have two large openings at the bottom of the house and a wren-sized hole at the top. Wrens do not like tenement houses so the sparrows have taken over the house.
>
> ——— reports: This morning, May 18, a pigeon flew onto my window ledge. It was a large bird, black and white. It nestled close to the pane and pecked and pecked at the screen, perhaps trying to get inside. It did not mind my watching it. I was wishing it would make a nest there, but the ledge was too narrow, so it finally flew away to a larger nesting place, or so I thought.
>
> A robin is nesting in the bird feeder just below my window. While she broods, the father bird sits on the edge of the birdbath nearby, chasing the sparrows away. Soon there will be young ones to feed and I can watch them come and go with food for their young. It used to be angleworms, but there don't seem to be any more to pull up. It is thought that the sprays have killed the angleworms.
>
> About May 5 the first young starlings were noticed out on the lawn, screaming to be fed. How do the parents know their own children? They all look alike to us.
>
> A pair of flickers have been noticed several times in the old tree at at the entrance driveway. Let's hope they are nesting there in spite of the quarrelsome starlings. . . .

Window watchers, residents, and bed patients alike, even though viewing only an alley, can find this lookout a resource. A patch of sky above the branch of a tree, the window ledge where bird life appears at a simple feeding station, or with better luck, a view of a lawn, a terrace, or walk offers interest to those confined, thus providing material for a study project.

Another sample of observation is given by the same writer.

> Now that the bird feeders on the front lawn have been reopened, the men of 1 East enjoy watching the sparrows gorging and quarreling. . . . Two or three different evenings just at dusk a small owl was spotted perched on the roof of the east feeder, perhaps looking for a fat sparrow that had stuffed himself so he couldn't fly away.
>
> Just a day or two before the last real cold spell three squirrels were noticed on the front lawn early in the morning searching for stray tree seeds to eat, and dry leaves to repad their nests in the hollow tree limbs against the coming cold.
>
> Also, fresh rabbit tracks were seen in the new-fallen snow close to the buildings.

The leader jots down an "observation" from each member. Each item can be developed into a paragraph resulting in a well-filled column for the Home newsletter.

Twenty-fourth Meeting

CHANGING THE SETTING for the club meetings, this club held their group in the lounge. The leader described their programs in an interview.

The club of twenty residents meets in the lounge every afternoon with the charge nurse, in project studies on nature, reporting new birds seen on the lawn. The group learned a poem about a robin which they recite together. A question is passed to each resident to answer:

What season of the year do you like best and why?

When do we say spring begins?

Tell something about the big black bears found in the north. What do they eat in the winter?

Tell a joke about nature.

Recite or read a poem about nature.

Tell what you know about nature study in this county.

Tell what is done at the Conservation Department.

What magazines do you like best and why? Newspapers?

How did the Indians collect maple sap and make maple syrup?

Why do we have Nature Study class? ("Become acquainted with one another"; "Pass the time"; "Help us get out of our rooms"; "The help one gets from physical therapy"; "I've learned a lot"; "One gets different ideas coming down here, talking about everything under the sun"; "You keep after us until we give an answer.")

A NATURE MUSEUM could come into being in the Home, with a resident committee able and willing to start with a few shelves or an old bookcase where unusual nature objects are displayed, each with the benefactor's name. Local merchants could donate space for a display of club specimens; children encouraged to contribute entries, too, could add to the collection.

BIRD EXTINCTION is discussed by residents listing all the birds the group has seen in previous years, now gone; they list also the birds which seem immune to DDT.

This could be a novel idea to most residents: a TURTLE RACE.
Equipment. Live turtles; cards for turtles' names; bets of play money.
A Home describes their contest.

> Bets were placed on the winner of the fantastic turtle race.
> The track ran from the middle of the table to the end. The race started with the touch of each turtle's tail and they were off; Joe moved his little legs quickly into the first place while Frank skidded into a close second even though his belly rubbed the table.
> I regret to say that Wayne took third but at least I can say he tried and that's what counts. The turtles at the time of the race were a week old.

TO READ ALOUD
(Set aside a limited time each meeting.)

Adamson, Joy: *Elsa, the Lioness*   917
Baker, Ray: *Under My Elm*   818
   Thoughts and experiences by a man who has found life good.
Baker, Robert: *When the Stars Come Out*   520
   Astronomy for the beginner.
Collis, John Steward: *The Triumph of the Tree*   574
   A history of trees, from the silent fern forests of millions of years ago to the present. (Paperback) $1.25; Viking X3

Dubkin, L.: *Natural History of a Yard*   574
How the author and his small daughter found a world of enchantment in a small city yard.

Krutch, Joseph Wood: *The Desert Year*   574
A naturalist and philosopher views the pattern of the desert world of the American Southwest. (Paperback)

$1.35; Viking X13

Lane, Ferdinand: *All about the Sea*   551
A book of the wonders of the sea.

Muir, John: *Story of My Boyhood and Youth*   92-M
The early years of a Wisconsin naturalist.

Parmenter, Ross: *The Plant in My Window*   92-P
Charming, warm, and wonderful.

Peattie, Donald: *Cup of Sky*   504
A book about the "common and lovely miracles of natural life," inspired by St. Francis of Assisi's Hymn to Creation.

Peterson, Roger: *Wild America*   571
The record of a 30,000 mile journey around the continent by a distinguished naturalist and his British colleague.

Rutledge, Archibald: *Santee Paradise*   917
A southern writer describes his home region.

Shippen, Katherine: *The Great Heritage*   333
Stories of the origin, discovery, and development of the treasures of the American earth.

Sloane, Eric: *Eric Sloane's Weather Book*   551
Presents the "human side" of weather for the layman.

Tazieff, Haroun: *Caves of Adventure*
The firsthand story of a famous expedition into the labyrinth of caves 2000 feet underground in the Pyrenees. (Paperback)

$1.45; Viking X7

Teale, Edwin: *Green Treasury*   808
A journey through the world's great nature writing.

Teale, Edwin: *North with the Spring*   507
                 Autumn across America   574
                 Days without Time   507

APPENDIX

BIBLIOGRAPHICAL RESOURCES FOR STUDY OF THE AGING

The Gerontologist (periodical).

Journal of Gerontology (periodical).

Kastenbaum, R.: *New Thoughts on Old Age*. New York, Springer, 1964.

Loeb, Pincus, and Wood (Eds.): *Social Problems of the Aging and the Aged*. A Book of Readings, Madison, Wisconsin University Extension, Department of Social Work, 1961.

Mathiasen, Geneva: The aging. In Lurie, Harry L. (Ed.): *Encyclopedia of Social Work*. New York, National Association of Social Workers, 1965, pp. 73-80.

McKinney and DeVyver (Eds.): *Aging and Social Policy*. New York, Appleton Century, 1966.

Social Security Bulletin. Washington, D.C., Department of Health, Education and Welfare.

Tibbitts, Clark (Ed.): *Handbook of Social Gerontology, Societal Aspects of Aging*. Chicago, University of Chicago Press, 1960.

Williams, Tibbitts, and Donahue (Eds.): *Processes of Aging*. New York, Atherton, 1963.

GENERAL APPENDIX

A Portable Hand Mike

A loudspeaker in a satchel the size of a doll's suitcase equipped with a handle for carrying, and a 10′ cord to be plugged into any wall socket. Of great use in a club circle whether in calling games, for featured performers, or to be used in general conversation when it can be passed from hand to hand and talked into. The common problem of the hard-of-hearing can best be solved with a mike.

At the close of the meeting, the cord is unplugged, the hand mike put in the case, snapped shut, and carried easily into another ward or area for use there.

Speaker-attached Game-Caller, $79.97, 8-watt speaker. Wholesaler Stewart-Games: Jerry Schewe, Point Sporting Goods, 1036 College Avenue, Stevens Point, Wisconsin 54481, who will tell you where it can be purchased.

Devices to Aid Handicapped

J. A. Preston Company
71 Fifth Avenue
New York, N.Y. 10003

Emblems

A and B Emblem Corporation
Box 695
Weaverville, N.C. 28787

Award Pins and Emblem Jewelry

Robt. Erffmeyer and Son
5300 West Clinton
Milwaukee, Wis. 53223

Old-fashioned Magazines

Sunshine for All the Family ($3 a year).
Sunshine Center
Sunshine Park
Litchfield, Ill. 62056

Grit (weekly) ($7 a year).
"America's Greatest Family Newspaper"
208 W. Third Street
Williamsport, Pa. 17701

A book to read aloud to all groups, written by a blind man in a county Home:
Adventures of a Wooden Eye ($3.95 plus 35¢ mailing cost and 16¢ sales tax).
Mr. Leslie R. Borer
c/o Wedgewood Orchards
4131 State Road
La Crosse, Wis. 54601

This resident dictated his adventures of blindness and life in the Home, the white cane his "wooden eye." A volunteer typed and prepared the material for publication, 122 vignettes in a paper cover book, short page or page-and-a-half accounts—amusing, courageous, and heartening for people with handicaps to read or be read to. (See "To Read Aloud" at the end of most club chapters.)

Holiday Handcraft Project Made of Folded Magazines (60¢)

Aleene's Inc.
9123 No. Tunas Drive
Temple City, California 91780

Free Films and Slides

The best free films and slides can probably be obtained locally, the source listed in the telephone directory.

1. Travel and nature slides from a local conservation department.

2. Travel agencies as well as conservation departments will either come to the Home or send the film there on request: skiing, fishing, hunting, sports, as well as beauties of other lands delight residents.

3. The local library.

4. State manufacturers of sport equipment.

5. State brewers with sport films.

6. Airline companies.

7. One Home finds the local camera shop a source for travel films and slides which, upon special request, they will bring to the Home and show.

8. The local county agricultural agents can be a good source for travel slides or can suggest a source.

9. A large catalogue (for $11.75) has literally 3000 listings of free films, and can be considered worth the price: Educators Progress Service, Inc., Randolph, Wisconsin 53956.

10. Local department of natural resources.

11. Universities or colleges.

12. Local chamber of commerce.

13. Local museums.

14. Examine the society page for people recently returned from trips who could be contacted for films or slides.

Free films available from the following sources must be ordered a month ahead of time, unless otherwise indicated:

Alaska Railroad. East of Mississippi address: Federal Railroad Administration, Dept. of Transportation, 6 and D Streets, S.W., Washington, D.C. 20591. West of Mississippi address: Alaskan Railroad, Mr. D. L. Allen, General Traffic Manager, 226 Federal Office Bldg., Seattle, Washington 98104.

Allstate Insurance Co. (Ask for your zone and regional office.) 808 North Third Street, Milwaukee, Wis. 33202.

AAA Foundation for Traffic Safety. (Obtain film from local AAA club.)

Aetna Life and Casualty. Public Relations and Advertising Dept. Film Library, 151 Farmington Avenue, Hartford, Conn. 06115 (2 months).

Alabama State Docks. P.O. Box 1588, Mobile, Ala. 36601.

American Angus Association. 3201 Frederich Street, St. Joseph, Mo. 64501.

American Bakers Association. Att. Miss Frances Drilloch, Suite 650, 1700 Pennsylvania Avenue, N.W., Washington, D.C. 20006 (8 weeks).

American Jr. Bowling Congress. 1572 East Capitol Drive, Milwaukee, Wis. 53211 (3 weeks).

American Red Cross. (Through your local Red Cross.)

Arkansas State Parks Recreation and Travel Comm. 149 State Capitol Bldg., Little Rock, Ark. 72201. (Films must be insured for $100 on return; 3 weeks.)

Babe Ruth Baseball. 524 Hamilton Avenue, Trenton, N.J. 08609 (2 weeks).

Bassist Fashion Inst. 923 S.W. Taylor Street, Portland, Ore. 98205 (2 months).

Bay State Film Production Inc. Box 129, Springfield, Mass. 01101 (6 weeks).

Colorado School of Mines. Mr. Charles S. Morris, Dir. Public Relations, Golden, Colo. 80401 (2 months).

Colorado Div. of Highways. Mr. Stanley K. Brown, Public Relations Officer, 4201 East Arkansas Ave., Denver, Colo. 80222.

Colorado Mining Association. 402 Majestic Bldg., 209 16th Street, Denver, Colo. 80202 (8 weeks).

Coco-Cola Co. (Available from your local bottler.)

Coffee Brewing Center. 120 Wall Street, New York, N.Y. 10005.

Chinese Information Service Pacific Coast. 3440 Wilshire Blvd., Los Angeles, Cal. 90005. (Must insure; distribute to West Coast, Hawaii, and Alaska.)

Chicago Board of Trade. Sterling Movies, 309 West Jackson Blvd., Chicago, Ill. 60606 (3 weeks).

Chicago Tribune. Motion Picture Bureau, 33 W. Madison Street, Chicago, Ill. 60602. (Distribution limited to Great Lakes Area; 2 months.)

Chanard Motion Pictures Inc. 2110 East 24th Street, Brooklyn, N.Y. 11290 (3 weeks).

Charleston Trident Chamber of Commerce. Travel and Visitors Dept. P.O. Box 975, Charleston, S.C. 29402 (3 months).

California Redwood Association. 617 Montgomery Street, San Francisco, Cal. 94111.

Chamber of Commerce of the New Orleans Area. Public Relations Dept., P.O. Box 30240, New Orleans, La. 70130.

Bureau of Reclamation. Office of Chief Engineer, Bldg. 37, Att. D841, Denver Federal Center, Denver, Colo. 80225 (2 months).

Bureau of Sport Fisheries and Wildlife. (Ask for your regional office.) Federal Bldg., St. Paul, Minn. 55111. (Serves Ill., Ind., Ia., Mich., Minn., Mo., Neb., S.D. , N.D., Ohio, Wis.)

Brunswick Corp. Bowling Div., Film Library, 69 W. Washington Street, Chicago, Ill. 60602 (6 weeks).

Bureau of Mines. U.S. Dept. of the Interior, Motion Pictures, 4800 Forbes Avenue, Pittsburgh, Pa. 15213.

Bell System Telephone Offices. (Write or call the manager of the nearest office.)

Other free films, according to title, include the following:

AEF in Siberia. 1963, 28 min. Story of Expeditionary Force which journeyed into Russia following World War I.

Dept. of the Army, Fifth U.S. Army, Att. Audio-Visual Support Center, Fort Sheridan, Ill. 60037.

American Battleground. 30 min. Visitor in N.Y. at historic houses, forts, and battlegrounds 1775-1783.

New York State Dept. of Commerce Film Library, West Mall Plaza, 845 Central Avenue, Albany, N.Y. 12206.

(The) Arboretum of the University of Wisconsin. 1965, 32 min. An outstanding cinematic record of the arboretum in all seasons showing the great diversity of plants, animals, and birds that makes the 1200 acres an important center for environmental study, research, and public enjoyment.

Audio Visual Aids, University of Wisconsin, 1327 University Avenue, Madison, Wis. 53706.

Alaskan Scout. 1962. Activity of Eskimo scouts, Alaskan National Guard in fishing village near the Arctic Circle. Dept. of Army (find your nearest Army headquarters and address: Att. Audio-Visual Support Center, Washington, D.C. 20315).

Aleutian Morning. 1962, 32 min. Radar outposts along the Aleutians. Dept. Air Force, USAF Central Audio-Visual Library, AF Audio-Visual, Norton AFB, Cal. 92409.

America's First Thanksgiving. 11½ min. Dramatization of first officially recognized Thanksgiving, 1619.

Virginia State Travel Services, 911 East Broad Street, Richmond, Va. 23219.

Frank Lloyd Wright. B&W, 30 min. Displays Wright's agile wit and eloquence as he discusses his theories of functional architecture. Includes pictures of some of his most famous buildings. Produced for NBC Wisdom Series, 1959, Encyclopaedia Britannica Films.

Public Relations Dept., 425 N. Michigan Avenue, Chicago, Ill. 60611.

More Oil and Gas for Today and Tomorrow. 25 min. A strong case for oil and gas reserves.

American Gas Association, Film Service Library, 1515 Wilson Blvd., Arlington, Va. 22209.

Open World of Glass. 31 min. Various methods of flat glass manufacturing narrated by Lowell Thomas.

Association Films, Inc., Executive Office, 600 Madison Ave., New York, N.Y. 10022.

(The) Rival World. 1956, 25 min. Story of the endless attack on insects.

Food and Agriculture Organization of the United Nations, Shell Film Library, 450 N. Meridian Street, Indianapolis, Ind. 46204.

Survival of the Pacific Salmon. 25 min. Creating the safe passage of adult salmon.

U.S. Army Engineer Div. Southwestern, 114 Commerce St., Dallas, Tex. 75202.

Trek to the Tetons. 23 min. Wild life: buffalo stampeding, whitetail deer, prairie dogs, giant bull moose, and so forth.

Association Films, Inc., Eastman Kodak Co., 512 Burlington Ave., La Grange, Ill. 60525.

Underwater Reflections. 30 min. World existing below surface of inland lakes and streams.

Wilkie Brothers Foundation, Film Dept., 254 N. Laurel Ave., Des Plaines, Ill. 60016 (3 months).

Valley and the Stream. 50 min. Beauties of the valley and a broad river. Wilkie Brothers Foundation (see address above).

What Is Medicare? 1968, 33 min. Social Security Administration (get the address from your local post office).

Wildlife in the Main Stream. 27 min. Missouri River range, closeups of antelope and eagles, hunting and fishing.

U.S. Army Engineer Div. Missouri River, 906 Olive St., St. Louis, Mo. 63101.

Wildlife World. 30 min. New Mexico quiet deserts, prairies, and timberland ridges, antelopes, mule deer, and mountain lions.

New Mexico Dept. of Development, Film Library, State Capitol Bldg., Sante Fe, New Mexico 87501.

Wood Duck World. 30 min. Fowl that pass through the Mississippi flyway each spring and fall, wood ducks from spring courting days to fall migration.

Wilkie Brothers Foundation (see address above).

Wondrous World of Sight. 28 min. The role the eye plays in life.

Modern Talking Picture Service, 1212 Avenue of the Americas, New York, N.Y. 10036.

APPENDIX FOR OLD-TIMERS CLUB

Old Farmer's Almanac. Weather forecasts and country things; can be purchased at most newstands. (50¢)

Yankee. Dublin, N.H. Small monthly magazine; everything in it, including the ads, is old-fashioned. ($3 a year)

APPENDIX FOR HOMEMAKERS CLUB

Focus on Living, Package Programs, Home Economics and Continuing Education of Women, Cooperative Extension Program, University Extension, University of Wisconsin, Madison, Wisconsin 53705. Or, any similar local university extension unit.

APPENDIX FOR AUTOMOBILE CLUB

Regata Kit, Space Derby (car racing) Official Cub Scout Space Derby Kit, Catalogue 1695. These can be purchased in any department store selling Boy Scout uniforms. The kit has eight blocks to a kit and a track plan to race the cars, using a plywood track 15′ 10″. Whittlers would enjoy working on these racing cars of balsa, easily done. $4 for eight.

A catalog of antique model cars—Mercer 1912, Cord 1936, Duesenberg 1931, First Race Car 1907, and so on—is available for 25¢ from Marbet Enterprises, 411 Stewart Avenue, Garden City, N.Y. 11530.

APPENDIX FOR MEN'S CLUB

One can play *chess-by-mail* by joining the USO's All Service Postal Chess Club. Write its director: Mr. Spencer Hurd, 1212 First Street S.W., Moultrie, Ga. 31768.

Voit Sports manufactures a *punching bag,* $10.50 plus shipping, which a nearby sporting goods store will order upon request. The punching bag is mounted on a board on the floor, wheelchair high, easy to assemble in three parts: the board on the floor, the rod attached to the bag, and the bag. No one passes this tantalizing exerciser without giving it a few swings with a fist or elbow, from a seated position.

APPENDIX FOR TRAVEL CLUB

Geographic School Bulletin. National Geographic Society, Washington, D.C. 20036. 30 issues a school year $2.75, $7.50 for three years. About 16 pages 6″ x 9″ color-illustrated articles. Mailed weekly, lends to educational discussion.

Free films (see preceding pages): Eastman Kodak Company, Modern Talking Picture Service, 1212 Avenue of America, New York, N.Y. 10036. Association Film, 561 Hillgrove Avenue, La Grange, Ill. 60525 ("The Carnival Under the Sea" and "Gods and Mountains").

Local travel agency—ask for travel posters, brochures, speakers, and other help.

Embassies and other offices that represent foreign countries are rich sources of free learning materials. However, their representatives say they are often swamped with questions that can be answered by checking encyclopedias or other library sources.

Many of the embassies contacted asked that whenever possible, requests be made for specific information instead of for "all the information you have available."

List of Sources *(The First Eight Were Particularly Helpful in Compiling the List)*

Canada. Embassy of Canada, 1746 Massachusetts Avenue, N.W., Washington, D.C. 20036.

France. Press and Information Division, French Embassy, 972 Fifth Avenue, New York, N.Y. 10021.

Germany (West). German Information Center, 410 Park Avenue, New York, N.Y. 10022.

Israel. Information Office, Embassy of Israel, 1621 22nd Street, N.W., Washington, D.C. 20008.

Japan. Information Service, Consulate General of Japan, 235 East 42nd Street, New York, N.Y. 10017.

Netherlands. Netherlands Information Service, 711 Third Avenue, New York, N.Y. 10017. (In the Midwest you may write to

The Netherlands Information Service, Netherlands Museum, Holland, Michigan 49423. Pacific coast readers may contact The Netherlands Information Service, International Building, 601 California Street, San Francisco, Calif. 94108.)

Poland. Polish Embassy, 2640 16th Street, N.W., Washington, D.C. 20009.

Sweden. Swedish Information Service, 825 Third Avenue, New York, N.Y. 10022.

Argentina. Argentine Cultural Office, 1600 New Hampshire Avenue, N.W., Washington, D.C. 20009.

Australia. Australian News and Information Bureau, 635 Fifth Avenue, New York, N.Y. 10020. (For eastern and midwestern states: Information Attache, Australian Embassy, 1001 Massachusetts Avenue, N.W., Washington, D.C. 20036. For western states: Australian Consulate-General, Crocker Plaza, San Francisco, Calif. 94104.)

Botswana. Embassy of Botswana, 825 Connecticut Avenue, N.W., Washington, D.C. 20006, Room 310.

Brazil. Embassy of Brazil, 3007 Whitehaven Street, N.W., Washington, D.C. 20008.

Cameroon. Embassy of the Federal Republic of Cameroon, 1705 New Hampshire Avenue, N.W., Washington, D.C. 20008.

Central African Republic. Embassy of the Central African Republic, 1618 22nd Street, N.W., Washington, D.C. 20008.

Chad. Embassy of the Republic of Chad, 1132 New Hampshire Avenue, N.W., Washington, D.C. 20037.

China (Nationalist). Chinese Information Service, 100 West 32nd Street, New York, N.Y. 10001.

Czechoslovakia. Secretary of the Embassy of the Czechoslovak Socialist Republic, 3900 Linnean Avenue, N.W., Washington, D.C. 20009.

Ecuador. Embassy of Ecuador, 2535 15th Street, N.W., Washington, D.C. 20009.

Greece. Royal Greek Embassy, Press and Information Service, 2211 Massachusetts Avenue, N.W., Washington, D.C. 20008.

Guatemala. Embassy of Guatemala, 2220 R Street, N.W., Washington, D.C. 20008.

Guyana. Embassy of Guyana, Suite 404, 1701 Pennsylvania Avenue, N.W., Washington, D.C. 20006.

Italy. Instituto Italiano de Cultura, 686 Park Avenue, New York, N.Y. 10021.

Jamaica. Embassy of Jamaica, 5th Floor, 1666 Connecticut Avenue, Washington, D.C. 20009.

Korea (South). Embassy of Korea, Information Office, Suite 312, 1145 19th Street, N.W., Washington, D.C. 20036.

Lithuania. Lithuanian Legation, 2622 16th Street, N.W., Washington, D.C. 20001.

Luxembourg. Economic and Tourist Department, 200 East 42nd Street, New York, N.Y. 10017.

New Zealand. Embassy of New Zealand, 19 Observatory Circle, N.W., Washington, D.C. 20008.

Niger. Embassy of Niger, 2204 R Street, N.W., Washington, D.C. 20008.

Norway. Norwegian Information Service, 825 Third Avenue, New York, N.Y. 10022.

Philippines. Philippine Embassy, 1617 Massachusetts Avenue, N.W., Washington, D.C. 20036.

Portugal. Casa de Portugal, 570 Fifth Avenue, New York, N.Y. 10036.

Saudi Arabia. Embassy of Saudi Arabia, 1520 18th Street, N.W., Washington, D.C. 20036.

Senegal. Embassy of Senegal, 2112 Wyoming Avenue, N.W., Washington, D.C. 20008.

Somali Republic. Embassy of Somali Republic, Room 1109, 1875 Connecticut Avenue, N.W., Washington, D.C. 20009.

South Africa. South African Information Service, 655 Madison Avenue, New York, N.Y. 10021.

Switzerland. Embassy of Switzerland, 1900 Cathedral Avenue, N.W., Washington, D.C. 20008.

Tunisia. Press Department, Embassy of Tunisia, 2408 Massachusetts Avenue, N.W., Washington, D.C. 20008.

Union of Soviet Socialist Republics. Embassy of the U.S.S.R., 1125 16th Street, N.W., Washington, D.C. 20036.

Venezuela. Information Service, Embassy of Venezuela, 2437 California Street, N.W., Washington, D.C. 20008.

Viet Nam (South). Embassy of the Republic of Viet Nam, 2251 R Street, N.W., Washington, D.C. 20008.

Yugoslavia. Yugoslav Information Center, 816 Fifth Avenue, New York, N.Y. 10021.

APPENDIX FOR HOBBY CLUB

Hobbies. A magazine devoted to all kinds of collecting. Lightner Publishing Co., 1006 S. Michigan Avenue, Chicago, Ill. 60606.

Coins

The American Numismatic Society, Broadway at 155th St., New York, N.Y.

American Numismatic Association, P.O. Box 2366, Colorado Springs, Colo. 80901. The Association maintains a lending library and publishes a monthly magazine "The Numismatist" which contains many worthwhile articles as well as advertisements of most professional numismatists in the United States. It will also be able to recommend a coin club in your area.

Post Cards

Post Card Collector's Magazine and Gazette. 2642 Ellendale Place, Los Angeles, Calif.

Playing Cards

Playing Card Collectors' Association, 3873 N. 37th St., Milwaukee, Wis.

APPENDIX FOR THE GARDEN CLUB

By posting a list on their bulletin boards, the leader asks volunteers and employees for discarded items which could be used by the club: mason jars, bowls and vases, a blackboard, simple garden tools, clay flower pots, discarded paint and brushes, work aprons and gloves, glass roller, discarded garden magazines and seed catalogues, beans, seeds and slips, lemon seeds, and almost any seeds, birdfeed, and peanuts for the squirrels.

1. Jiffy peat pellets, for about 10¢ apiece, are used for potting soil and can also be used as one unit for easy storage and handling of a plant. A small net-enclosed wafer expands into a pellet upon adding water. Seeds may be started in it. It saves the cost of soil, is clean to use, saves filling pots, prevents transplanting, and insures faster growth for young plants.

2. Grass seeds sprinkled on top of a piece of cork coaster, if soaked, will grow almost before one's very eyes. A bean or a lemon seed soaked overnight and then planted an inch from the surface in soil in a paper cup, will grow rapidly.

3. A plastic tray which holds seed, sowing trays, and peat pots will accommodate an electric heating cable. It has durable light green plastic that will last for many seasons, 12″ × 18″. It costs $1.45 (the 6′ cable is $1.95) advertised in most seed catalogues.

4. A seed-starting kit for $3.50 includes the plastic tray for holding seed-sowing trays and peat pots, won't leak, will last for years. It includes two bags of planting formula for starting seeds, fifteen label stakes for identifying the plants, the instructions for starting seed indoors and bringing plants to mature successfully.

5. A more expensive appliance is a timer to be set for the hours the plants want heat; a "night guard" turns lamps on automatically. Minimum "on" time is 15 minutes, maximum is 23 hours.

6. Crocuses that grow without sun, soil, or water: House of

295

Wesley, Nursery Division, RR 1, Dept. 1575-99, Bloomington, Ill. 61701. Five for $1, twelve for $2.

7. Vegetables "can be grown without soil all year long (tomatoes, peppers, strawberries, cucumbers), Hydroponic starter sets include growing bed, growing granules, soluble nutrients, seed, instructions." For $2.98 plus mail costs. Order from Graham's of Florida, 3273 N. Dixie Hwy., Ft. Lauderdale, Fla. 33307.

APPENDIX FOR FIN AND FEATHER CLUB

Trade Periodicals Concerned with Animals and Birds

Game Bird Breeders, Pheasant Fanciers and Agriculturists' Gazette. (Monthly, 50¢ a copy; $4.50 a year.) Allen Publishing Co., Inc., 1328 Allen Park Dr., Salt Lake City, Utah 84105.
All Pets Magazine Inc. 245 Cornelison Ave., Jersey City, N.J. 07002.

Associations Concerned with Animals and Birds

American Rabbit Breeders Association, 4323 Murray Avenue, Pittsburgh, Pa. 15217.
American Pheasant and Waterfowl Society, Mr. Thane Earle, Pres., Box 219, Whitewater, Wis. 53190.
Giant Chinchilla Rabbit Association, North Highland Ave., Pearl River, N.Y. 10965.
American Belgian Hare Club, Secy., J. Ed Shanaberger, 113 Floy St., Spartanburg, S.C. 29301.
National Wildlife Federation, 1412 16th St., N.W., Washington, D.C. 20036.
Wildlife Management Institute, 709 Wire Bldg., Washington, D.C. 20005.
Free films are available from state departments of natural resources, on such subjects as conservation, pollution, game birds, and fish. The same source often has display sets available for exhibition use, photos on loan on 16″ × 20″ boards ready to mount, including waterfowl and upland birds and mammals, state songbirds, wild flowers, state forests and roadside parks, upland game birds and waterfowl, state recreation and hand-tinted state scenic prints.
Slide sets with a descriptive booklet are free from the Department of Natural Resources, too: birds of field and meadow, home and garden, woodlands, fish identification, game birds, Na-

tional Audubon Society, state game farms and parks, state mammals and forests, and so on.

Free films for sportsmen are available through National Shooting Sports Foundation, Inc., 1075 Post Road, Riverside, Conn. 06870.

Free material is available from the Fisherman's Information Bureau, 20 North Wacker Drive, Chicago, Ill. 60606.

APPENDIX FOR NATURE CLUB

Sounds of Nature. Free records from the American Printing House for the Blind, P.O. Box 6065, Louisville, Ky. 40206. These will be enjoyed by all residents whether visually handicapped or not.

Readers Digest Book, Amazing World of Nature, Its Marvels and Mysteries. A large book filled with colored illustrations.

The following records may be purchased through a record store, for about $7 apiece:

African Birds. (2 discs) Cornell University.

American Bird Songs. (2 discs) Cornell University.

Songs of Insects. Cornell University.

Swamp in June. Hawkes, Droll 17.

Sounds of Spring. F.O.N. 1.

Day of Algonquin Park. F.O.N.